*The quiet continent.
Australia and its people
was a land that waited.
For many centuries it
lay undisturbed. The
Endeavour's landfall
in April 1770 tolled the
bell of change. From a
watercolour by William
Westall, 1804.*

THE FATAL IMPACT

THE INVASION OF THE SOUTH PACIFIC
1767–1840

ALAN MOOREHEAD

HAMISH HAMILTON

THE FATAL IMPACT was first published in 1966 by Hamish Hamilton. It was published in paperback by Penguin in 1968 and reprinted six times. This edition has been enhanced by the inclusion of approximately 150 paintings, drawings and etchings which illustrate the events, people and places written about in this tragic story of a great adventure.

The boxed information and captions were researched and written by the historian Ann Moyal, whose broad knowledge has added further insights to Alan Moorehead's colourful text.

Alan Moorehead died in September 1983.

This edition created and produced in 1987 by
Mead & Beckett Publishing
139 Macquarie Street Sydney Australia

First published in Great Britain 1966 by
Hamish Hamilton Ltd
27 Wrights Lane London W8 5TZ

This edition published simultaneously in
London and Melbourne

Additional text by Ann Moyal
Designed by Leonie Bremer-Kamp
Edited by Amanda Bilson
Picture research by Don Chapman
Typeset by Asco Trade Typesetting, Hong Kong
Colour separations by Bright Arts, Hong Kong
Printed by South China Printing, Hong Kong

ISBN 0 241 12346 1

CONTENTS

Author's note   8

Part One: Tahiti

1. *The landfall*   13
2. *Venus observed*   32
3. *The noble savage*   59
4. *The familiarity*   69
5. *Arcady reformed*   89
6. *Nevermore*   105

Part Two: Australia

1. *Botany Bay*   118
2. *Australia observed*   132
3. *The Aborigines*   143
4. *The settlement*   160
5. *The spreading out*   181
6. *The acclimatization*   198

Part Three: The Antarctic

1. *The Resolution*   212
2. *The bloodstained ice*   226

Bibliography   244
Source of Illustrations   246
Index   249

TO
ALWYN LEE

The corvettes L'Astro-labe *and* La Zelee *free themselves from the ice during a voyage to Antarctica led by Dumont d'Urville in the years 1837–40. Painting by Louis Le Breton.*

PREFACE

NOT LONG after the publication of Alan Moorehead's *Cooper's Creek* in 1964 he came to our house in Canberra for a talk. We soon found we had much in common. We both believed history was an art in which the writer imposed an order on the chaos. We both believed that the historian should have the art of the story teller. We both believed history was the bible of humanity, and that the historian should tell his story both to entertain and to add his own mite to the store of human wisdom. We had much to say to each other, and parted in the hope of continuing the exchanges of mind and heart.

So when the first edition of *The Fatal Impact* was first published in 1966 I devoured it. Once again Alan Moorehead displayed superbly the gifts in his earlier works – the art of reader preparation, the skill of holding the reader, and above all the one essential thing for a writer, having something to say. Alan Moorehead always had the gift to anticipate the groundswells in public opinion. In *Cooper's Creek* he was out in front of that huge swell of interest starting in the history of Australia. Hitherto, with exceptions, Australian history was written and taught as a branch of British colonial history. Alan Moorehead helped to make it Australian centred: Alan Moorehead helped to show it was interesting to explore the minds of the heroes and heroines of Australian history.

In *The Fatal Impact* he told the story of how the white man came to dominate the people in the islands of the south Pacific, New Zealand, Tasmania and Australia. He wrote it not as a caricature or a cartoon or a comic strip but as a tragedy in which no one was to blame except possibly the human situation. Alan Moorehead was not a man to allot praise or blame. He was not the historian as judge and punisher. He was the historian with the eye of pity, and the eye of understanding.

The publishers are to be congratulated on their decision to have this new edition. As long as there is a reading public for a story teller such as Alan Moorehead we can be sure the age of the human ant-heap has not arrived in Australia.

MANNING CLARK
1987

AUTHOR'S NOTE

AN ATTEMPT has been made here to give a short account of the penetration of the Pacific over a period of eighty years, from the late 1760s to the 1840s. I have taken three examples to illustrate what happened at this first contact between the white man and the inhabitants of that hitherto uncharted ocean: Tahiti, the tropical island, with its lush forests and flowers, a place where there is neither winter nor summer, and where the days are varied merely by sunshine and warm showers; next, the temperate eastern coast of Australia where there are lightly timbered plains and hills, and the seasons exist in all their variety; and finally, the south polar regions where hardly anything will grow in the perpetual cold, and where the short summer with its continuous daylight is succeeded by a long winter of unbroken night.

In these three regions you have the difference between abundance, moderation and nothing, between lethargy, energy and death.

I have naturally followed Captain James Cook on his Pacific voyages, since nearly everywhere he was the first on the scene, and he seems to me to have understood, better than any other explorer, what was happening at that special moment and what the consequences were going to be.

But this is a brief sketch; for a fuller account of Captain Cook, the student will turn to the splendid volumes of Dr J. C. Beaglehole, of the Victoria University of Wellington, New Zealand; indeed his masterly editing and annotation of Cook's original journals have illuminated Pacific travels as nothing else has done before, and it is not too much to say that any account of Cook's discoveries can hardly hope to be more than an appendage, if not a plagiarism of his work. My only excuse for trespassing upon ground that Dr Beaglehole has made so very much his own is that I have concentrated upon one aspect of Cook's voyages, namely that fateful moment when a social capsule is broken open, when primitive creatures, beasts as well as men, are confronted for the first time with civilization; the moment which is not so much one of truth, nor even of recognition, as of an eager, awkward fumbling to try and understand.

Another work which is invaluable in the study of these matters is *European Vision and the South Pacific*, by Bernard Smith. I have particularly relied on Dr Smith for his account of Omai, the Tahitian boy who was transported to England.

Since, in the pursuance of my theme, I have not been able to relate events in chronological order, it may be useful here to remind the reader that Cook made three separate voyages. The first, in the *Endeavour*, took him to Tahiti, New Zealand and Australia, and lasted three years, from 1768 to 1771. After barely a year in England he set out again, this time with two ships, the *Resolution* and the *Adventure*, and this was the voyage on which he crossed the Antarctic Circle and circumnavigated the South Pole. Again he was away three years, from 1772 to 1775, spending the summer months in Antarctic waters and the rest of the year either in New Zealand or cruising among the tropical islands in the Pacific. On this second voyage he twice visited Tahiti. Again he had another twelve months' respite in England before setting out on his third and final voyage with the *Resolution* and the *Discovery*. It began in 1776, and its principal object was to search for a passage from the Pacific to the Atlantic through north polar seas. He visited Tahiti for the last time in 1777, and then sailed north to the western coast of America and to Hawaii, where he met his death in 1779. His lieutenants brought the two ships safely back to England.

It is the first two voyages that mainly concern us here.

I must extend my very great thanks to Dr Beaglehole, Dr Smith and Mr Robert Hughes who read and corrected my manuscript before publication, to Mr Edouard A. Stackpole of the Whaling Museum, Mystic, Connecticut, who kindly consulted his records for me, and to my wife, whose help has been essential.

The compilation of the book required extensive travelling and I am most grateful for the assistance given me by the United States Navy in the Antarctic, by Qantas Airways and The British Petroleum Company. Most of the books I obtained from the London Library.

ALAN MOOREHEAD
1966

James Cleveley, a carpenter to the expedition, did this watercolour of the Resolution and Adventure anchored at Moorea, Tahiti in September 1772. It was Cook's third voyage of exploration.

PART ONE

TAHITI

I

The landfall

WHEN COOK SAILED the *Endeavour* into Matavai Bay on 13 April 1769, it was by no means the first time the Tahitians had encountered white men. Bougainville in *La Boudeuse* had been there, or at any rate a little further round the coast, the year before; Wallis in the *Dolphin* had arrived in 1767, and Quiros was in these seas as early as 1606. But Quiros had long since been forgotten, Bougainville had stayed in Tahiti only thirteen days and Wallis five weeks. Cook was to be here three months, he was to live ashore and make meteorological observations, he was to chart the coast; this landfall was the first great object of his journey.

It might be fairly said, therefore, that with the *Endeavour*'s arrival the penetration of the Pacific was only just beginning. From now on it was going to be no great wonder for the islanders to see a sailing ship beating into land; Cook himself was to return three times, and he was soon to be followed by the Spanish, and Bligh in the *Bounty*, and the English missionaries, and the Nantucket sealers and whalers calling in for 'refreshments' on their way south, and then the French. All these visitors – perhaps intruders is a better word – were going to make their separate contribution to the transformation of the Tahitians, whether by firearms, disease or alcohol, or by imposing an alien code of laws and morals that had nothing to do with the slow, natural rhythm of life on the island as it had been lived up till then.

It was perfectly true that the Europeans were also going to import the antidotes to their poisons and diseases – the doctors, the priests, the administrators and the policemen – but the Tahitians had had no need for these people before; if they had been left undisturbed they might have gone on forever without them, and at the time of Cook's arrival they were probably happier than they were ever to be again.

Naturally neither Cook (at first) nor the Tahitians themselves saw things in this light. Cook was acting under orders from the British Admiralty, and he had no evil designs on these people; indeed his whole desire was to make friends with them and to interfere as little as possible with their customs. The Tahitians, on their side, were quite unable to stifle their curiosity; they were delighted to greet these fascinating strangers with their great sailing ship, their extraordinary clothes, their wonderful trinkets and gadgets. Even if they had known the evil that was in store for them they would still have welcomed the *Endeavour*.

Thus this early contact between the white-skinned sailors and the dark islanders, this first real shock of recognition, was a momentous occasion, a sharp and irrevocable turn in the history of the Pacific; and it was going to make its impact on Europe as well.

Let us consider Tahiti for a moment as it was in 1769 in the light of the knowledge that we now possess. It was only a small dot in the vast ocean, a

ABOVE
Tahiti offered the En-deavour party idyllic tranquillity. Beneath towering peaks, the native huts were scattered under the shade of the plantations.

BELOW
Sydney Parkinson's sketch of the neat, well constructed Tahitian huts sheltering beneath the palms.

The Endeavour *riding at anchor in Matavai Bay. The ship would spend some four months there from April to August 1769 on its scientific mission, while Cook and his men developed their absorbing and far-reaching relationship with the Polynesians. In this sketch by natural history artist Sydney Parkinson, the sturdy converted collier is dwarfed by the spreading boughs of a breadfruit tree on One Tree Hill.*

James Cook, navigator, man of action and distinguished cartographer, was the Admiralty's choice to lead the expedition to observe the transit of Venus across the sun at Tahiti in 1769, and to search for a 'great south land'. Cook, painted here by Nathaniel Dance, was practical and courageous, and first on the scene nearly everywhere in the Pacific. He, more than any other explorer, sensed what was happening at the moment of contact and what the likely consequences might be.

tiny parcel of land some 53 km (33 miles) in length and covering an area of barely 1,000 km² (400 sq miles), but its central mountains, rising above 2,100 m (7,000 ft), could be seen from 96 km (60 miles) away at sea. The slopes of the mountains were covered with a thick tropical forest, and on the flat shores below the Tahitians moved among groves of coconuts and breadfruit trees. There were no villages; the huts, open on all sides to the breeze, were scattered about under the deep shade of the plantations, each hut about 45 m (50 yds) from its neighbour and connected with it by a well-worn path. There were other islands visible on the horizon, but Tahiti was the largest of the group and its curious coastline, shaped like a top-heavy hourglass and protected by a coral reef, provided safe anchorages from the prevailing wind. Although it lay in the tropics of the central Pacific, just north of Capricorn, its hot, damp climate was not oppressive, there was fresh water in abundance in the moun-

ABOVE, LEFT
*The Tahitians seemed
exceedingly beautiful;
only their broad noses
gave them a less than
European air. Tainamai,
robed in a toga with a
crown of flowers in her
plaited hair, was the
daughter of a chief.*

ABOVE, RIGHT
*Oedidee was a young
man of about seventeen or
eighteen years from Bora
Bora. Fastidious in their
personal habits, the men
plucked their moustaches
and both sexes removed
the hair from their arm-
pits. For their part, they
thought the English visi-
tors, with their disinclina-
tion for bathing, less than
clean.*

A view of Queen Obarea's house on Tahiti, by Captain Samuel Wallis, 1767.

tain torrents, and flowers and fruit grew everywhere. Like Capri in the Mediterranean, Tahiti had a quality of lushness combined with sudden, unexpected grandeur that set it quite apart, and it would not have been unreasonable to have described it as the most beautiful island in the world. If it lacked the ruins and the reassurance of older civilizations at least it was the heart of Polynesian culture in the Pacific.

In Cook's time the population may have numbered about 40,000, and to the eye of sailors, weary of the cramped ship and the endless sea, the people seemed every bit as beautiful as their surroundings, the men tall and well-proportioned with fine smooth skins, often not much browner than that of a southern European, and the women in some cases lovely beyond dreams. The diarists aboard the *Endeavour* speak of their dark liquid eyes and perfect teeth, of the sprays of jasmine and hibiscus in their long black hair, and of their smiling welcoming faces. They wore brightly coloured toga-like robes which, in the evening, or in the presence of important people, they dropped to the waist, revealing in the young girls beautifully moulded breasts and arms and shoulders.

There were, of course, imperfections in these paragons. Their noses were just a little too flat for the European taste, they tended to grow fat with age, and tattooing, done with lamp-black pricked into the skin with a sharp bone, disfigured large areas of their legs, their buttocks and their torsos (though not their faces). They tended also to anoint themselves with coconut oil which turned rancid after a time. However, they were a cleanly people. The men plucked their moustaches and both sexes removed the hair from under their armpits. They washed in running water when they rose in the morning, again at noon, and before they slept at night, and their clothes were spotless.

They did little hard work, and there was no real necessity for it; the food was all around them, the fish in the lagoons, the breadfruit and the coconuts in the branches above their heads, bananas, yams and sugarcane grew wild, and little pigs and fowls, roasted in underground ovens, provided their occasional banquets. They sometimes brewed an intoxicating drink from a pepper root named *ava*, but they had no tobacco and did not feel the lack of drugs. A few were afflicted with a skin disease, but those beautiful teeth did not decay, childbirth came easily, and in the main they knew no sickness except the decline into old age and death. They made no journeys into the mountains – it was too

The dance in Tahiti.

fatiguing – and in their arts and crafts they seemed to have all they wanted: bark from the trees was beaten into cloth and coloured with natural dyes, palm leaves were woven into mats and roofs for their huts, coconut shells were their drinking cups, and their canoes, elaborate affairs with sails and outriggers, and sometimes 18 or 21 m (60 or 70 ft) long, were constructed out of the local timber. They slept and sat on the ground and therefore had no need of furniture in their huts. Since there was no winter they were never cold, and even on the hottest day the sea breeze blew. There were no snakes or dangerous animals to threaten them, and natural disasters such as earthquakes and hurricanes seldom came their way. They were illiterate and did not care.

Apart from a few carved images they kept no records of the past and they had very little interest in it. However, they acknowledged in a vague mystical way the existence of a supreme being, they had their temples – the *marae* – courtyards with raised platforms built of stone in a clearing or near the shore. They kept alive by word of mouth their ancient legends, and they had their religious festivals which were conducted by a special sect known as the *arioi*. For their distractions they loved to surf in the long Pacific rollers, to dance and sing to the music of drums and flutes, and to enact plays and engage in wrestling matches. They divided their year into thirteen lunar months, but years signified nothing very much; they lived from day to day in an endlessly repeated cycle, controlled only by their hunger and their desires, ashamed of nothing, eating, sleeping, dancing, fishing, cooking, talking and making love, always together and always in the open air.

Thus far the idyllic life, the life that revealed itself to an explorer on a casual visit. But on a closer view it had its complications, as Cook and his crew were soon to find out. This was a society which was divided into tribal groups, each with a ruling family surrounded by an upper class. Below them were the general mass of the people and the servants or serfs – a division in fact not so unlike the class structure in Europe in the eighteenth century. Promiscuity was fairly generally practised, at least in youth, but no woman of the ruling or upper class would have thought of offering herself to the English sailors except in the most unusual circumstances, and among the middle class the bonds of marriage – and the Tahitians were monogamous – were observed with some strictness. It was true that the young girls from the age of ten or thereabouts would very readily make love and had no modesty at all about it (they were

17

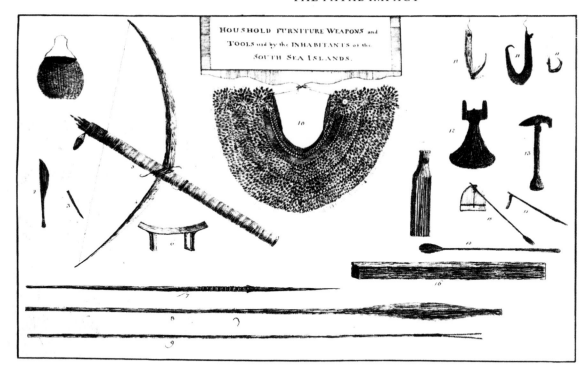

Household objects, weapons and tools of the Tahitians depicted by Parkinson and others include the traditional Tahitian basket, a mallet, a chisel and bow, a quiver of arrows, a carved stool, a heavy 'gorget' made of finely matted feathers and used as an ornament of war, assorted fish hooks, a stone pestle for beating breadfruit into paste, a wooden mallet for beating tapa cloth, and the long-handled instruments with which they carried out the extensive tattooing of their bodies.

Tahitian musicians. Singing and dancing to the music of drums and flutes was a passion of the Tahitians. There was a large concourse of people round this band which consisted of two flutes and three drums.' The flute was played by blowing through one nostril, the other nostril being stopped with the thumb.

amused that the sailors wanted to retire privately into the woods), but most of them came from the lower strata, and directly they became pregnant a marriage normally followed. Nor did the apparent good nature and amiability of the Tahitians prevent them from engaging in tribal wars. Six months before Cook arrived there had been a devastating battle between Big Tahiti (the larger end of the hourglass) and Little Tahiti, and although their weapons were limited to clubs, spears and slings, both women and children as well as men had been killed and injured in the general slaughter. These engagements were often preceded and followed by human sacrifices at the *marae*, one of the prisoners or some luckless serf being used as the victim. The *marae* platforms were piled with human skulls.

The privileged priesthood, the *arioi* (which included both men and women), was also a long way from Arcadian innocence when judged by European standards. Except for the very highest among them (whose offspring were de-

'Te Atua' – arbiter of life and death

Tahitian religion acknowledged one supreme god – 'Te Atua', meaning the godhead. Te Atua could not be personified, but was the arbiter of life and death. The only demands made by this supreme being were reverence to the divinity and kindness to each other. Tahitians believed in the existence of a heaven, but no hell. Lesser gods, however, were also worshipped, known by personal names, and there were innumerable spirits including the spirits of their ancestors who were revered. The *maraes* were holy places used for formal worship and presided over by the priestly *arioi*. There, on the raised altars, a steady flow of sacrificial and propritiary offerings of pigs and fruit were served up to the gods, with an occasional human sacrifice to support an urgent prayer. The *maraes* were also used for funerals of chiefs and other members of the elite. Essentially, the Tahitians enjoyed an uncomplex religion. Since society was based on communal ownership and kindness to each other, they held no concept of sinful man. Only unkindness was *taboo*, a Tahitian word that passed quickly into the English language.

'View of a Tomb'. Commoners were not allowed into the holy maraes, *and women for only one special ceremony. The dead were deposited under a hut or shed where their bones were left to rot. The robed figure here represented the person who conducted the funeral ceremony. Engraved by William Woollett after Barralet from Hawkesworth, 1773.*

clared to come from the gods) they were childless. This was not because they were celibate – the very reverse, they practised indiscriminate free love – but because they strangled their children at birth. This was their drastic method of keeping the sect exclusive, and it bears some resemblance to the customs of the contemporary Mamelukes in eighteenth-century Egypt who preferred to train Georgian slaves as their successors rather than have children of their own. Possibly too, infanticide was a means of preventing overpopulation on so small an island. No one knows how many children were thus dispatched every year but it must have been a considerable total since the *arioi* themselves were very numerous. They were a revered and complicated hierarchy, with six different grades or orders, each distinguished by different dress and different tattoo marks, and it was their habit to travel about in consecrated canoes celebrating the seasonal and religious festivals.

There were, of course, back-slidings in this feudal society – an influential woman could take a lover with impunity – but most of the taboos were very strictly observed: no woman, for instance, could eat in a man's presence, and a member of a ruling family could not help himself to his food but had to be fed by his attendants. A chief was treated with semi-divine honours which no one would have dared to dispute; when he travelled about he had to be carried on another man's shoulders since the land immediately became his wherever his foot touched the ground. Curiously, when an heir was born a chief at once abdicated in the child's favour and became regent instead. All these rules and many more were immutable.

This then, very briefly described, was the confined little community, cut off from all the rest of the world by thousands of kilometres of ocean and centuries of time, into which the Europeans were now about to import their own utterly different scale of values. If it was a good deal less than perfect at least it had established a balance with itself, it had a certain gaiety and well-being, it was intact. Despite the wars, the sacrifices and the stranglings it was not decadent, and it was not yet subject to the curse of a mass restlessness. In the absence of firearms it was not easy for a dictator to emerge, there were no great riches to stir ambition, and the sense of fundamental guilt could hardly be said to exist. Bougainville, with his recent memories of the destitution caused by the Seven Years War in Europe, had compared the island to the Garden of Eden, and had renamed it New Cythera after the Peloponnesian island where Aphrodite (or Venus) had first emerged from the sea. This may have been a little fanciful (he did not know about the sacrifices), but at all events it would be hard to imagine any greater contrast than that which existed between the easygoing lives of the Tahitians in 1769 and those of the ninety-odd Englishmen in the *Endeavour* who were now sailing into Matavai Bay.

Cook had been given two missions, the second of which was secret; he was first to observe from Tahiti the transit of Venus across the disk of the sun which was due to occur seven weeks hence, on 3 June; and then, having charted the island and its neighbours, he was to proceed to the south Pacific to discover whether or not a large continent existed there. It was only by chance that Tahiti had been chosen. As a point of observation six other stations in the Pacific might have done as well, and in fact no one in England had even heard

Samuel Wallis, Cook's precursor

Samuel Wallis had sailed from England in August 1766 on HMS *Dolphin* with instructions from the Admiralty to look for islands and a continent west of Cape Horn. Rounding the Horn, winds drove him north-westerly and he struck shore in Tahiti in June 1767. He called it King George the Third's Island and annexed it for his monarch. Fortunately for England, Wallis was able to sketch in both the latitude and (difficult at that time) the longitude of the island and fix it on the map. His arrival back in England in May 1768 gave the Admiralty a well located and identifiable island on which to site observations for the transit of Venus.

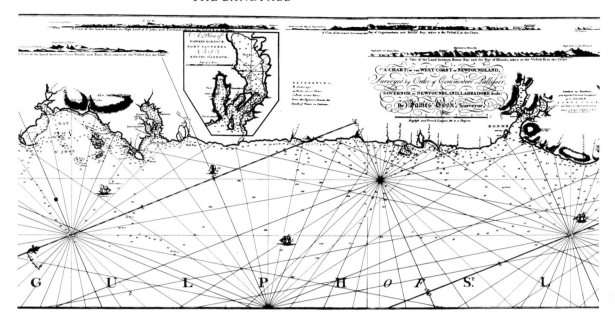

of the island until a few months before Cook's departure from England. But then Wallis in the *Dolphin* had sailed into the Downs with the news of this new hospitable refuge, conveniently sited for the work in hand, and the *Endeavour*'s orders had been altered at the last moment.

Cook at this time was thirty-nine years of age, and it was surprising that he had been given the command of so important and adventurous a voyage as this; he was the son of a Yorkshire labourer and it was not until the late age of eighteen, having worked as a farmer's boy and a grocer's assistant, that he had taken to the sea in the Whitby coal trade. At twenty-seven he had joined the Navy, stepping down from mate to be an able seaman. Even after seeing service in Canada and Newfoundland, he had not reached commissioned rank. But if the Admiralty was slow in recognizing merit it was by no means adverse to putting it to use. Year after year it had become apparent that this tall, solid, unpretentious Yorkshireman was altogether exceptional, not only as a navigator but as a commander of men as well. He might not have been a scholar or a gentleman but he was absolutely reliable, and his charting of Newfoundland had brought him to the notice of the practical men who exercised the real control inside the Admiralty. Thus when all the other candidates had been considered and passed over, this unknown sailor from the ranks, who was soon to become the greatest explorer of the age, was given the command and elevated to the rank of lieutenant.

It is a strange thing about Cook that one has the sense of knowing him very well, and yet at the same time it is difficult to describe him, to build up a picture of all those idiosyncrasies and peculiar qualities and attitudes of mind that make us feel we are really intimate with a man. We hardly know what he looked like. The portrait of him painted by Nathaniel Dance in 1776 and now in the National Maritime Museum at Greenwich is a posed and formal study, showing him at the height of his fame, with his wig, his white breeches and blue coat ornamented with gold lace and brass buttons, and his formal hat; a big man, with a large, steady face, and rather a tight and determined mouth,

A section of the map of the west coast of New-foundland surveyed by Captain Cook.

The painter of this portrait of Captain Cook is uncertain; it has been attributed to both William Hodges and Zoffany, artists respectively on his second and third voyages of discovery. In its strength and informality it conveys the seaman who could be stern and hot-tempered; the wry, open-minded observer of other cultures; the adventurer, and the practical, far-seeing navigator. It is the face of a man undaunted by the immensity of the Pacific or by the incalculable challenges of the unknown.

not a particularly brilliant officer, one would say, or one with any artistic accomplishments. But the eyes are patient and understanding, and while one might not have been very easy in his company he certainly inspires confidence.

The other accepted portrait attributed to Hodges, but possibly painted by Zoffany, is quite a different matter. Here we see an immensely attractive character, a suggestion of humour in his rugged face, a youthful out-of-doors man, an adventurer with a touch of wildness. Zoffany, if he really was the artist, may have made him a shade too theatrical, but his portrait is alive, one responds to it as one fancies one would have responded to Cook himself; with candour and with liking.

Turning from these conflicting impressions to the written records we are not much more enlightened. Not many of Cook's personal letters have survived, his logs are nearly always non-committal, at any rate as far as his own emotions and feelings are concerned, and surprisingly little was written about him by his shipmates and others who knew him well. Yet this very absence of testimony is possibly an indication of his strength; unlike Captain Bligh later on he is not a controversial figure whom everyone wants to talk about, no one challenges his authority, no one questions his decisions, and at the same time no one is his enemy. He sits so squarely in command of his ship, and

Some account of Georges Island

care that her country people should not know what she had done, so that what ever may be the reason for this Custom, it certainly affects their outward manner more than their principals.

Of their Persons

With respect to their Persons the Men in general are tall, strong limb'd & well shaped one of the Tallest we saw measured 6 feet 3 Inches & a half the superior women are in every respect as large as Europeans, but the inferior sort are in general small owing possibly to their early Amours which they are more addicted to than their superiors. they are of various colours those of the inferior sort who are obliged to be much exposed to the Sun & Air are of a very dark brown the Superiors again who spend most of their time in their Houses or under Shelter are not browner than people who are born or reside long in the W.t Indies, nay some of the Women are almost as fair as Europeans, their Hair is almost universally black thick & strong but the Women wear short cropt round their Ears, the Men on the other hand wear it different ways the better sort let it grow long sometimes tying it up on the top of their Heads, or letting it hang loose over their Shoulders, but many of the inferiors & such who in the Exercise of their professions, fishing &c. are obliged to be much upon or in the Water wear it cropt short like the Women, they always pluck out a part of their beards & keep that, that remains neat & Clean, both Sexes eradicate every hair from under their Arm pits & look upon it as a Mark of uncleanliness in us that we do not do the same, they have all fine White Teeth & for the most part short flat noses & thick Lips yet their features are agreable, & their gate graceful & their behaviour to Strangers & to each other is open Affable & Courteous & from all I could see free from Treachery only that they are thieves to a Man & would steal but every thing that came in their way & that with such dexterity as would shame the most noted pick Pocket in Europe, they are a very cleanly people both in their Persons & Diet always washing their hands & mouth immediately before & after their Meals & wash & bathe themselves in fresh Water three times a day, morning, noon, & night, the only disagreeable thing about them is the Oil with which they annoint their heads, Monoë as they call it this is made of Cocoa nut oil in which some sweet herbs or Flowers are infused the oil is generally very rancid which makes the wearer of it smell not very agreable. another custom they have that is disagreeable to Europeans which is eating Lice a pretty good stock of which they genr-ally carry about them however, this Custom is not universal, for I seldom saw it done but among Children & common people & I am per-

Extract of a page from Cook's journal describing the physical aspect of the Tahitians. Cook's entries showed a consistent objectivity and control. But, off the page, he could give way to vigorous expression and bursts of rage. His midshipman referred to them as 'heivas' after the expressive Tahitian dance.

its adventures, he is so fair, so undemonstrative and so unafraid, that he is accepted and respected by his contemporaries as a matter of course and no comment is necessary; he is simply there, an older and steadier man than all the rest, almost a father-figure to his crew; they cannot think of the *Endeavour* going anywhere without him.

He himself writes like a commander. He has a practical workmanlike style, nothing really shocks him or amazes him, and he is interested in everything from the last detail about the weevils in the ship's biscuits to the more esoteric habits of the Patagonians. He is simply concerned to cover all the facts and to get them right, and when occasionally he does speculate about his discoveries he always prefaces his remarks by saying that it is possible that he may be wrong. But he is not often wrong, nor does much escape the dragnet of that steady commonsense. Beyond this it is entertaining to see from his writings how, as the voyage goes on, his interests expand with it. From the practical navigator he begins to develop into the amateur naturalist and anthropologist, and always when he is dealing with coloured people he is without prejudice. He has his own code for himself and his ship, and he sticks to it, but he does not attempt to lay down this code for anybody else. He takes people as he finds them, and he is deeply interested in them. He possesses that fundamental curiosity of the real explorer who does not necessarily want to arrive at some goal but who is driven on and on, always eager to see the other side of the next hill, and only infinity is the end.

About his private life one wonders. As with Livingstone in Africa it virtually ceased to exist and his passion for exploration took over almost entirely. Yet like Livingstone he married, and although their existence grows fainter and fainter as he retires into the distance, he loves his family, he works for them, he wants them to be there in the background. His wife was Elizabeth Batts of Shadwell, the only daughter of a modest provincial family, and he had married her six years before this present voyage began. In her seventeen years of marriage to Cook she was only to see him at intervals of several years and barely for a year at a time. All her six children as well as Cook himself predeceased her. But of these distresses we hear from Cook himself not a word.

The crew of the *Endeavour* was much as one would have expected; men of humble backgrounds who had either volunteered or had been impressed into the Navy, and most of them were already experienced in the fearfully hard life at sea. Zachary Hicks, the second in command, was ten years Cook's junior, John Gore, the third officer, had already sailed in the *Dolphin* with Wallis, and the rest of the company of seventy included a surgeon, a clerk, forty able seamen, a number of midshipmen and eight servants. Twelve marines were added to protect the crew on shore. Then there were the scientists appointed by the Royal Society: the astronomer Charles Green and a group of naturalists and artists led by Joseph Banks. Now we know a great deal about Banks. In later years he was to become a very celebrated man indeed, the virtual dictator of scientific affairs in England, the president of the Royal Society for nearly half a century, the rich and generous patron of innumerable activities, the confidant of a fashionable and intellectual world in London that was perhaps more brilliant than it was ever to be again. He was painted many times, his correspondence was enormous, he had a finger in every scientific pie; in short, he was a public man.

The indefatigable Joseph Banks

Banks's influence on the planning of the *Endeavour* voyage has been under-estimated. Educated at Oxford, he had already been on one journey of exploration on HMS *Niger* in 1766 collecting rocks, plants and fauna in Labrador and Newfoundland, and he was elected a Fellow of the prestigious Royal Society of London that year. He was one of four Fellows to petition the king to provide a vessel for a voyage to the Pacific and it was Banks who convinced, first the Royal Society's Council and secondly the Admiralty, that the thrust to biological exploration and anthropological investigation should be added to the prime aims of the expedition. His private fortune and recruitment of his own scientific and artistic team made these purposes possible. Throughout the long journey he took responsibility for the company's 'watering' and for much of its communication with the native inhabitants. His journals became a major source of information on the historic voyage. 'Banks as usual,' Cook scribbled of him, 'explored, botanized, conversed.'

Joseph Banks, the youthful botanist and naturalist whose personal and financial investment in the Endeavour *expedition brought a treasure-trove of scientific findings back to England. Portrayed here by Benjamin Wise, he is surrounded by trophies of the voyage, the native artifacts, collecting net, and flower illustrations at his feet.*

What we have to consider here, however, is Banks as he was when all this lay in the future. He was only twenty-five when the *Endeavour* sailed from England, and great wealth (he had £6,000 a year from his country estates) had combined with good looks and a buoyant, affable nature to turn him into the very prototype of the *beau jeune homme* setting out on the grand tour from eighteenth-century England. He had the easy likeable manners of Eton and Oxford, but he was not a fop in any way, nor yet an intellectual nor a coming politician; he was an immensely enthusiastic amateur botanist, a genuine dilettante of natural history. His energy was inexhaustible, and his wealth gave him the opportunity to spread his wings. He had contributed £10,000 to the expedition, so it was said, and he had brought on board the *Endeavour* a personal

Sydney Parkinson, draughtsman and prolific writer

Sydney Parkinson was the first European painter to land in Tahiti. Born in Edinburgh in 1745, the son of a Quaker, he had been apprenticed to a wool draper, but his keen interest in botanical drawing took him to London and into the employment of Joseph Banks. Banks chose him as botanical draughtsman for the *Endeavour* voyage but, with the death in Tahiti of the expedition's topographical draughtsman Alexander Buchan, the youthful Parkinson assumed responsibility for the entire record of plants, places, people and fauna. His sketches and drawings totalled some 1,300 and he also compiled vocabularies of the natives of Tahiti and New Holland. Parkinson died at sea on 26 January 1771, one of the many victims of the fever that struck the homewardbound *Endeavour* company at Batavia. All his work was marked by a lightness and precision of detail and colour, as unique as his written observations.

A VIEW of the ENDEAVOUR'S Watering-place in the Bay of GOOD SUCCESS

suite of no fewer than eight persons: his Swedish friend Dr Daniel Carl Solander, who was a pupil and correspondent of Linnaeus and a botanist of distinction; two artists, the landscapist Alexander Buchan and the natural history draughtsman, Sydney Parkinson; a scientific secretary named Herman Spöring and four servants, including two Negroes; and two greyhounds. The party was accompanied by such a mass of equipment, of scientific books and general baggage, that it is something of a wonder how they all managed to stow themselves away in the *Endeavour*. Banks had a cabin to himself alongside Cook on the main deck.

All this was very grand, and there was no question whatever about the social hierarchy on board: Banks and his young friends were the travelling gentlemen, they supplied the social *chic* and the elevated conversation; Cook was the sailor who sailed the ship. It was a situation that could have been explosive, but from the first all went well; a genuine liking sprang up between the young dilettante and the steady Yorkshire captain who was fifteen years his senior. Cook soon made his authority felt, and the exciting nature of the voyage itself left little room for dissension. In any case, it was the navigation and the handling of the ship that were going to count on this enterprise, and here Cook's ability was beyond all dispute. His experiences in the coal trade on the east coast of England had made him an expert at dealing with unbuoyed, unlighted

ABOVE
A view of the Endeavour's *watering place in the Bay of Good Success, Patagonia, en route to Tahiti, drawn by the topographical artist Alexander Buchan. Buchan died from an epileptic fit soon after the ship's arrival at Tahiti.*

LEFT
The ship that stamped an ocean. Originally it was a Whitby collier, the Earl of Pembroke, *which the Admiralty aptly renamed the* Endeavour. *Among her advantages was the large cabin midships – the 'Great Cabin' – she provided for Banks and his scientific party. This oil painting is supposedly by Thomas Luny.*

tidal waters, and it was no accident that the Admiralty had chosen for his ship a three-masted Whitby collier. She was of 373 tonnes (368 tons), 31.8 m (106 ft) long, 8.7 m 7.5 cm (29 ft 3 in) in the beam and she had been specially fitted for the work of exploration. She could make seven or eight knots at the best, but speed hardly mattered on a voyage which was to last two or three years. The things that counted were that she was sturdy, she had a relatively shallow draught – 4.2 m (14 ft) – she had been sheathed against the boring worm, the *Teredo navalis*, of tropical waters, and she carried twelve swivel guns.

It is, of course, growing increasingly hard in this machine age to understand what it was like to be on a long voyage under sail in the eighteenth century; the monotonous uneventful days, the absence (in the Pacific) of *any* other European ships at sea, the sense of leaving civilization far away behind, perhaps never to be regained. They sailed from Plymouth in August 1768, and towards the end of the year they called at Rio de Janeiro. That was their last contact with the known world. The days drifted away, punctuated by storms, by the catching of sharks and dolphins, by the shooting of birds, by the minutiae of the little happenings on board that make a ship a world in itself. Officers and gentlemen messed together in the Great Cabin which lay directly over the high, square-built stern (it reminded one a little of a Spanish galleon), and here from 8 a.m. to 2 p.m. and then again after dinner until dusk Banks and his party worked at classifying and drawing the specimens they were constantly gathering from the sea and from their various landfalls along the route. Whenever there was a calm they put out in the ship's boats to net marine life and to fish, but for the most part they sailed steadily southward, moving out of the northern winter into the tropics and down into the southern summer. Banks notes in his journal:

'Christmas Day all good Christians, that is to say all hands, got abominably drunk so that at night there was scarce a sober man in the ship; wind, thank God, very moderate or the Lord knows what would have become of us.'

(Cook's own reference is more laconic: 'Yesterday being Christmas Day the People were none of the soberest.')

Then they were in the gales and the bitter cold of Cape Horn, the region of whales, penguins and seals, and the men put on their woollen Fearnought jackets. It was discovered on landing on Tierra del Fuego that Buchan, the artist, was rather a liability – he had an epileptic fit – and Bank's two Negro servants, Richmond and Dalton, got drunk on an excursion ashore and were frozen to death – an event they all seem to have accepted very philosophically. Then they were moving north, back into the vast unexplored tropics of the Pacific, with the albatrosses swinging about in the wake of the ship.

They ate tolerably well. A goat that had already circumnavigated the world with Wallis in the *Dolphin* provided the wardroom with a little fresh milk, they had wine (picked up in Madeira) and spirits, and occasionally they caught fish or slaughtered one of the pigs or cows they had brought with them. The basic diet was salt pork and biscuit, and they got heartily sick of it, especially when the weevils began to multiply, but Cook went to great lengths to keep the ship free of scurvy by forcing the men to eat vegetables – chiefly preserved sauerkraut – and by the regular airing and washing out of the sleeping quarters.

Naturally there were some discontents on board. One young sailor accused of theft was so harried by his shipmates that he threw himself overboard, and the midshipman, Bootie, was not altogether happy. We find him heading his private log with 'By John Bootie, Master's Brute'. Elsewhere he writes, 'Evil communications corrupt good manners. N. Young is a son of a bitch.' Poor young Bootie, he was to die like so many others before the journey's end.

Every few weeks Cook ordered the punishment of twelve lashes for some misdemeanour. But this was no hell-ship of impressed men, they were all young (the average age was under thirty), and if we are to judge by the log-books and the letters that have survived they were all eager for the adventure that lay ahead. Whether or not they were going to comprehend it was, of course, another matter. One has to remember the background of most of the *Endeavour*'s crew: the cold dark dockyard streets of the English ports, the frigidities of poverty, the coarseness and insecurity of the working man's life in the eighteenth century. Certainly they had seen nothing like Tahiti before. The blacks – the Indians – were for them rather closer to animals than to human beings, Protestant and English conventions were a fixture in their minds, and nothing in their education, such as it was, had prepared them for the relaxed conditions of a tropical island. Banks himself, in his frogged waistcoat and white breeches, and with all his enthusiasm and his open-mindedness, was removed by ages of sophistication from the scene that now lay before him, and even for Cook this was his first experience in the tropics.

He was ahead of time; early in April 1769 he was cruising through the Tuamotu archipelago, and on 11 April Tahiti was sighted from the topmast. They spent the next two days beating up to the island and then, in a fever of impatience to get ashore, they were on their goal at least. 'The land,' Parkinson says, 'appeared as uneven as a piece of crumpled paper.'

Fern trees, part of the rich vegetation that skirted Matavai Bay, rising like pennants on the wind. From a drawing by George Tobin.

The flat site Cook would develop at the end of the Bay as Fort Venus. Painting by William Hodges.

So now we must envisage the storm–battered little ship edging her way into Matavai Bay in the hot morning light, with the crew gazing ashore at the bright green hills and valleys, the mountain peaks rising behind with clouds about them, and on the calm water in the lagoon the native canoes coming out to meet them. The *Endeavour*'s men had been cooped up on board, entirely deprived of women and almost continuously out of sight of land, for eight

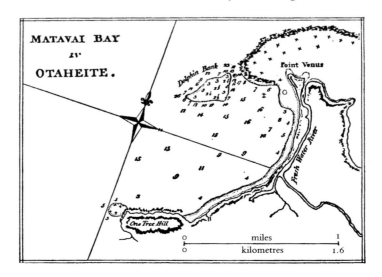

months, and it must have been a wonderful thing at that moment to anticipate the feel of ground beneath their feet again, and to have the prospect of fresh food and perhaps even (no doubt they had discussed the matter a good deal) the possibility of making love to the voluptuous Tahitian girls. Nor can there have been much less of a commotion among the Tahitians themselves. They might perhaps have been compared to village children at the arrival of a travelling circus; they came forward to the encounter with a sort of timid, wondering excitement, eager to see the show, ready to be amazed, but a little fearful of approaching too close until they were sure that all was well.

Dr J. C. Beaglehole, of Wellington University, writes:

'It is difficult for us now to measure the impact on a Polynesian island in that day of a European vessel with its iron, and its physically repressed prostitute-accustomed sailors. Many a more modern community has been rocked in wartime and in peace by the presence of a visiting fleet.'

As in all moments of true drama, there was an element of doubt and hesitation in the air, a last hanging-back from the actual impact. Cook approached the shore very cautiously, sending his pinnace ahead to reconnoitre, and closely watching the oncoming canoes. Soon Gore, the lieutenant who had sailed with Wallis, saw several acquaintances among the natives, notably an old man named Owhaa. They were waving and smiling – they recognized him. Cook had them on board and 'made much of them'. Without incident the *Endeavour* anchored quietly off the beach.

The superb haven of Matavai Bay, Tahiti. Cook's biographer, Beaglehole, writes: 'One sees a perfect curve, beyond and above it the cleft uneven lines of the nearer ridges; beyond them again, the great form of the mountain, its shoulders and steep flanks falling away still hung with green, the peak of Orofena.' In this painting by William Hodges, the site of Fort Venus established for observing the transit is seen on the point to the left; the foreground contains a variety of Tahitian canoes, large single and double sailing canoes, the small outrigger paddling canoe, and war canoes with their warriors in ceremonial dress.

Venus observed

MATAVAI BAY has altered somewhat in the last two centuries. The river, 3.6 m (12 ft) wide, that fell into the sea at the eastern end in Cook's time has since become a backwater, and on Venus Point a road now leads down to a light-house and a group of modern huts. They give the place the vague air of a picnic ground. But for the rest the scene is marvellously unchanged. One sees the same empty black-sand beach, fringed with coconut palms, the *Endeavour*'s anchorage, and beyond the lagoon the long Pacific swell breaking on the reef. It agitates the heavy air with a light thunder that never ceases; it is the last thing you hear at night and it is still there in the morning.

The palms are extraordinarily tall and are not straight but curve far out over the beach and the lagoon, and it is a wonder that their thin tangled roots, constantly washed by the tide, can ever support them. The cats that Cook landed on Tahiti seem to have done no good since every tree is encircled with a metal band to prevent the local rats from getting at the coconuts. The bread-fruit grows a little further inland, and these are fine, big trees with broad, waxy leaves shaped like a man's hand. The fruit is a green globe about the size of a small watermelon, and it hangs down from the branches like a Chinese lantern. Everywhere bright green grass spreads away and one is never out of the sight of flowering shrubs and creepers – the red hibiscus, the frangipani, the little white *tiare Tahiti*, the yellow jasmine. There is no end to the flowers, and always you see them against the deep tropical green of the jungle.

This jungle, split by the flash of cataracts and waterfalls, rises up the sides of the valleys inland until it vanishes in the drifting clouds of the mountains 2,100 m (7,000 ft) above. Sometimes a rainstorm will blow up from the sea and it blots out the neighbouring island of Moorea. But it is gone in a few minutes and in the sunshine, heavily scented perfumes come up from the wet earth. The bay itself is a shallow curve only 1.6–3.2 km (1–2 miles) in length, but a

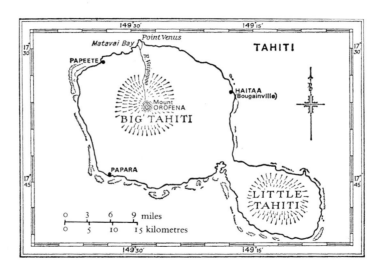

hill at its western end blocks the view of the modern port of Papeete, and the traveller standing on the beach can be quite alone. Thus he can very easily be transported back to 1769 and in imagination see the *Endeavour* riding in the lagoon.

Cook had every reason to be cautious, since Wallis in the *Dolphin* had had a very rough reception here two years before. The Tahitians had at first pretended to be friendly, but when two of the *Dolphin*'s boats had gone ahead to find an anchorage they had been set upon with stones and spears, and Wallis had been forced to open fire, killing one man and wounding another. That was the first gunfire the Tahitians had ever heard, and it must have been a terrifying and miraculous thing for them to have seen men struck down at a distance. Yet for several days more they had opposed the *Dolphin*'s landing with a force of 500 canoes and 4,000 men and had attempted to get possession of the ship. It had been a curious business, the Tahitians by turns making a show of peace and offering to trade and then hauling off to renew the attack. According to George Robertson, the *Dolphin*'s Master, they had tried to lure the crew of the ship's cutter ashore by displaying 'a good many fine girls' on the beach and in their canoes. This sight, he says, 'attracted our men's fancy a good deal, and the natives, observing it, made the young girls play a great many droll, wanting (*sic*) tricks.' In the Homeric tradition the sailors had stuck to their oars, but the *Dolphin*, following the cutter in through the coral reef, had run aground, and still further skirmishes had ensued before the ship had been safely anchored and the islanders had accepted defeat. Among their wounded had been a young man named Omai of whom we are to hear a good deal more later on.

Thereafter the *Dolphin*'s stay had been indescribably pleasant, and Wallis had

Captain Samuel Wallis received a rough reception by the Tahitians when he entered Matavai Bay two years before Cook. Their hostility, however, soon turned to friendship and the frail and sickly Wallis enjoyed a five-week reprieve from his journey tenderly ministered to by Queen Obarea.

Queen Obarea and her ladies present a frond, the emblem of friendship, to Captain Wallis and his officers. 'Thereafter the Dolphin's stay had been indescribably pleasant.' Engraving by J. Hall.

made a particular friend of a woman named Obarea who was apparently the queen of the island.

So now Cook warned his crew to be on guard, but at the same time to 'endeavour by every fair means to cultivate a friendship with the natives and to treat them with all imaginable humanity'. Then with a party of officers and scientists he disembarked. Banks tells us:

'As soon as the anchors were well down the boats were hoisted out, and we all went ashore, where we were met by some hundreds of the inhabitants, whose faces at least gave evident signs that we were not unwelcome guests.'

But the Tahitians were afraid at first. They came creeping forward almost on their hands and knees to offer green boughs, their token of peace. Very soon, however, they became more confident and conducted the strangers up the beach and into the plantations. Banks goes on:

'In this manner, we proceeded for four or five miles [6–8 km], under groves of coconut and breadfruit trees, loaded with a profusion of fruit, and giving the most grateful shade I have ever experienced. Under these were the habitations of the people, most of them without walls; in short, the scene that we saw was the truest picture of an Arcadia, of which we were going to be king, that the imagination can form.'

So far so good. The opening scene is set: the gentlemen go strolling through the tropical garden distributing beads and small presents to the respectful, smiling natives, and there were to be no two minds about who were to be masters on the island. But complications were to follow. Let us for a moment follow Cook's log. On 14 April, the day after the *Endeavour*'s arrival, we get this entry:

'This morning we had a great many canoes about the ship, the most of them came from the westward but brought nothing with them but a few coconuts etc. Two that appeared to be chiefs we had on board together with several others for it was a hard matter to keep them out of the ship as they climb like monkeys, but it was harder still to keep them from stealing but everything that came within their reach, and in this they are prodigious expert.'

It was the same when they were ashore:

'Here the natives flocked around us in great numbers in as friendly a manner as we could wish, only that they showed a great inclination to pick our pockets. We were conducted to a chief who I shall call Lycurgus. This man entertained us with broiled fish, bread-fruit, coconut etc. with great hospitality, and all the time took care to tell us to take care of our pockets, as a great number of people had crowded about us. Notwithstanding the care we took, Dr Solander and Dr Monkhouse each had their pockets picked, the one of his spy-glass and the other of his snuff-box.'

One envisages the scene in that warm enervating air: the food spread out on banana leaves on the ground, the Englishmen in their heavy uniforms squatting awkwardly on their mats, and endeavouring with their smiles and gestures to put themselves and their hosts at ease; and all around them among the coconut palms the islanders staring and staring, following their every move and intonation of voice with the rapt absorption of children at a pantomime. Then the quick, deft snatch of the spy-glass and the snuff-box.

It was extremely provoking. Banks in particular had been very liberal; in exchange for a present of a length of cloth he had taken off his laced silk neck-cloth and had given it to the chief together with his linen handkerchief. Beads and hatchets had been distributed galore, and in return they had had this excellent lunch where Banks had felt so much at ease that he had been able to entice a pretty girl 'with fire in her eyes' to sit beside him. He now got up, made a threatening gesture with his gun and angrily demanded the return of the stolen belongings. In an instant all smiles vanished; most of the crowd fled in panic and the chief, with great emotion, took Banks by the hand and led him to his store of precious cloth in one of the huts, indicating by signs that the Englishmen were to take all they wanted. But no, Banks insisted, they wanted the spy-glass and the snuff-box, and after a confused series of dealings they eventually got them back. Now all was harmony again, and in an excess of cordiality both sides pressed further presents upon one another.

'About six o'clock in the evening,' Cook says, 'we returned on board well satisfied with our little excursion.'

This incident was to be repeated again and again, and on more serious occasions than this and on other Pacific islands as well as Tahiti – indeed, it was just such an affair that, eventually, was going to lead to the death of Cook himself on Hawaii. A point of principle, or, if you like taboo, was involved. It was no more possible for the islanders to keep their hands off the Europeans' belongings than it was for the Europeans to abandon their rule that private property was sacred. Like small boys the Tahitians wanted to rob the orchard; felt, in fact, that they *had* to rob the orchard, almost as a matter of personal pride, and somehow not get found out. Only the force of firearms could stop them, and when those firearms were inevitably used, the Tahitians were hurt, bewildered and reduced to crying for forgiveness. This was the first step in the tragedy that lay ahead.

However none of this was as yet apparent, and Cook felt secure enough to establish himself on shore. He had seven weeks in hand before the transit of Venus, and he decided to build a fort where his instruments could be set up and where he could trade with the natives for the fresh food he so badly needed. He chose a site on the beach at the north-east end of Matavai Bay which seemed to be of no value to the Tahitians – there were no huts close by – and at the same time, in the event of trouble, it could be covered by the *Endeavour*'s guns. The river, the Vaipopoo, that ran into the sea at this point would provide them with all the fresh water they wanted.

On the morning of 15 April a party was sent ashore, and they erected a tent and marked out the ground that was to be occupied. Cook tried to explain to the crowds of Tahitians who were watching in a transport of curiosity that they should not trespass on this area, and even if they did not quite understand they seemed to take the matter with good humour. Leaving a petty officer and a squad of marines on guard Cook then set off with Banks, Solander and the astronomer Green for another walk through the plantations. The crowds followed. We have several accounts of what next occurred. Here is Cook's:

'We had but just crossed the river when Mr Banks shot three ducks at one shot, which surprised them [the Tahitians] so much that most of them fell down as though they had been shot likewise. I was in hopes this would have had some good effect, but the event did not prove it, for we had not been gone long from the tent before the natives again began to gather about it, and one of them, more daring than the rest, pushed one of the sentinels down, snatched the musket out of his hand and made a push at him, and then made off, and with him, all the rest. Immediately upon this the officer ordered the party to fire and the man who took the musket was shot dead before he had got far off from the tent, but the musket was quite carried off.'

Hastening back to the beach Cook found the Tahitians had decamped in a body.

Sydney Parkinson was also ashore and he tells a somewhat different and grimmer story:

'A boy, a midshipman, was the commanding officer, and, giving orders to fire, they [the men] obeyed with the greatest glee imaginable, as if they had been shooting at wild ducks, killed one stout man and wounded many others. What a pity that such brutality should be exercised by civilized people upon unarmed ignorant Indians!' He adds: 'The natives fled into the woods like frighted fawns . . . terrified to the last degree.'

Banks's account is as follows:

'The midshipman, maybe imprudently, ordered the marines to fire, which they did, into the thickest of the flying crowd, some hundreds in number, and pursuing the man who had stolen the musket, killed him. Whether any others were killed or hurt no one could tell.'

One rather fancies that Cook, with his official version of the incident, was

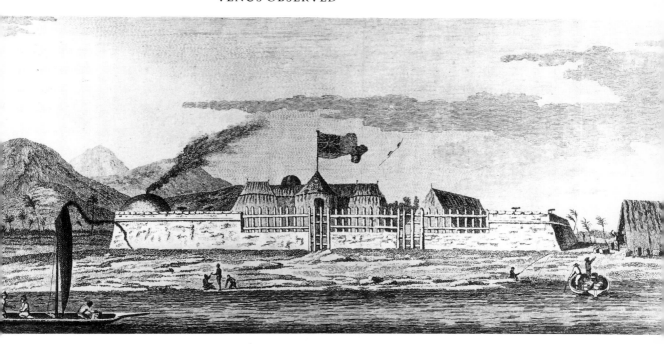

ABOVE
*Fort Venus, built by the
Endeavour's company to
secure the astronomical
and measuring instru-
ments for recording the
transit of Venus across
the sun on 3 June 1769.
From an engraving
by S. Middiman after
Parkinson.*

LEFT
The plan of Fort Venus.

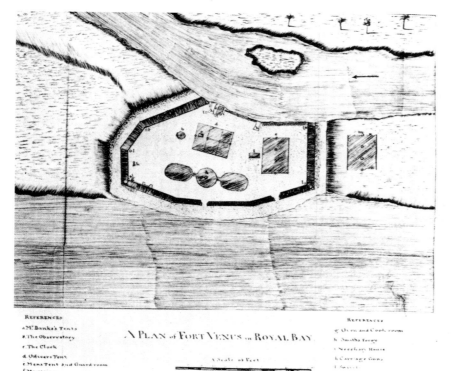

REFERENCES
a M.ʳ Banks's Tents
b The Observatory
c The Clock
d Observers Tent
e Mens Tent And Guard room
f Magazine

A PLAN of FORT VENUS in ROYAL BAY.

A Scale of Feet

REFERENCES
g Oven and Cook room
h Smiths Forge
i Necesary House
k Carriage Guns
l Swivels
m Coopers and Sailmakers tent

covering up for the midshipman and his men, and that, out of fear perhaps, as
well as a certain arrogance, the guard lost their heads. At all events it was the
worst possible thing to have happened at this fragile moment, and Cook and
his companions had great difficulty in persuading the terrified Tahitians to
come out of hiding and to parley. Using old Owhaa as a go-between, they

explained that the stealing of the musket was a serious thing, that the shooting would never have otherwise occurred, that there was no longer any danger. At length about twenty of the islanders were induced to come and sit in the tent and peace was made. Towards nightfall the tent was struck and without further incident the *Endeavour*'s men came back on board.

But the shock had not quite subsided as yet. No canoes put out to the ship next day, an apprehensive silence hung about the beach, and it was not until the evening when Cook went ashore that the islanders began to reappear. The breach was finally healed on the following day when several of the chiefs came out to the *Endeavour* with banana branches and a present of two pigs and breadfruit. Cook handed out two more hatchets and now felt that he could get on with his plans for the fort. With Green and a party of men he came ashore and again erected his tent. In it they spent the night without disturbance.

Quite apart from the shooting it had been a trying few days; Alexander Buchan, the landscape artist, had been seized with another epileptic fit, and after lying unconscious for forty-eight hours without regaining consciousness had died. His body was committed to the sea, a surprising procedure to the Tahitians whose own dead man had been laid out in a special hut, there to rot until his bones were dry, surrounded by offerings of food. Since Parkinson was more of a scientific draughtsman than an artist in general, the chance of our seeing competent pictures of Cook and his men on Tahiti were gone for ever.

But now the building of the fort went briskly forward. As many men as could be spared from the ship, about forty-five of them, were brought on shore and put to work. Not realizing that it was designed against themselves, the Tahitians offered to help. On the western-seaward side a 1.2 m (4 ft) bank was thrown up with a palisade of posts on top (and Cook paid for the trees he cut down). On the north and south there was a similar bank with a ditch outside, 3 m (10 ft) wide and 1.8 m (6 ft deep), and on the east, fronting the river, a double row of ships' casks was planted. Since this eastern side was the weakest, two 1.8 kg (4 lb) guns were established there. In the fort itself six tents were set up, one for the ship's company, another for Cook and the officers, others for an observatory and for Banks and his party. A large copper oven was brought from the ship, together with a forge, and equipment for the cooper and the sailmaker.

The work was impeded by daily showers of rain, but by 1 May all was finished and a quadrant and the other astronomical instruments were brought on shore.

These must have been wonderful days. Banks had set himself up as the expedition's liaison officer with the natives, and every morning at the gate of the fort he purchased with nails and beads quantities of coconuts, breadfruit and occasionally pigs and fowls. Relations with the islanders had so much improved that one of the chiefs moved his hut close by so that he and his women could dine regularly with the Englishmen. The *Endeavour*'s crew were delighted to be on land and everyone was busy and healthy. And now, securely ensconced in his fort, with his ship anchored alongside, fresh water at his front door and food in abundance, Cook was as snug and as safe from attack as Robinson Crusoe. Banks in fact felt so secure that he thought nothing of spending the night among the Tahitians. He notes in his diary:

'I lay in the woods last night as I often do. At daybreak I was called by Mr Gore and went with him shooting. We did not return till night . . .'

There had been just one incident. The chief Tubourai, whom Banks and Cook had originally called Lycurgus, and who had now become a fast friend, came to them one day in great distress saying that the *Endeavour*'s butcher, a certain Henry Jeffs, had threatened to cut his wife's throat with a reaping hook. She had apparently refused to part with a stone axe that Jeffs wanted, and he had whirled the hook about her head. Cook took a very serious view of this. He brought Tubourai and his wife on board and in their presence the butcher was stripped and fastened to the rigging. At the first stroke of the cat-o-nine tails the Tahitians burst into tears and implored Cook to let the man off the rest of his punishment – 'A request,' says Banks, 'which the Captain would not comply with.'

Nearly three weeks had now elapsed since the *Endeavour*'s arrival, and the sailors and the Tahitians were entering a much more intimate relationship. Cook drove his men hard and they were only off duty on Sunday afternoons after divine service, but that left them sufficient time to meet the very willing Tahitian women, even though they had to be back inside the fort or on board ship at nightfall. 'Queen' Obarea had appeared and had become a favourite of Banks and the *Endeavour*'s officers; she seems always to have been about the fort with her retainers. Cook found her 'very masculine', by which he probably meant aggressive, Parkinson thought she was 'a fat, bouncing, good-looking dame', and Banks, who had his eye on her young handmaidens, describes her as,

'about forty, tall and very lusty, her skin white and her eyes full of meaning; she might have been handsome when young but now few or no traces of it were left.'

Heads of Tahitians from a lost drawing by Sydney Parkinson. The top three beauties may well have been Obarea's 'hand-maidens', so appealing to young Banks. Engraving by Thomas Chambers after Parkinson.

A woman and a boy from an engraving by Thomas Chambers after Parkinson. It shows the poncho or draped shirt worn over the upper part of the body. The poncho frequently glowed crimson and gold.

Natives fishing on the shore looking towards Matavai.

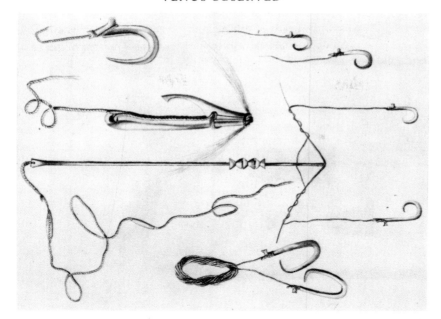

Fish hooks from Tahiti. The Tahitians developed a great variety made from shells and human bones.

Then there was the mass of the common people, never less than about 300 of them, clustering around the fort like camp followers, and always wanting to attract attention whether by their songs and dances, by offering themselves as guides and companions or by bartering their goods.

It was a scene of crimson and gold – those were the colours in which the Tahitians most liked to dye their clothes; the *pareu*, the sarong-like skirt which they draped round their waists and the *tiputa*, the poncho or shirt which was worn over the upper part of the body. Only the children were naked.

Banks loved to watch these people swimming in the sea and he gives us the first known description of surfing in the Pacific:

'Whenever a surf broke near them they dived under it with infinite ease, rising up on the other side; but their chief amusement was being carried on by an old canoe; with this before them they swam out as far as the outermost beach, then one or two would get into it, and opposing the blunt end to the breaking wave, were hurried in with incredible swiftness. Sometimes they were carried almost ashore . . . We stood admiring this very wonderful scene for fully half an hour . . .'

Banks is a mine of information about the artifacts and the small daily habits of the Tahitians. He tells us of the fish hooks that were made from shells and human bones, and of the lines that were woven from jungle creepers. Then there were the nets and traps for lobsters and crabs. The food of the island was very good and varied: at an average meal a chief would consume two or three breadfruit, several fish and twelve or more bananas, and this was served to him with some ceremony. First he would wash, then fresh leaves would be spread upon the ground with a half coconut shell of fresh water on one side and another of salt water on the other. During the meal a man would drink about half a litre of salt water, taking sips between each mouthful and dipping each morsel of his food into it. The fish would be served to him wrapped in leaves and would be eaten cooked or raw. Then, at the end, he would again rinse his mouth and wash his hands.

Breadfruit, drawn here by George Tobin, was the staple diet of the Tahitians, with fish and bananas. Its soft flesh was both filling and refreshing and was often dipped into salt water before eating. The Tahitians, surprisingly, consumed 0.25 litre ($\frac{1}{2}$ pint) of salt water with their meals.

The *Endeavour*'s crew thought the baked dishes were more delicious than any they had ever eaten. The oven consisted of a hole in the ground into which hot stones were placed with a layer of green leaves on top. The meat, usually a small pig, was then placed in the hole and overlaid with another layer of leaves and hot stones and the oven was then sealed with earth. The roast that emerged an hour or two later contained all its natural juices. There was then (but now no more) a race of native dogs on Tahiti, and Cook and his companions fell back a little when they were offered roast dog for dinner one day. Yet when they tried it they found it delicious, no doubt because the animals were vegetarians. 'There were few,' Cook wrote, 'but allowed that a South Sea dog was next to an English lamb.' There was also a little apple growing on the island and the *Endeavour*'s cook produced passable apple pies.

And so little by little the sailors and the islanders, eating the same food, seeing the same scenes, and caught up together in the routine of the long hot day, were beginning to know one another. The Tahitians found it impossible to pronounce Cook's name but 'Toote' served well enough, and Banks was known as 'Tapane'. The English on their side never grasped that in Tahitian the sound of 'o' was the article sometimes affixed to proper names, and so the correct spelling was not Otaheite or Otahiti as they thought, but simply Tahi-ti. But this hardly mattered. It still seemed to the Tahitians that the Englishmen were rather dirty people since they did not pluck the hair under their armpits or bathe enough. To the Englishmen such practices as tattooing were bizarre and inexplicable – the covering of the skin with all kinds of dark designs, zigzags and arc-like lines drawn across the stomach (of which the Tahitians were particularly proud) and their buttocks disfigured entirely with a

The ritual of tattooing

The greatest subject for artistic bodily adornment in Tahiti was the skin itself. Tattooing was virtually compulsory for males and females and served a number of purposes. It denoted the arrival of puberty or that someone had gone through certain childhood rituals. It was an expression of beauty by marking the skin with birds, circles, trees and crescents. 'The ornaments follow the curvature of the body so gracefully,' Charles Darwin noted some eighty years later, 'that they have a very elegant effect.' Banks became so interested in the practice that he had a small tattoo sketched on the inside of one arm. The actual technique of tattooing remained the preserve of the priests. Tattooing combs (as seen on page 61) were precision instruments made of flat pieces of bone or shells with fine sharp needles (some fifteen or so), carved across the end. This working edge varied to create different designs. A stick-like handle was attached to the tattooing comb. To make a tattoo, the tips of the needles were dipped into a solution of water and fine carbon derived from the smoke of candlenuts. The needled edge was then placed against the skin and the wooden handle tapped with another stick driving the blackened points into the flesh. For the more extensive tattooing of the buttocks, the pain of the operation required that sections be done at a time. 'The arches upon the loins,' Banks noted, 'upon which they value themselves much . . . caused more pain.' Having observed a young girl undergoing this 'beautification' amid screams of suffering, he prudently reflected, 'Our European ladies have found the conveniences of patches!' The tradition of buttock-tattooing is no longer widely practised.

Tattooing design on buttocks. The designs were used on both men and women.

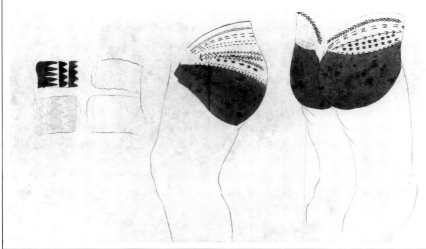

An example of buttock-tattooing, from a painting by William Hodges. 'To the Englishmen such practices were bizarre and inexplicable.

heavy impregnation of lamp-black. Banks one day came upon a fourteen-year-old girl spread out on the ground undergoing this operation upon her buttocks. The pain caused by the jabbing of the sharp bone was evidently excruciating, for the girl screamed and screamed; and days would elapse before her skin, now covered in blood, would be healed. But sailors it seems will try anything, and several of the *Endeavour*'s crew had their arms tattooed, thus becoming, as Dr Beaglehole points out, the founders of the time-honoured tradition of the tattooed sailor. Banks, of course, could not be left out of this and he had a design pricked into his arm.

It was not exactly a paradisical life they were all living; the men were worked very hard (as Cook afterwards confessed), everyone suffered from the flies and the unaccustomed heat, and no doubt there were squabbles and punishments which are not mentioned in the records. But it had been a good landfall, better than they could have hoped for; Fort Venus – the name was chosen with an eye on the planet rather than the goddess – was functioning well, and all around them the extreme beauty of the island must have had its effect on even the most hard-bitten and recalcitrant of the *Endeavour*'s crew.

These happy circumstances were abruptly shattered on 2 May. On making his rounds in the morning Cook discovered that the quadrant was missing. It was a very heavy instrument encased in a box about 45 cm (18 in) square, and it had been placed in the observatory tent with a sentry on duty all night. This man had seen and heard nothing. Now it was one thing for the Tahitians to make off with spy-glasses and snuff-boxes (and on one occasion they had even succeeded in prising out two of the ports from the *Endeavour*), but the theft of the quadrant was quite a different matter; it was absolutely essential for the astronomical observations they had come all this way to carry out. The alarm was raised at once, and one can imagine the beating of the drums, the comings and goings in the fort, the furious questionings of the Tahitians gathered at the gate. Cook gave orders that no canoe should be allowed to leave the harbour, and was preparing further reprisals when Tubourai drew Banks aside and revealed that he knew the thief and that he had taken to the hills. With Tubourai and some of his men as guides Banks, Green and a midshipman set off in pursuit. Banks says:

'At every house we passed Tubourai inquired after the thief by name, and the people readily told which way he had gone, and how long it was since he passed by, a circumstance which gave us great hopes of coming up with him. The weather was excessively hot, the thermometer before we left the tents was ninety-one degrees, which made our journey very tiresome. At times we walked, at times we ran, when we imagined (as we sometimes did) that the chase was just before us, till we arrived at the top of a hill about four miles [6.4 km] from the tents; from this place Tubourai showed us a point about three miles [4.8 km] off, and made us understand that we were not to expect the instrument till we got there.'

Here was a predicament. They were now entering the country of a quite different group of islanders whom they did not know, and they were armed only with a brace of pocket-pistols. It was resolved to send back the midshipman to Cook for reinforcements while the others pushed on. They had all but covered the 4.8 km (3 miles) when Banks was immensely relieved to see some of Tubourai's men who had gone on before them, hastening back with a part of the quadrant. A large party of the hill people were at their heels. Banks continues:

'We now stopped and many Indians gathered round us rather rudely; the sight of one of my pistols, however, instantly checked them, and they behaved with all the order imaginable, though we quickly had some hundred surrounding a ring we had marked out on the grass.'

The joke – and perhaps to the Tahitians it was no more than a joke – was now over and they realized it; one after another the missing parts of the quadrant were brought in and a quantity of other stolen property besides – reading glasses, a pistol case and so on. The quadrant was slightly damaged but it could easily be repaired. And so in high spirits they began the return and had covered about 3.2 km (2 miles) when at sunset they met Cook coming up the track with a squad of marines, and ready to do battle. When they all got back to the ship they found that Hicks had imprisoned as a hostage one of the chiefs, a man named Tootaha, and there was great lamentation among his followers who believed he was to be shot. Cook had him instantly released.

The next day there was an uneasy quiet around the fort and no one came to barter at the gate. But it was not in the Tahitian nature to keep up a grudge for long. Childlike, they wanted to be forgiven and to make friends again. An invitation arrived for the Englishmen to attend a banquet at one of the entertainment houses about 6.4 km (4 miles) up the coast, and Cook gladly accepted this chance of a reconciliation. He set off on foot with Banks and Solander. A huge concourse of people, some 500 in all, was making for the place and they had to be beaten back to make a path for the Englishmen. On arrival they found Tootaha, their erstwhile captive, sitting under a tree in a circle of old men, and there was an exchange of presents. This was followed by a wrestling match, a strange affair in which twelve men wearing only waistcloths paraded slowly round a courtyard making a loud booming noise by striking their left arms with their right hands. Presently the actual wrestling began, each man seeking any opponent who was convenient. The challenge was delivered by the contestants joining their fingers together and moving their elbows up and down, whereupon they clutched one another, either by the hands, the hair or the waistcloth, and struggled until one was flung down. This was the signal for the old men to break into a sort of laudatory chorus, and then the proceedings, says Cook, were always 'resumed again with great good humour'. The performance went on for two hours, and the only women allowed to be present were Obarea and her attendants. With so many people pressing around them the Englishmen found it excessively hot, and they were glad to get away at last. A banquet of roast pork was eaten with the chiefs back on board the *Endeavour*, and that evening the people flocked back to trade at the fort as before.

The performances of the *arioi* were not always as innocent as this wrestling match – innocent, that is to say, in the European sense. Their dancing displays were just as common and these were an uninhibited expression of sex. The band consisted of two instruments, a drum made of wood and sharkskin and a flute that was blown through one nostril, the other nostril being stopped with the thumb. The players never seemed to achieve more than six notes and they were accompanied by singers who repeated the same tune over and over again. Cook found this monotonous, the actual dancing rather less so. It was performed by young girls in groups of eight or ten:

'a very indecent dance which they called Timorodee, singing the most indecent songs and using most indecent actions in the practise of which they are brought up from the earliest childhood. In doing this they keep time to a great nicety.'

The girls, Cook adds, on growing older or on getting husbands abandoned dancing to the younger generation. But:

'both sexes express the most indecent ideas in conversation without the least emotion and they delight in such conversations beyond any other.'

This was a matter that was going to bedevil the reputation of Tahiti from that day to this. Were the Tahitians really licentious, and if so what harm did it do them? Robertson, the *Dolphin*'s Master, declared that the girls were prepared to make love at any time for the most trifling gifts; most of all they preferred ordinary carpenter's nails which they seemed to value as the Europeans value gold. There had been a commotion on board the *Dolphin* when it was discovered that the sailors were not only withdrawing nails from the ship's planks but had even filched the nails from which their hammocks were suspended so that most of them were sleeping on the deck.

Bougainville, in the previous year, had been captivated by the beauty, the innocence – and the willingness – of the Tahitian girls, and Philibert Commerson, the naturalist he had on board, had echoed his commander's enthusiasm. The Tahitians, Commerson declared, were '*sans vice, sans préjugés, sans besoins, sans dissensins*'; a people who '*ne connoissent d'autre Dieu que l'amour*'.

Distortions of the mouth used in Tahitian dancing. As Cook observed, the young girls and men danced singing 'most indecent words using most indecent actions and setting their mouths askew in the most extraordinary manner.'

Bougainville describes a lively incident that occurred when he first arrived at the island. The Tahitian men, he says,

'*pressed us to choose a woman and come ashore with her; and their gestures, which were nothing less than equivocal, denoted in what manner we should form an acquaintance with her. It was very difficult in such conditions, to keep at their work four hundred young French sailors who had not seen a woman for six months. In spite of all our precautions a young girl came on board and placed herself upon the quarter-deck near one of the hatchways, which was open in order to give air to those who were heaving at the capstan below it. The girl carelessly dropped a cloth which covered her, and appeared to the eyes of all beholders such as Venus showed herself to the Phyrgian shepherd, having, indeed, the celestial form of that goddess. Both sailors and soldiers endeavoured to come to the hatchway, and the capstan was never hove with more alacrity than on this occasion. At last our discipline succeeded in keeping these bewitched fellows in order, though it was no less difficult to keep command of ourselves.*'

Then, when the French had come ashore, they were

'*invited to enter the houses where the people gave them to eat; nor did the civility of their landlords stop at a slight collation: they offered them young girls. The hut was immediately filled with a curious crowd of men and women who made a circle round the guest and the young victim of hospitality. The ground was spread with leaves and flowers, and their musicians sang an hymeneal song to the tune of their flutes. Here Venus is goddess of hospitality, her worship does not admit of any mysteries and every tribute paid to her is a feast for the whole nation. They were surprised at the confusion which our people appeared to be in as our customs do not allow of these public proceedings. However I would not answer for it that every one of our men found it impossible to conquer his repugnance and conform to the customs of the country.*'

Bougainville's classical references were deliberate: here on this wonderful island, he claimed, nature really had maintained its pristine simplicity and purity; freed from hunger, disease and toil, unrestricted by false modesty or artificial conventions of any kind, the people lived at peace with one another and were genuinely happy. It was the Arcadian age come to life in the Pacific.

Now all this was very engaging, but it was quite impossible for Bougainville, despite his gifts as an explorer and a scholar, to know much about the Tahitians during a stay of thirteen days; and although Wallis was longer on the island he was ill most of the time, he could not speak the language, and neither he nor his officers could lay much claim to be historians or anthropological observers. We have to wait for Cook's arrival for a more balanced account.

Cook was no prude (it has to be remembered that the Victorian era still lay more than half a century in the future); he allowed his men to mingle with the native girls whenever they could, even to the extent of permitting the girls to spend the night on board his ship, and in general he seems to have been more amused than shocked at Tahitian morals. Admittedly he knew very little about them as yet, but he was learning fast, and as opposed to the romanticizing of Bougainville he took a detached but sympathetic view. We find him writing, even at this early stage:

'Upon the whole these people seem to enjoy liberty in its fullest extent, every man seems to be the sole judge of his actions and to know no punishment but death, and this perhaps is never inflicted but upon a public enemy.'

Banks was much more exuberant:

'On the island of Otaheite where love is the chief occupation, the favourite, nay, the sole luxury of the inhabitants, both the bodies and the souls of the women are moulded into the utmost perfection . . .'

It was a question of course of just how far one insisted on judging the Tahitians from a European point of view. Towards the middle of May two incidents occurred which must certainly have been outlandish to European eyes. Cook describes the first of these thus:

'Mr Banks was as usual at the gate of the fort trading with the people, when he was told that some strangers were coming and therefore stood to receive them. The company had with them about a dozen young plantain trees (bananas) and some other small plants. These they laid down about twenty feet [6 m] from Mr Banks. The people then made a lane between him and them. When this was done the man (who appeared to be only a servant of the two women) brought the young plantains singly, together with some of the other plants and gave them to Mr Banks, and at the delivery of each pronounced a short sentence, which we understood not. After he had thus disposed of all his plantain trees he took several pieces of cloth and spread them on the ground. One of the young women then stepped upon the cloth, and with as much innocency as one could possibly conceive, exposed herself entirely naked from the waist downwards. In this manner she turned herself once or twice round, I am not certain which, then stepped off the cloth and dropped down her clothes. More cloth was then spread upon the former and she again performed the same ceremony. The cloth was then rolled up and given to Mr Banks, and the two young women went and embraced him which ended the ceremony.'

Banks was a gay and handsome young man and there could be no doubt about the meaning of this pantomime; it was a proposal from the two girls that he should make love to them. The phallic symbol of the banana was presented, the dowry in the form of cloth was offered, the sexual parts and the tattooed thighs and buttocks were displayed, and to make their meaning clear beyond all doubt the girls came and embraced him. Banks himself is very circumspect about all this but there does not seem to be much doubt that he succumbed –

if not on this same day then on a number of occasions later on. We hear of Obarea and other women sleeping in his tent, and one day there was a violent row between him and William Monkhouse, the surgeon, over one of the girls. There is no evidence that Cook took a mistress,★ but he too was clearly charmed by the warmth and naturalness of the Tahitians. His attitude seems to have been: why should this innocence be destroyed? Where there was no thought of evil how can you talk of modesty or immodesty on Tahiti? It is the girls' function to have children and it is natural that they should entice men by displaying themselves. Perhaps too, it might have been argued that this little ceremony had rather more dignity and grace about it than the usual Christian hypocrisy about the sexual act. In any case it was normal practice on the island, as normal as it was for the girls to put flowers in their hair, to smile at men who attracted them, to perform with the swaying of their buttocks the sort of dances that would lead men on, and, when the time came, to make love completely without shame or concealment.

Two days later, on 14 May, an even more explicit incident occurred. It was a Sunday and divine service was performed in one of the tents. Banks brought in two of the natives and they sat quietly watching the sailors and rising and kneeling when they did. Then, Cook relates,

'the day closed with an odd scene at the gate of the fort where a young fellow above six feet [1.8m] high lay with a little girl about ten or twelve years of age, publicly before several of our people and a number of the natives. What makes me mention this is because it appeared to be done more from custom than lewdness, for there were several women present, particularly Obarea and several others of the better sort, and these were so far from showing the least disapprobation that they instructed the girl how she should act her part, who, young as she was, did not seem to want it.'

Other witnesses of the scene say that Obarea went further than this; they say that she commanded the couple to make love, that they were too frightened to succeed, and that afterwards she was very strongly criticized by her own people for her part in the affair. Obviously this could be true. It may not be impossible that Obarea, fat and ageing as she was, was eager to sleep with the English sailors and thought to attract attention to herself by this public display. However, it is interesting that Cook was not really shocked, even though his indulgence did not quite extend to seeing his ship's discipline endangered: he ordered a seaman, Archibald Wolf, twenty-four lashes, an unusually severe penalty, for stealing a large quantity of nails from the store room. (The girls had increased their prices and were now beginning to demand two or even three nails instead of one.)

Then there was the serious matter of venereal disease. Bougainville later declared that it was introduced by Wallis; Wallis denied it and put the blame on Bougainville. It was a dispute that raged at long distance in the explorers' books for many years. The Dolphin preceded Bougainville's ship, La Boudeuse, in Tahiti by ten months, and it seems hard to believe that 100-odd British

---

★ One of his officers on a later voyage wrote: 'It has always been supposed that Cook himself never had any connexion with our fair friends; I have often seen them jeer and laugh at him calling him old and good for nothing.' Cook appears to have accepted this reputation with good humour.

sailors, many of whom must have consorted with the prostitutes at Plymouth or by the Thames at Wapping, were entirely free of infection. Yet we have Robertson, the *Dolphin*'s Master, denying the charge absolutely. 'No venereal,' he writes in red ink in his journal. 'The doctor affirmed upon his honour that no man on board was affected with any sort of disorder that they could communicate to the natives of this beautiful island.' Bougainville, however, was insistent that the disease was prevalent on his arrival. It is highly likely that he mistook the symptoms caused by yaws for those of syphilis, for they are similar in appearance, and once again one is left wondering if it was really possible for 400 young Frenchmen to have escaped infection in their own country.

Be all this as it may, Cook's doctor, after a special tour of inspection, gave the *Endeavour* a clean bill of health a month before the ship arrived in Matavai Bay, and yet no less than twenty-four of the seamen and ten of the marines – a third of the ship's company – were down with the disease within a few weeks of going ashore. Venereal disease, Cook notes sombrely in his journal, 'may in time spread itself over all the islands in the South Seas to the eternal reproach of those who first brought it among them'. This was to be all too brutally accurate.

But in 1769 the excitement of the first contact overrode all thought of the disasters that were to follow, and it was a honeymoon of a kind between the coloured people and the whites. Even Cook trusted himself to sleep in the Tahitians' huts at night, though he had sometimes cause to regret it. He writes:

'Notwithstanding all the care we took, before twelve o'clock the most of us had lost something or other. For my own part I had my stockings taken from under my head, and yet I am certain that I was not asleep the whole time. Obarea took charge of Mr Banks' things and yet they were stolen from her, as she pretended.'

This was the occasion on which Banks lost his white jacket and waistcoat with silver frogs.

Showery weather continued, and towards the end of May it built up into a tremendous thunderstorm. Then the air cleared and as the vital day – 3 June – approached it was fairly settled. The object in observing the transit of Venus across the disk of the sun (an event which would not occur again until 1874), was to determine the distance of the sun from the earth. Cook, with his quadrant and his telescopes, could never have made this calculation – other methods had to be employed – but in the eighteenth century no one was aware of this, and so he set about his arrangements with some confidence. Three parties were to take observations from three different points: Green was sent off a little further round the coast, Banks, Gore and Monkhouse crossed to the nearby island of Moorea, while Cook himself remained at Fort Venus. There was some little anxiety when the night of 2 June clouded over and a 'dusky shade' was still hanging about Venus the following day, but all three parties had an adequate view and there was every reason to believe that when the calculations had been worked out the experiment would prove itself to be a success.

There was still a good deal to be done before the *Endeavour* could get away; the longboat was found to be riddled with worms and had to be repaired, the ship itself had to be careened and restowed, and it was necessary for Cook to gather all the fresh provisions he could before he committed himself to the

Louis de Bougain-ville, distinguished captain and scholar

Louis de Bougainville had set out in command of the frigate *La Boudeuse* and the store-ship *L'Etoile* some ten months after the British expedition under Wallis. They arrived on the eastern side of Tahiti by accident. A mathematician, classicist and an aristocrat, he had fought against the British at the siege of Quebec and, as a naval officer, would also fight against them during the Napoleonic Wars. Bougainville believed that he had been transported to the Garden of Eden in Tahiti and named the island 'Nouveau Cythère' after the island in Greece where the goddess Venus first emerged from the sea. During his short stay on the island, Bougainville befriended Aotourou who helped him compile a Tahitian dictionary which he later published. Aotourou was so captivated by the Frenchman that he decided to accompany the expedition back to Europe – the first of four Tahitians who were to make this dramatic departure from their homeland in the next three years. For a while, Aotourou was an object of interest in learned circles in France. But the scholars soon tired of him and he led a lonely life in Paris, unable to learn the language or concepts of a new culture, his only pleasure being to go to the cheapest seats at the opera and peer at the stage through windows at the back of the boxes. Bougainville himself finally paid £1,500, said to be a third of his fortune, to have the Tahitian taken home. Bougainville subsequently became a great name in France under Bonaparte and a bust of his fine, cultivated face now stands on the waterfront at Papeete. His name is enshrined in the brilliant climbing shrub bougainvillea which he found in South America and brought back to adorn the houses of the Mediterranean.

Tahitians, with their customary show of hospitality, presenting fruits to Captain Louis de Bougainville and his officers when he called at Haitaa on the east coast of the island aboard La Boudeuse *and* L'Etoile *in 1768.*

unknown ocean once again. Another month went by before he was ready. The rain delayed him, and so did the Tahitians; he was obliged to break off relations with them for a few days in order to stop the continuous thefts. One also suspects that there was a general reluctance among the crew to depart from the indolent and happy island. This perhaps was a fortunate thing for the understanding between the two peoples; Banks and Solander began to speak the Tahitian language fairly well and they greatly extended their collection of South Sea island fauna and flora. Parkinson was busy executing his excellent

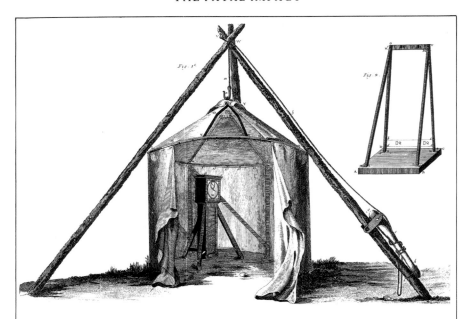

Portable observatory used by Cook on his voyages. This equipment was pressed into service when short stops were made. Engraving by R. Benard.

The transit of Venus, an event of rare importance

First observed in 1639 by the twenty-one-year-old astronomical prodigy, Jeremiah Horrocks. The astronomer Edmund Halley predicted that it would occur again on 6 June 1761 and on 3 June 1769 and then not again until the years 1874, 1882, 2004 and 2012. Calculations from the 1761 observations had not been a great success and the British were determined to take a lead in 1769, scattering observers at Hudson Bay, Newfoundland, the North Cape and the South Seas. The purpose of Cook's journey was to measure the distance of the earth from the sun. If the distance could be discovered it would be a base-line for all other measurements of astronomy. The presence of a planet in a direct line between earth and sun offered (in the absence of sophisticated instruments) the best chance of obtaining such a measurement, and accuracy depended on simultaneous observations from widely scattered places around the earth. But the Tahiti experiment proved a failure through no fault of Cook or the other members of the company scattered with their telescopes in three places around the island. The reason for the failure was unforseen by astronomers. Viewed through the telescopes against the light of the sun, the planet Venus had no sharp edges but was surrounded by a dark ring which looked like an atmosphere, about an eighth of the radius of the disc itself. Cook saw this 'dusky shade' clearly, as did Green, Banks and Solander. It was impossible to record the exact time when the disc of the planet touched the disc of the sun or when it left again. 'We differ'd from one another in observing the time of the Contact much more than could be expected,' Cook wrote in his journal. And, after all the preparation, this was all he wrote. Probably he knew then the results were useless and their labour wasted, though he would take responsibility for incorporating the astronomer Green's results in his final report to the Admiralty. The same method of calculation would, nonetheless, fail again in 1874 and 1882.

drawings of hundreds of new specimens of plants and birds and tropical fish. As for the Tahitians, the *Endeavour* had become a fixture in their lives; every day disclosed the ship riding there at anchor in Matavai Bay and the crew at work about the fort. The *Endeavour*'s supply of nails, hatchets and beads appeared to be inexhaustible, and life was more amusing than it had been before. They may still have been frightened of the Englishmen but they had also grown fond of them.

Towards the end of June Cook set out with Banks in the ship's pinnace to circumnavigate the island. It was the pleasantest of voyages; Little Tahiti, the smaller end of the hourglass, pleased them just as much as Matavai Bay and all the places that have since become tourist haunts were then a scene of pristine waterfalls, of mountainous tropical forests where no one ever went, and of huts and burial grounds with carved images never before seen by a white man. Obarea's great coral *marae* in the Papara district, 13.4 m (44 ft) high, 80 m (267 ft) long and 21.6 m (71 ft) broad (Banks measured it) must have been a remarkable sight, a more impressive structure than any on the island today.

Since they possessed no contrivance for exploring beneath the surface of the sea the *Endeavour*'s men missed the prettiest sight of all – the bright festoons of coral there, yellow, pale heliotrope, pink and blue, and the myriads of fish,

Charles Green, astronomer

Charles Green was a Yorkshire farmer's son who had become an accomplished astronomer serving two royal astronomers at Greenwich Observatory before being chosen by the Royal Society to accompany Cook. He accepted a fee of 200 guineas for the voyage, with the promise of 100 guineas a year if it lasted more than two years. It proved hard-won pay. Green was indefatigable in making observations and calculations. 'Mr Green's assistance,' Cook early assured the Admiralty, 'has been very great.' But as the journey wore on, Green became less scrupulous in his recording and the disappointment of the Venus observations was clearly demoralizing. The young astronomer died of dysentery, along with many other members of the company, en route home from Batavia.

Cook's paper on the transit of Venus published in Philosophical Transactions of the Royal Society, *1771, included his and Charles Green's drawings of the phenomenon.*

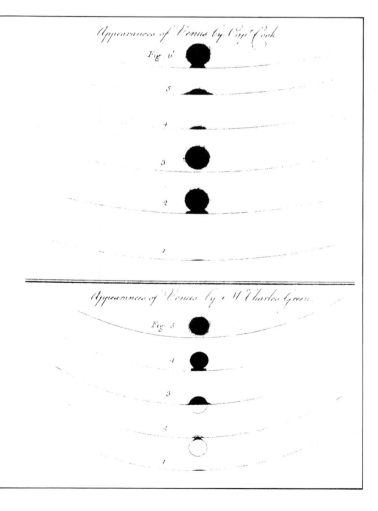

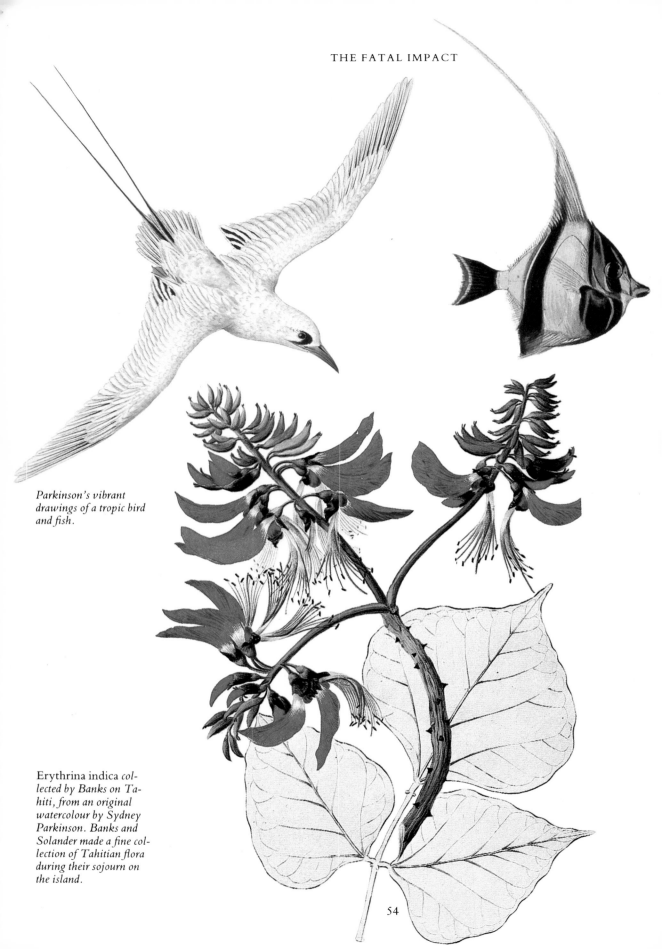

Parkinson's vibrant drawings of a tropic bird and fish.

Erythrina indica *collected by Banks on Tahiti, from an original watercolour by Sydney Parkinson. Banks and Solander made a fine collection of Tahitian flora during their sojourn on the island.*

54

A plant used by the Tahitians to dope the fish. This greatly facilitated catching them, and did no harm to the consumer.

The gold-throated bird of paradise brought back to England by Joseph Banks.

After the main goal of the expedition was complete, observing the transit of Venus, Cook circumnavigated the island with Banks in a pinnace. Despite Wallis's earlier naming of the island King George the Third, Cook took formal possession of Otahiti, Huahine, Otaha and Bora Bora in July 1769 and baptized the archipelago the 'Society Islands' in honour of the Royal Society which was responsible for launching the expedition. A view of the Matavai River, from a painting by George Tobin, shows it to be one of the beauty spots of their exploration.

brighter and more fantastic even than the coral itself, some with streaming ribbon-like tails, others streaked and coloured like butterflies, shoals of minute minnows that advance and retreat in a pale blue cloud, the occasional turtle, the slimy water-snake, crabs that inhabit shells and clams with scarlet and cerulean lips that close upon their prey and never let it go.

However, they charted the coast with Cook's usual thoroughness and wherever they made a landfall at night they were welcomed by the inhabitants; the fame of the English sailors had long since become known throughout the island. On their way they passed Bougainville's anchorage of the year before at Haitaa. Bougainville's visit had been puzzling them a good deal, and until the *Endeavour* returned to England they never did clear the matter up. They knew that *some* ship or ships had called at Tahiti after Wallis – the Tahitians had shown them pieces of iron and trinkets that could never have come from the *Dolphin* – but from the Tahitians' description they thought they were Spanish. They were also mystified by a reference to a white woman who had been on board. In fact this was perfectly correct. It was an odd story. Philibert Commerson had engaged a valet named Jeanne Baré or Baret at Brest, and since this valet was dressed as a man and behaved like a man no one on board had any idea that he was a woman. The Tahitians were not so easily deceived; the instant Baré came ashore they gathered round her, and instantly deduced her

Tupia, 'man of genius'

Tupia (Tupaia), Tayeto's master, was a priest, 'a man of real genius' and 'encyclopedic knowledge', who, coming from a family of famous sailors, provided Cook with a long list of islands from which it was possible to construct a map. He had, Cook notes of him in his journal, 'been with us the most part of the time we had been upon the Island, which gave us an opportunity to know something of him: we found him to be a very intelligent person and to know more of the Geography of the islands situated in these seas, their produce, and the religion, laws and customs of the inhabitants than any one we had met with.' Even so, Cook had been initially averse to the idea of transporting Tupia and Tayeto from their homeland and was prevailed upon to do so by Banks. Banks's adoption of the distinguished Tupia is more disconcerting since he confides to his journal: 'Thank heaven I have a sufficiency and I do not know why I may not keep him as a curiosity, as well as some of my neighbours do lions and tygers at a larger expense than he would probably ever put me to.' Despite misgivings, Tupia was to prove most valuable to Cook in New Zealand and Australia. He was always among the party who first went ashore in the pinnace. The Maoris understood him perfectly, though Tupia was full of warnings about them and greatly objected to their cannibalism. He was also able to communicate with the Australian Aboriginals at Botany Bay and the Endeavour River. His natural pride and dignity, however, did not endear him to the *Endeavour*'s crew who thought themselves degraded

by 'bending to an Indian'. Tayeto, however, became the darling of the ship's company being, as one of the seamen John Marra reported, 'of a mild and docile disposition, ready to do any kind of office for the meanest in the ship, and never complaining, but always pleased.' The Maoris also clearly fancied him and tried to kidnap Tayeto in October that year off Cape Kidnappers. Unfortunately both Tayeto and Tupia died at Batavia within a few days of each other from the fever contracted there en route to England.

The boy Tayeto, native of Otaheite, in the dress of his country. He is playing the flute through his nose, in traditional fashion. Engraving by R. B. Godfrey after Parkinson.

true sex. Commerson, a respectable and serious man, was much embarrassed.

It was now early July. Fort Venus was dismantled, and the guns were carried back on board the *Endeavour*, together with as many provisions as could be got, mostly live hogs, breadfruit and coconuts. Banks as a gesture to the Tahitians planted the seeds of melons, oranges, lemons and limes he had brought from Rio de Janeiro, and he went for a last walk among the plantations behind

Matavai Bay. The last thief got away with some pieces of ironwork, and the sailors on liberty sought out their girls for the last time. When the Tahitians realized that the *Endeavour* was really about to depart they implored Cook to remain a little longer, and Obarea and her friends came to live on the beach so that they should be with him day and night. Hardened though they were to departures, the sailors had seldom seen such genuine distress as this, such a sad, clinging reluctance to let them go. Cook was besieged by young Tahitians who wanted to sail with him, and at length he agreed to take 'a chief and a priest' named Tupia (or Tupaia) who would be useful as an interpreter and as a guide on the other islands. Tupia was allowed to bring with him a servant, a boy named Tayeto.

In the midst of these friendly and moving scenes the last *contretemps* occurred; on the night of Sunday, 9 July, two marines, Clement Webb and Sam Gibson, deserted from the fort. It had been known that all hands still ashore were to go on board the *Endeavour* on the following day, and so the two young men had seized this last chance to get away. Cook was told that 'they were gone into the mountains and that they had got each of them a wife and would not return'.

This was a serious business; every man in the *Endeavour* was vitally needed. Since there was no possibility of getting the men back without the help of the Tahitians, Cook's first act on the morning of 10 July was to seize Obarea and six chiefs and hold them as hostages in the fort. The Tahitians were deeply resentful – after all, they had not abducted the two marines – but they agreed to help in the search. The affair was soon over. A midshipman and a party of marines set off for the hills, and at nine o'clock that night Webb was brought in by some Tahitians. They reported that the midshipman's party had been seized by the natives in the mountains and that Gibson was with them. Hicks, the second officer, now went out with a strong bodyguard and was back with all the missing men before morning.

When Cook questioned the two deserters they said that they had become so strongly attached to two girls they could not bear to leave. Cook confined them until 14 July (when the *Endeavour* was already at sea), and they were then given twenty-four lashes each and the incident was forgotten.★

The departure was a painful affair. All past agitations and disturbances were forgotten. Obarea and the chiefs bore no grudge for their confinement; they came on board the *Endeavour* to say goodbye, overwhelmed with tears, and when the ship weighed anchor at 10 a.m. on 13 July she was surrounded by canoes filled with lamenting men and women. Banks climbed up to the masthead as they sailed away and stood there waving for a long time.

Something like half the ship's company were now suffering from venereal disease, and Cook decided to cruise for a while in the tropics to give them time to recover before he turned again to the cold south. On the whole he could congratulate himself. The chief object of his mission was accomplished. He had made firm friends of the Tahitians, he had established a valuable port of call in the Pacific, and he had gathered some notable information about the South Sea island way of life. On Tahiti the first shock of contact was over. The slow and more penetrating shocks of familiarity still remained to come.

★ Gibson sailed with Cook on his two subsequent voyages and never again deserted. He learned to speak Tahitian and became useful as an interpreter.

3

The noble savage

And now rose up, indeed, within Natural History, something new, something incomparably exciting, Man in the state of nature; the Noble Savage entered the study and the drawing room of Europe in naked majesty, to shake the preconceptions of morals and of politics.

BEAGLEHOLE

EVERY AGE presumably dreams of escaping its bonds, but Europe in the 1770s seems to have been specially ripe for the notion of an earthly paradise. Rousseau had written his *Discours sur les arts et sciences* in 1749, and for twenty years the theory of the simple and unsophisticated man living in Arcady had intrigued philosophical imagination. The discovery of Tahiti was the perfect denouement, the apparent reality of the preconceived idea. The island was like one of those unseen stars which eventually come to light after the astronomers have proved that it must exist.

We are dealing here with a time when the Far East was almost a closed book, when Africa was known only in outline, and, most mysterious of all, the immense Pacific offered the possibility of anything. It could be haunted by demons and monsters but it could also be the abode of the blessed. And now Cook brought back the proof that it really did exist, this golden island inhabited by happy, healthy, beautiful people whose every want was supplied by the tropical forest, and who, best of all, knew nothing of the cramping sophistries of civilization.

It was not until July 1771 – two years after she had left Tahiti – that the *Endeavour* returned to England, having explored New Zealand and the eastern coast of Australia on the way. She had had an appalling time on the voyage home; more than a third of the crew had died of dysentery, malaria and other diseases, among them Monkhouse the surgeon, Tupia and Tayeto, the two Tahitians, Parkinson the artist, Green the astronomer, Molyneux the Master, and Lieutenant Hicks. Yet the journey had been so remarkable that no one was much disposed to count the cost. Everyone wanted to hear about this new strange world in the Pacific.

Banks and Solander – and it was generally regarded as *their* voyage, not Cook's – were very much fêted. They were carried off to George III for a royal interview, Oxford granted them both honorary degrees and Banks sat to Reynolds for his portrait. Banks with his wealthy and influential connections was soon away on the social round, and one can imagine the guests at a dinner party sitting enthralled around the exuberant young man while he displayed the tattoo on his arm and recounted his adventures. Johnson had him to lunch and was persuaded to write a distich on Wallis's famous goat that had imperturbably returned from its second voyage round the world. It ran:

Perpetua ambita bis terra praemia lactis
Haec habet altrici Capra secunda Jovis. ★

The Royal Society was particularly gratified. Quite apart from the results of the observation of Venus, Banks and Solander had brought back 1,000 new species of plants, pressed or preserved in spirits, 500 fish, 500 skins of birds, and 'insects innumerable'. Then there were the drawings of the unfortunate Parkinson to be worked up and engraved, hundreds of them depicting with a clear and beautiful line the plants, the fruits, the fish, the animals and the strange people of the Pacific. Then again there were all the native weapons and artifacts, the shields, spears, drums and fishing nets, Tahitian cloth, carvings and ornaments, seashells and coral. For the etymologists there were the vo-

RIGHT
The native implements illustrated here, from an engraving by W. Darling, are as follows: 1. A sling made of plaited twine formed from the fibres of the bark of a tree; 2. A paddle made of wood used to strike the instruments 3&4 to indent or mark the skin in tattooing; 3&4. Tattooing instruments; 5. A cloth beater; 6. A basket; 7. An ebupa or stool, used as a pillow; 8. A flute made of bamboo and ornamented with plaited twine; 9. A hatchet; 10. A figure of the stone paste-beater; 11. A fly-flap. The handle is made of hard wood; 12. A feather ornament for the head; 13&14. Mother-of-pearl ornaments for the ears; 15. A decoy used for fishing, made of shells; 16. Bone plummets for fishing lines; 17. Another plummet, this one made of spar; 18–25. A selection of fish hooks made of wood, shell and mother-of-pearl; 26. Three pearls tied together with plaited hair, worn as an ornament for the ears; 27. Sting of a stingray, used to point their lances and arrows.

Joseph Banks, man of influence

From the moment the *Endeavour* docked in England, Banks found himself the centre of scientific interest. His house in New Burlington Street and later Soho Square, London, became the repository for the *Endeavour* collections along with collections made earlier in Newfoundland, Labrador and Great Britain. The illustrations from the *Endeavour* voyage, totalling some 1,163 depictions of flora, fauna and native inhabitants, were assembled and others commissioned on the collected material. Banks himself, to the disappointment of some naturalists, contributed little from his journeyings to the scientific literature and his grand plan for the botany of the expedition did not mature. But he opened his remarkable collections to the scientific world. Generous, responsive to all calls on his time and finances across the public and private board, he became one of the most active and diversely engaged figures of the age. A year after his return, Banks was nominated director of the King's Royal Gardens at Kew, a post from which he exercised a powerful spur to impe-

rial botanical science. His collectors spanned the world. In 1778 he became president of the Royal Society of London, a post he held uninterrupted for the next forty years, and in 1781 he was knighted for his services to science. A year into his presidency, Banks gave important evidence before a Select Committee of the House of Commons for the choice of a penal settlement at Botany Bay, and for thirty years after settlement in 1788, he inspired and dominated scientific investigation in the Australian colonies until his death. With honours heaped upon him and with a swift and amicable farewell to his mistress of one year, in March 1779 he married the heiress Dorothea Hugessen. Banks had no children but he scattered largesse, explorers and collectors to the far corners of the globe. From the agreeable, independent-minded companion and colleague of 1769–71, Banks became a major 'backroom boy' of his age. For the last decade of his life until his death aged seventy-seven in 1820, he suffered acutely from gout and had to be carried to his appointments in a chair. A statue of him sitting in reflective pose was later erected in his honour in the Natural History Museum, London.

★Thus translated in Boswell:

In fame scarce second to the nurse of Jove,
This goat, who twice the world had traversed round,
Deserving both her masters' care and love,
Ease and perpetual pasture now has found.

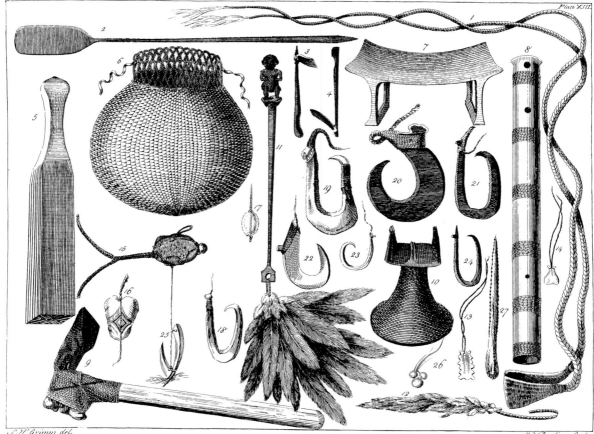

Various Instruments, & Utensils, of the Natives of Otaheite, & of the adjacent Islands

cabularies of new languages to study and for the geologists the specimens of many rocks.

It was enough for Banks to launch himself as the pundit of the new age of scientific exploration, enough to set up a great herbarium in his house in New Burlington Street, enough to lead on to a general stirring up of interest in the Pacific and all its other mysteries that yet remained.

Cook was not altogether overlooked. He too had an hour with the King, and he must have been elated to have heard from the Admiralty that 'their Lordships extremely well approve of the whole of your proceedings and . . . have great satisfaction in the account you have given them on the good behaviour of your Officers and Men . . .' His geographical and meteorological observations and his reports on the management of a ship in tropical waters were of the utmost value, and made it certain that he would be employed again.

It was true that he had failed to find a southern continent (Australia was not regarded as such), but his traverse of the Pacific had filled in a great blank space and had added many new islands to the map.

But it was the philosophical aspects of Cook's discoveries that especially intrigued people: if the Tahitians really were living such an idyllic life had one any right to disturb them? This was a matter that had already been taken up in

Cook's single-minded act of possession

Although Cook took possession of the whole east coast of Australia naming it New South Wales, he did not regard this as the long-looked-for great south continent. The idea of this continent dated back a very long time. Marco Polo spoke of it in the thirteenth century. It was believed that a large mass of land had to exist in the south to balance the great continents of the Northern Hemisphere – otherwise, scholarly men maintained, the world would have turned over on itself. Australia did not immediately qualify. It was not large enough and not far enough south. Cook's action, however, was somewhat arbitrary. In his official instruction, the Admiralty had stressed that he might take possession of 'convenient situations in the country', only 'with the consent of the natives'. Cook did not follow these instructions and no consultations with any Aborigines were held. To a friend he wrote, 'A man would not accomplish much in discovery who only stuck to orders.' His act of possession was never officially endorsed in his lifetime.

France where Bougainville's account of his voyage in *La Boudeuse* had just come out. It had instantly attracted the attention of the intellectuals, notably Diderot, the friend of Rousseau. In his *Supplément au voyage de Bougainville*, Diderot raged against the wilful intrusion into pagan simplicity and happiness. What possible good, he demanded, could be brought to these people by Christian civilization with its overload of guilt, its hypocrisy, its cold-climate strictures, its physical sickness and its ambition? He warned the Tahitians that,

'one day they [the Christians] will come, with crucifix in one hand and the dagger in the other to cut your throats or to force you to accept their customs and opinions; one day under their rule you will be almost as unhappy as they are'.

And he goes on to speak of the ravages that will follow the 'wretched caresses' of the European sailors.

Bougainville, as we have seen, was hardly in a position to supply the philosopher with all the facts about the island, and this was nothing more than the intellectual's heart's-cry for a return to natural innocence. But Bougainville's romantic enthusiasm was infectious, the Rousseauian fervour took fire again, and Tahiti was a useful peg on which to hang an argument against Christian society. Why should not love govern all? Was it not natural sometimes for the brother to desire his sister, the father his daughter? Were we not, all of us, the incestuous descendants of Adam and Eve? Did we not constantly break the Christian commandments by committing adultery, by hating our neighbours, by piling up riches? Better to do away with all this cant and learn from the Tahitians how to live the simple communal life in which no one starved, children were loved and the aged were never neglected.

It was a powerful argument and it entirely overlooked the facts that the Tahitians were not necessarily incestuous, that they practised infanticide, that they were just as capable of hating their neighbours as anybody else and that in the breaching of at least one of the Christian commandments – thou shalt not steal – they were experts. Yet it was true, or at any rate true enough, that they appeared to be living without guilt, and that compared to the Europeans they were an amiable and amorous people who were now in danger of inheriting all the afflictions of the civilized world. Could you really blame the European sailors – or the philosophers for that matter – for succumbing to the delights, both real and imagined, of the enchanted island?

Dr Beaglehole has an apt comment on these matters. Writing of Webb and Gibson, the two marines who tried to desert from the *Endeavour*, he says:

'The 18th century sailor was confronted by the obvious contrast between his foc's'le and his work on one side, the unremitting demands of virtual imprisonment with hard labour at sea, and on the other what Bougainville had called New Cythera. Is it too fanciful, that name having been mentioned – is it to labour the point too much, to consider in that century the attractions of the art of escape? Consider the nostalgic and sentimental magic of Watteau's L'Embarquement pour Cythère, the sophisticated longing for the unreal, the transmutation of classical mythology in the age of reason. But the unsophisticated Webb and Gibson did not need classical mythology, they were standing on the beach of the dreamworld already, they walked straight into the golden age and embraced their nymphs . . .'

Thus on both levels, the actual and the philosophical, the island, or rather the idea of the island, seemed to fulfil a need of the time.

These issues were vigorously taken up in England when the official account of the *Endeavour*'s voyage came out in 1773. The circumstances in which this publication – three massive volumes illustrated with engravings and maps – was produced, were unusual. It was thought that Cook, a rough sailor, was not quite up to the business of writing up his own journal for general readership, and so Dr John Hawkesworth, one of the literary figures of London and a friend of Dr Johnson, was commissioned to do the work. In addition to Cook's journal, he was given access to Banks's papers, and for good measure he appended an account of Wallis's and other explorers' voyages in the Pacific. Hawkesworth was paid a handsome fee of £6,000 for these labours, and in the main he carried them out as well as might be expected. But he was given somewhat to animadverting on his facts, and he was decidedly of the Diderot-Bougainville school – he was all for the noble savage. Banks, particularly, supplied him with details of Obarea and the enticing Tahitian girls, and Hawkesworth made the most of them.

Now a London which in addition to Johnson and Boswell contained such figures as Horace Walpole, Fanny Burney, Burke, Gibbon, Garrick, Sheridan, Fox and any number of highly sceptical wits, was hardly likely to let all this romanticism go by the board. Walpole was one of the first in the field. He wrote in a letter to the Countess of Ossory:

'Captain Cook's voyage I have never read or intend to read. I have seen the prints – a parcel of ugly faces, with lubber lips and flat noses, dressed as unbecomingly as if both sexes were ladies of the highest fashion; and rows of savages with backgrounds of palm-trees. Indeed I shall not give five guineas and a half – nay, they sell already for nine, for such uncouth lubbers; nor do I desire to know how unpolished the north or south poles have remained ever since Adam and Eve were just such mortals.'

Soon too Hawkesworth's 'luscious descriptions' of free love on Tahiti brought out the moralists and satirists – it was not easy to say which was which – in full cry. Banks's amours were an obvious target, and the law of libel in England in the eighteenth century was not what it is now. In 'An

Epistle from Mr Banks, Voyager, Monster-Hunter and Amoroso', Banks is made to speak to Obarea of the children she is supposed to have borne him –

> '. . . blest produce of thy charms,
> My image lives and prattles in thy arms.'

and Obarea replies:

> 'The children grow in stature and in grace,
> While all their father blooms in either face . . .
> And when I weep I almost hear them say
> Why, cruel, went our Father far away;
>
> 'Yet think at least my copious tears you see,
> And spare one thought from Botany for me . . .
> Think on the raptures which we once have known,
> And waft one sign to Otaheite's throne.'

Then there was the damaging effect upon British morals of Hawkesworth's frank account of Tahitian promiscuity:

> 'One page of Hawkesworth, in the cool retreat,
> Fires the bright maid with more than mortal heat:
> She sinks at once into the lover's arms,
> Nor deems it vice to prostitute her charms;
> "I'll do," cries she, "What Queens have done before";
> And sinks, from principle, a common whore.'

It was the old business, not unknown at the present time, of purveying lubricity while pretending to denounce it, but no doubt these effusions – and there were a number of them printed anonymously – were a kind of corrective to over-sentimentality. Hawkesworth did, in fact, rather over-egg the pudding, Banks's high-flown descriptions of Tahitian life were a little too ecstatic, and Bougainville had been carried away by his own eloquence. But there was more than envy, more than moral indignation, more even than aesthetics, involved in the attack on the explorers; by praising Tahitian manners so highly they were making a criticism of Christian Europe and of Christian education. If Tahiti was so perfect a place as they claimed it was, then the idea of progress was nonsense; and this was intolerable. Unregenerate luxury of the South Sea island kind was immoral and had to be denounced – otherwise how was one going to endure the hard humdrum life of the West?

It was suggested, moreover, that the rich shared the essentials of life with the poor on Tahiti, and in these pre-French Revolution, pre-Marxist days this was a reproach to the established order of things in Europe where the most wretched poverty was accepted – perhaps enforced is the better word – as inevitable. From his safe and privileged perch at Strawberry Hill, Horace Walpole could afford to speak of 'uncouth lubbers', and there were as yet no artists like Gauguin in the world to reveal his embarrassing provincialism. Johnson's stand was what you would have expected from a man who liked to find his whole world in London, or at all events no further off than the Mediterranean. He was not impressed by the noble savage; he thought one learned very little from a journey around the world, and he wondered why Banks had bothered to bring back with him innumerable insects when there were already plenty for him to study in England.

But Boswell was much impressed by Cook. He met him at Sir John Pringle's house some time after this, and he says he found him to be

'a plain, sensible man with an uncommon attention to veracity. Sir John gave me an instance. It was supposed that Cook had said he had seen a nation of men like monkeys and Lord Monboddo had been very happy with this. Sir John happened to tell Cook of this. "No," he said, "I did not say they were like monkeys. I said their faces put me in mind of monkeys." There was a distinction very fine but sufficiently perceptible. I talked with him a good deal today, as he was very obliging and communicative. He seemed to have no desire to make people stare, and being a man of steady moral principles, as I thought, did not try to make theories out of what he had seen to confound virtue and vice. . . . He said that a disregard of chastity in unmarried women was by no means general at Otaheite. . . . It was curious to see Cook, a grave, steady man and his wife, a decent plump Englishwoman, and think he was preparing to sail round the world.'*

A few days later Pringle, Boswell and some others were again with Cook at the Mitre, and Boswell sat next to the Captain and talked to him throughout the meal. He was gratified to find that Cook was quite ready to admit that any study he and his shipmates made of the religion, government and traditions of the South Sea islanders was likely to be superficial. Boswell permitted himself an atrocious pun on rising from the table: 'I have had a good dinner,' he said, 'for I have had a good *cook.*'

The fact was that Cook had been much embarrassed by Hawkesworth. He had not been able to correct the text before publication (though Hawkesworth said he had), and many of the observations and descriptions that had been ascribed to him were not his own at all. Now that Dr Beaglehole has produced for us Cook's own journal, few people will bother to read Hawkesworth's volumes; the rough sailor's account is incomparably the better of the two. Banks suffered just as much. His fresh and lively journal was not published until long after his death and then in a form so bowdlerized by the editor, the eminent botanist Joseph Hooker, that Dr Beaglehole has been moved to comment that the work was not so much a journal as a scene of carnage.

Yet despite all this, Hawkesworth's book was an immense success. It was reprinted twice in 1773, an edition came out in America, and there soon followed translations into French, German, Italian and other languages. For the next ten years or more it was regarded as a sort of classic of South Sea island literature. So far as the world was concerned Hawkesworth *was* Cook and the engravings he printed were illustrations of what Cook had seen. This last was a serious aberration. It was not merely that no photographs were available – the camera was not to appear for more than half a century – but it was a question of whether or not the artists could depict what they actually saw. No one could quarrel with Parkinson's splendid illustrations of plants – these were scientific studies especially made for Banks and the botanists – but when the European landscapist and portraitist got to work it was a different matter. The temptation to paint the idea of Tahiti rather than the reality was very strong,

---

*On his third and last voyage to his death in Hawaii in 1779.

and it was an idea interpreted in a European manner. In the Pacific the artist had no precedent to guide him, everything was new, the light, the strange vegetation, the colour of the sea, the Polynesian face and figure, the whole menagerie of outlandish animals and birds. To see these objects accurately, to divest himself of the European attitude, to refrain from the temptation to paint a pretty composition – this was the artist's problem if he was going to represent the Pacific without prejudice, and it is hardly surprising that the weaker brethren fell along the way so that their breadfruit trees grew up into English oaks and their Tahitian girls were transformed into nymphs surrounded by classical waterfalls in a soft English light.

But it was not the artists alone who, with the best of intentions, were depicting scenes that were half European and half Tahitian: the engravers of their works added their own refinements, they tended to Europeanize the originals even more; and from the public point of view it was the engravings which counted.

So then on both counts – in the written word and in the illustrations – a false, idealized impression of Tahiti was being built up, and not all Cook's scientific data could correct it. It is never very easy to stamp out a popular vogue; when the satirists had had their way and the fashionable derision had spent its force, people still wanted to know more about Tahiti, they still clung to the romantic dream, they wanted it to be true.

Fortunately for his peace of mind Cook, for the moment, knew little or nothing of all this. Long before Hawkesworth's book came out he was making plans to sail again. This time he was to have two vessels. The *Drake* was another converted Whitby collier of 469 tonnes (462 tons) and twelve guns and she had a company of 118 men. This was to be Cook's ship. Her companion, the *Raleigh*, 341 tonnes (336 tons) and ten guns, had a crew of 83 and was commanded by Lieutenant Tobias Furneaux, whose chief qualification was

---

Beaglehole and Captain Cook

John Cawte Beaglehole (1901–71)'s production and editing of Cook's journals, *The Journals of Captain James Cook on his Voyages of Discovery*, Vols 1–2 (1955 & 1961) and his two-volumed *The Endeavour Journal of Joseph Banks, 1768–1771*, (1962) gave the New Zealand historian an unrivalled knowledge of these great undertakings in the Pacific and Antarctic and provided him with an intimate understanding of the cast of characters. Of his work on Cook's journals, Beaglehole himself wrote: 'It became necessary to find out everything that could possibly be found out about Cook, his companions, the science of the age, the administrative background, innumerable personal relations and tensions as well as matters of geography, navigation and handwriting . . . Nothing was as simple as it seemed.' So lucid and perceptive is his response to the tranquil settings of the Pacific, the frozen blue landscape of the Antarctic, and to the joys and challenges that the expeditions met that, reading these works, one comes to believe that Beaglehole was there! In the last seven years of a life that also spanned wide scholarship on New Zealand, Beaglehole devoted his energies to *The Life of Captain Cook*, the definitive biography of the navigator which he left in typescript and which was published in 1974. He was awarded the Order of Merit for his work on Cook, the second New Zealander to receive this highest of British honours.

that he had sailed with Wallis in the *Dolphin*. The Spaniards still made general claims to the Pacific, and since there was no point in upsetting them unnecessarily the names *Drake* and *Raleigh*, which were anathema in Madrid, were altered to *Resolution* and *Adventure*.

Banks was also eager to sail again, and he arranged to take with him a suite of fifteen which was to include Solander, two horn players, and the celebrated painter Zoffany, who was engaged at £1,000 for the voyage. Cook had to be turned out of the main cabin to accommodate them all, and a separate round-house was built on the *Resolution*'s deck for his own use. This was the cause of a major setback; on sailing down the Thames the ship proved to be top-heavy and in danger of capsizing. This left no alternative but to remove the round-house and for them all to pack into the original deck space as best they could. Banks was furious when he heard the news; his equipment was already stowed on board, he had spent £5,000 on it, and he was determined to have his horn players. We are told that he stamped his foot with rage on the dock, and when his protests to the Admiralty proved unavailing he withdrew from the expedition altogether. Zoffany, much disappointed, went off to Italy instead, a sound move in Walpole's opinion: 'This . . . is better than his going to draw naked savages and be scalped by that wild man, Banks.' Dr Beaglehole remarks, 'What this master of the theatrical and domestic conversation piece would have made of icebergs and Tahitians it is hard to say.' (But we have an idea. Zoffany lived to paint his 'Death of Captain Cook', and it is a composition in the historico-classical manner that fits in perfectly with the prevailing mood of the 1770s.) Banks himself went off on a private expedition to Iceland.

William Hodges, the painter chosen to replace Zoffany, was a man of very considerable talents whose seascapes were to prove something of a milestone in the aesthetic struggle to come to terms with the colour and the light of the Pacific. Then there was a formidable team of scientific observers. John Reinhold Forster, the *Resolution*'s naturalist, a man of mixed Scottish-Prussian descent, was as unlike Banks as anyone could possibly be: he was a tiresome, rather mean-spirited pedant and a prude. Dr Beaglehole speaks of his 'miscellaneous low-powered scientific writing'. Yet he was widely read, he examined

HMS Resolution *and* Adventure, *Cook's two newly named ships which were to take him on his second expedition to the Pacific. In this oil painting by Francis Holman, the ships are at anchor in the Downs, 26–7 June 1772.*

everything he saw with a grammarian's precision and his curiosity was endless. His son, George Forster, who accompanied him on the voyage, was an excellent draughtsman as well as a natural philosopher of sufficient calibre to become in later years a strong influence on Alexander von Humboldt.

The *Resolution*'s astronomer, William Wales, might be described as an urbane provincial, he stood square on his Yorkshire background, he looked in later life like Mr Pickwick and he read the classics; a likeable man on the whole, and he was a precise and able scientist. A second astronomer, William Bayly, was carried in the *Adventure*, and Banks's two hornplayers were replaced by a Scottish marine who could play the bagpipes.

Among Cook's officers there were Charles Clerke who had sailed with Cook on the first voyage, a sprightly man and a very competent navigator, Richard Pickersgill, who was also in the *Endeavour* and who is described as 'a good officer and astronomer but liking ye grog'. Fanny Burney's brother James, who had been at sea since the age of ten, George Vancouver, who later was to become a notable explorer in his own right, Richard Grindall, an able seaman who was to rise to the rank of admiral and command the *Prince* at Trafalgar, and six midshipmen aged around fourteen, several of whom were to make their names in the years ahead. It was already a great thing to sail with Cook. Among ordinary seamen, however, in this age of the press-gang, voyaging in the Pacific still had no very strong appeal; no less than fifty-eight deserted from the *Resolution* and another thirty-seven from the *Adventure* before they sailed, and replacements had to be found.

Profiting from the experiences of his last voyage, Cook took with him, in addition to the usual biscuit and salt beef and pork, large quantities of salted cabbage, marmalade of carrots, and extract of oranges and lemons. Meat was served three or four times a week, and every day each man had 450 g (1 lb) of biscuits, as much small beer as he could drink, and 0.5 litre (1 pint) of wine or 0.25 litre (½ pint) of brandy, rum or arrack. The ships were also able to distil a small quantity of salt water.

Cook's orders this time were to penetrate as far south as possible towards the undiscovered Pole, and he was to retire to the tropics during the long Antarctic winter so as to continue his search for the elusive southern continent and to recruit his vessels in 'some known place to the Northward'. This meant Tahiti. On 13 July 1772, precisely a year after the *Endeavour*'s return, they sailed from Plymouth.

At Madeira, their first port of call, a strange matter came to light, and it indicated that perhaps the satirists had not been too hard on Banks after all. Cook wrote to a friend:

'Three days before we arrived a person left the island who went by the name of Burnett. He had been waiting for Mr Banks's arrival about three months. At first he said he had come here for the recovery of his health, but afterwards said his intention was to go out (on the voyage) with Mr Banks. To some he said he was unknown to this gentleman; to others he said that it was by his appointment he came here as he could not be received on board in England. At last when he heard that Mr Banks did not go, he took the very first opportunity to get off the island. He was about thirty years of age and rather ordinary than otherwise, and employed his time botanizing etc. Every part of Mr Burnett's behaviour and every action tended to prove that he was a woman.'

4

The familiarity

COOK WAS to make three more visits to Tahiti. On this second voyage he called at the island twice; for sixteen days in August 1773, and then for three weeks in April and May 1774. On his third and last journey to the Pacific he stayed at Matavai Bay for six weeks in August and September 1777. Thus we have a fairly full record of the island during this early period when it hovered in a sort of social adolescence, still clinging to its safe and familiar ways and yet drawn forward to the hard awakening that lay ahead.

On the voyage down to the Cape the *Resolution* lost one man overboard, two of the midshipmen in the *Adventure* died, probably of pneumonia, and a stowaway from Madeira was discovered. It was a great source of confidence for Cook to have two vessels, and whenever they were becalmed alone there in the empty Atlantic the *Adventure*'s officers rowed across to pass the day with him. They spent nearly a month refreshing at Capetown, and then in November plunged directly down into the unknown frozen south, gradually edging their way around the polar ice from west to east. By March 1773 the winter was closing in on them, and Cook turned north, at first to New Zealand, and then into the tropics of the Pacific. They picked up the trades and made over 160 km (100 miles) a day. A little more than a year out from England they were sailing up to the south-eastern coast of Tahiti. It was a most beautiful morning and the sun was just coming up.

'A faint breeze only,' George Forster tells us, 'wafted a delicious perfume from the land and curled the surface of the sea.'

It was soon evident that the Tahitian flair for sensuous melodrama with comical undertones was as strong as ever. Directly the ships were close enough a swarm of naked girls, aged mostly around nine or ten, the Tahitian age of puberty, swam out through the surf and climbed on board. Presently a chieftain with his wife and two sisters came alongside the *Resolution* in a canoe, and there was much inquiry after Banks (though a strange indifference to the fate of Tupia and his poor boy Tayeto). Forster relates:

'*One of the sisters took a particular fancy to a pair of sheets which she saw spread on one of the beds and made a number of fruitless attempts to obtain them from her conductor. He proposed a special favour as a condition; she hesitated for some time and at last with seeming reluctance consented; but when the victim was just led to the altar of Hymen the ship struck violently on the reef and interrupted the solemnity.*'

What had happened was that the land breeze had dropped and a strong current had drifted them on to the coral. For a while the two ships rocked helplessly together in the swell in imminent danger of colliding and of holing themselves on the reef, but providentially the breeze sprang up again and they were able to stand off. It was so bad a crisis that Cook, hoarse with shouting and weak from strain (he was suffering from a stomach disorder at the time), had

The Resolution *and* Adventure *in Matavai Bay – painted by the second expedition's artist, William Hodges – surrounded by a variety of Tahitian canoes. The Tahitians were delighted at the return of Cook and 'swarmed on board to embrace him and to swathe him in folds of coloured cloth . . . There was much enquiry after Banks though a strange indifference to the fate of Tupia and . . . Tayeto.'*

to revive himself with brandy. When it was all over the young officer who had attempted to seduce the chieftain's sister hurried back to his cabin but both the girl and the sheets were gone.

This incident occurred on the east coast of the island, and soon afterwards Cook moved his ships round to his old anchorage at Matavai Bay. Here he was instantly recognized and the Tahitians swarmed on board to embrace him and to swathe him in folds of coloured cloth. Trussed up like a cocoon he was forced to stand for hours, sweltering on his quarter-deck, while the welcoming ceremony went on. Forster says:

'A great number of women of the lowest class, having been engaged by our sailors, remained on board at sunset . . . The evening therefore was as completely dedicated to mirth and pleasure as if we had lain at Spithead instead of O-Taheite.'

The girls danced to the flute, the sailors responded by performing the hornpipe to the music of the bagpipes, and then all retired below.

Cook was disposed to be lenient. His men had had a fearful time among the icebergs, and in the *Adventure*, where Furneaux had not enforced a vegetable diet, many were suffering from scurvy. Like stricken insects they crawled around the decks and they were desperately in need not only of fresh fruit and meat but of all the kindness the islanders could show them. In the morning Cook began to get his sick ashore, once again the officers and gentlemen bathed in the mountain streams and strolled through the plantations with the sapphire-blue parakeets flying overhead; and it seemed that the island was as beautiful, as hospitable and as peaceful as ever.

They were soon disillusioned. Since the *Endeavour*'s visit four years before two disastrous civil wars had been fought between Greater and Little Tahiti, venereal disease had added to the general destitution, and now many of Cook's old friends were dead. The breadfruit tree was not in season and hardly any fresh provisions were offered for sale. Cook wrote in his journal:

'This fine island, which in the years 1767 and 1768 swarmed, as it were, with hogs and fowls, is now so scarce of these animals that hardly anything will induce the owners to part with them.'

He sought out Obarea, that 'fat, bouncing, good-looking dame' of other days and found her miserably poor and wretched. In the reshuffle for power she and her immediate family had been superseded by her nephew, a young man named Tu. It was also revealed that during the time Cook had been away a Spanish ship, the *Aguila*, had called at Tahiti and had imported a form of gastric influenza into the island.

Now while the Europeans were undoubtedly to blame for the diseases, the war at first sight could hardly be laid to their account. Wars – and of a particularly bitter kind involving the killing of women and children and the sacrifice of prisoners – were no rarity in the island, and up to this time no firearms had been introduced. Yet there was a stirring here of something new. It had been a valuable thing in 1769, a matter of prestige, for Obarea and her friends to have had a great ship like the *Endeavour* with its guns anchored off their coast, and to be on intimate terms with its crew. It may well have given them political ambitions and have encouraged the desire for war. Already we find Cook writing in his journal:

'. . . we debauch their morals already prone to vice and we introduce among them wants and perhaps diseases which they never before knew and which serve only to disturb that happy tranquillity they and their forefathers had enjoyed. If any one denies the truth of this assertion let him tell what the natives of the whole extent of America have gained by the commerce they had had with Europeans.'

So now, despairing of provisioning his ships, he did what he could to cement his friendship with young Tu, and then sailed off to Huahine and the other islands in the Society group where conditions were more settled, and hogs and other supplies were still to be had. Furneaux took with him in the *Adventure* the young man Omai who had been wounded six years before in Wallis's initial skirmishes with the Tahitians.

Eight months later Cook was back again from his second tremendous sweep through the south polar seas – and one pauses here to note the extraordinary circumstances of this voyage. He was moving between the two extremes of nature, Tahiti, one of the most luxurious places on earth, and the Antarctic with its frightening icy perfection, between the green jungle and the white abstraction. Neither place holds him for very long. The Antarctic, seen from the tropics, exerts its challenging attractions, its excitement, its dangers, its serene isolation and its detachment – but then, after a few months in the outrageous cold, he is driven north again to the food and companionship of the lovely island. And this time it does not fail him. Almost miraculously everything had changed. Provisions were to be had in abundance, new huts and canoes were everywhere in building and Obarea was her old self again. There was nothing in particular to which one could ascribe this return to prosperity; a spell of peace and the natural resilience of the tropics had apparently done the work, but the change must have been very great since we find Cook writing about the island with all the exuberance he and Banks had had when he first arrived there five years before.

The *Resolution* was now badly in need of a respite. She had parted company with the *Adventure* in a storm off New Zealand, scurvy had broken out, Cook himself had been dangerously ill with an acute infection of the gall-bladder, and all the crew were weary and eager for rest. Tu did everything he could to help. Once again the tents were set up for the sick at Fort Venus, crowds appeared every morning with fresh fruit, and so many hogs were offered for sale that a sty had to be set up on shore. In the *Resolution*, according to the younger Forster, 'the excesses of the night were incredible'. So many girls came on board there were not enough sailors to go round, the dancing was continuous and the 'gorging' by the girls of the roast pork provided by their lovers, a wonder to behold. Prices had gone up. Having got all the nails they wanted to Tahitians began to ask for clothing, and Cook remarks wryly that the girls left the ship in the morning dressed in the sailors' shirts only to return in the evening wearing rags. Soon even shirts were not enough, but Cook by a lucky chance had obtained on the voyage a quantity of red parrot feathers which were sacred objects in Tahiti. For these feathers the Tahitians were ready to sell anything or indeed do anything; in the hope of obtaining just one of them the wife of a chief, with her husband's approval, offered herself to Cook. ('My spirits,' says the senior Forster, 'were damped by this unexpected scene of immorality and selfishness.')

There were the usual disturbances: when a thief stole a water-cask Cook managed to persuade Tu and the chiefs that he should be punished with twenty-four lashes of the cat-o-nine tails – an ordeal which the Tahitian crowd watched with horror but which the man bore 'with great firmness'. Cook was increasingly confident in his dealings with the islanders; as he grew to know them better he treated them almost as though they were white men and his equals. He was well aware that in a crisis only his guns and his firearms made him safe, and that even these would be ineffective if used too frequently: 'they

Head of Tu, sometimes called Otoo, the sovereign of Tahiti when Cook returned on his second voyage in 1773 and 1774. In Tu, Cook found a staunch supporter. It was an act of compromise. Tu had fought a war against Little Tahiti and been defeated. He now deliberately cultivated Cook for the prestige it would give him on the island.

(the Tahitians) were very sensible of the superiority they have over us in numbers and no one knows what an enraged multitude may do'.

In Tu he had a considerable supporter. At first he had described him as a 'timorous Prince', but the young man was a good deal more than that. He had fought in the war against Little Tahiti and had taken to the mountains when his side had been defeated. But he had reappeared at the right moment to take advantage of the peace, and although he was still no more in the ruling hierarchy than chief among equals, he was politically astute, he was one of those men who have the power of survival because they have the ability to wait for their opportunities, and now he very deliberately cultivated Cook for the prestige it would give him on the island. For both sides it was a question of compromise and synthesis, and if the Tahitians were changing so were the Englishmen as well.

For men like the astronomer William Wales the bloom of the noble savage idea was wearing off, and it was being replaced by a much more matter-of-fact approach. Wales derides Bougainville and his 'warm imagination' for making the island sound like 'Mahomet's Paradise'. It was no more beautiful, he claims, than England (and perhaps it has to be conceded that the England of the eighteenth century was a much more beautiful place than it is now). He thought too that the physical attractions of the inhabitants had been much exaggerated: their women were too small, their features too masculine, their complexion was 'a light olive or rather a deadish yellow', their black hair 'cut short in the bowl-dish fashion of the country people in England', their eyes lively but 'rather too prominent for my liking', their noses flat, their mouths wide and their lips thick. Their teeth were good and 'the breasts of the young

Scenes of Tahitian dancing greeted the enthusiastic ship's company. The combination of grace and sensuousness gave a distinctive piquancy to these colourful scenes. Here, again, the flute is characteristically played through the nostril.

women before they have had children are very round and beautiful, but those of the old ones hang down to their navels'. As for the Tahitian dancing – 'The wriggling of their hips, especially as set off with such a quantity of furbelows, is too ludicrous to be pleasing and the distortion of their mouths is really disagreeable.' Nor was he much beguiled by the Tahitian *heavas* – the plays enacted by the *arioi* – in which 'the intimacies between the sexes were carried to great lengths'. On the other hand, he defends the women's virtue; wives, he says, were seldom offered by their husbands to the British sailors, and most of the unmarried girls were very careful as to whom they slept with. It was only the prostitutes who came on board – and where was the difference in all this to the women of Plymouth docks or of the Thames-side at Wapping?

This, to some extent, is the dyed-in-the-wool attitude of the conservative Englishman, and Wales no doubt would have been more indulgent if the Tahitians had been less eulogized by the early explorers. Yet his remarks are interesting because they are the beginning of a more critical approach to the south Pacific legend; he is no longer caught up in the wonder of discovery, he makes judgements about what he sees. The *Resolution*, moreover, on this long voyage had taken the British to other Pacific islands, and it was now possible to make comparisons. Wales, for instance, was inclined to think (and with some reason) that the inhabitants of the Marquesas to the north-east of Tahiti were better-looking people than the Tahitians, just as the New Zealand Maoris were more advanced in their carving and other crafts. Little by little too it was beginning to emerge that there were at least two distinct races inhabiting the Pacific islands, the Polynesian or Tahitian type, and the Melanesians living in the archipelagos to the north-east of Australia. The Melanesians were darker and more thick set than the Polynesians, their hair was woolly and they lacked the Polynesian grace; they opposed, as it were, a Teutonic heaviness to the Latin ebullience of the Tahitians. One could afford to be comic about the Melanesian primitiveness. We find Clerke writing of the New Caledonians:

'*When we found them they were totally naked to the penis which was wrapped up in leaves, and whatever you gave them, or they by any means obtained, was immediately applied there . . . I gave one of them a stocking – and he very deliberately pulled it on there – I then gave him a string of beads; with it he tied the stocking up – I then presented him with a medal which he immediately hung to it – in short, let that noble part be well decorated and fine, they're perfectly happy and totally indifferent about the state of all the rest of the body.*'

Such bawdiness would never have been applied by the *Resolution*'s diarists to the sophisticates of Matavai Bay.

The Forsters were also able to make a more scientific appraisal of the island-ers than any of their predecessors had done; indeed, it is only fair to acknowl-edge the father as a pioneer in the social anthropology and comparative study of native peoples in the Pacific. The son was inclined to think that the excesses that occurred when the *Resolution* put in to the island were more the fault of the bestial British sailors than of the Tahitians, and he reinforces Wales's point that only the lowest class of women were involved. However, he permitted him-self this lyrical and less than scientific note:

'*A kind of happy uniformity runs through the whole life of the Tahitians. They rise*

74

The Forsters, father and son

Being displaced Europeans, the Forsters were not so influenced by the deeply held belief that British civilization had received the Almighty's special nod. Johann Reinhold Forster (1729–98), a Polish Prussian scholar, had gone to live in England where several of his publications on entomology, flora and fauna won him the acquaintance of Banks and Solander. With his broad expertise and knowledge, he emerged as a natural and ready substitute when Banks was dropped by the Admiralty for Cook's second expedition in 1772. Voted £4,000 by Parliament, Forster was the best paid ship's naturalist to set forth and he took his seventeen-year-old son George (who was already a talented botanist and natural history illustrator) along with him as his assistant. Both men were excellent linguists as well as scientists and, with their range of skills, they acquired a considerable body of natural history, anthropological and geographical knowledge on what proved to be Cook's most extensive voyage of the south Pacific. George (1754–94) published *A Voyage Round the World in His Britannic Majesty's Sloop Res-*olution in 1777, and his father followed with *Observations made during a voyage around the World on Physical Geography, Natural History, and Ethnic Philosophy*, the next year. The books, published also in German, were to have a profound effect on German literature and science, George's more popular account becoming one of the most widely read and best scientific travel books of the time. His views on the South Sea islanders were said to have influenced Goethe's ideas on law in Nature. With three visits to New Zealand, the Forsters also laid the foundations for all subsequent studies of the natural history of the southern island. 'Whenever we landed,' wrote George, 'we all set about collecting with all our might, birds, plants, fish and shellfish.' Back on board, Forster the elder assigned zoological classifications to the new and exciting material while George drew and annotated each new specimen they had collected. Johann Reinhold Forster was later appointed professor of Natural History, Medicine and Mineralogy at Halle, while George left England at the age of twenty-four to become professor of Natural History in Cassel and, later, took the Natural History Chair in Wilna, Polish Lithuania.

with the sun, and hasten to rivers and fountains, to perform an ablution equally reviving and cleanly. They pass the morning at work, or walk about until the heat of the day increases, when they retreat to their dwellings, or repose under some tufted tree. There they amuse themselves with smoothing their hair, and anoint it with fragrant oils; or they blow the flute, and sing to it, or listen to the songs of the birds. At the hour of noon, or a little later, they go to dinner. After their meals they resume their domestic amusements, during which the flame of mutual affection spreads in every heart, and unites the rising generation with new and tender ties. The lively jest, without ill-nature, the artless tale, the jocund dance and frugal supper, bring on the evening; and another visit to the river concludes the actions of the day. Thus contented with their simple way of life, and placed in a delightful country, they are free from cares, and happy in their ignorance.'

This is taking us right back to the enthusiasm of Bougainville and Banks, and with embellishments, and one hastens to add that young Forster was not always as ecstatic as this. Yet it was perfectly true that there was still much to admire in the Tahitian civilization, not only its primitiveness but its accomplishments as well. At the time of this second visit of the *Resolution*, Tu and his advisers were preparing an expedition against the neighbouring island of Moorea, and the Englishmen were treated to an astonishing spectacle, a review in which no fewer than 330 canoes took part, some of them almost as long as the *Resolution* herself, and it was estimated that they were manned by nearly 8,000 men. The painting by Hodges now in Admiralty House gives one an idea of the scope of this display – the banners floating from the immensely high, carved prows, the *arioi* and the chiefs riding in the stern and got up in fantastic feathered headdresses and coloured robes, the myriad warriors brandishing their spears, the multitude of people watching from the shore. It was a high moment in the island's history, a demonstration of what purely native art could achieve without the aid of Europeans. And in fact the synthesis with the West had not gone far in 1774. The handful of foreign ships that had visited the island in the previous seven years may have created an underlying unrest, but there were no real inroads on Tahitian culture as yet. Nails and hatchets had been distrubuted, together with a few clothes and harmless trinkets such as beads. European liquor had been offered to the chiefs and most of them had turned away from it in disgust. They had stolen muskets which they did not know how to use and which in any case they were forced to return. Except for a few pumpkins and melons none of the seeds imported by Banks had flourished, and of the livestock only some goats left behind by Furneaux were breeding. Cook now, rather whimsically (perhaps he wanted to get rid of them), landed twenty cats, but roast cat was never to be a Tahitian delicacy as roast dog was.

Except for one man whom Cook had taken down to the Antarctic, no Tahitian had returned from the outside world to regale his countrymen with the wonders he had seen: Tupia and his boy were dead, another man taken off by Bougainville had died of smallpox at Madagascar when he was being brought back from France, and Omai, the Tahitian who had sailed with Furneaux in the *Adventure*, had not yet reached England. No white man had yet taken up permanent residence on the island. Thus the long downslide into western civilization had still not really begun, and the Tahitian virtues as well as their vices remained peculiarly their own. Yet the mutual attraction between the islanders and the Englishmen was very great and obviously was going to become stronger. When the *Resolution* was about to leave, a number of young Tahitians came to Cook and begged to be allowed to go with him, and at the same time many of the English sailors longed to stay on the island. One of them, an Irishman named John Marra, actually attempted to do so.

Marra was an interesting case. He was a particularly troublesome and footloose character whom Cook had picked up in Batavia in 1770 when he was returning to England in the *Endeavour*. He had sailed again in the *Resolution* – had probably been forced to sail – and on the voyage had been constantly confined or flogged for insolence, drunkenness and mutinous behaviour. But he was quite a literate character and a good seaman. Now, as the *Resolution* sailed away from Matavai Bay, he jumped overboard and swam to a canoe which, by previous arrangement, had come out to meet him. One of the *Resolution*'s boats was launched and picked him up, but again he jumped and again was recovered. Cook was much less severe with him than he had been with Webb and Gibson, the two marines who had attempted to desert on his

European offering Tahitian a drink, from an engraving by R. B. Godfrey after Parkinson.

first visit to the island; he merely put him in irons for the night. And now he wrote in his journal:

'I know not if he might not have obtained my consent if he had applied for it in proper time. I never learnt that he had either friends or connexion to confine him to any particular part of the world, all nations were alike to him; where [could] such a man spend his days better than at one of these isles where, in one of the finest climates in the world, he can enjoy all the necessaries and some of the luxuries of life in ease and plenty?'

George Forster also spared a thought for the unhappy Marra:

'It was highly probable that, immediately on his return to England, instead of indulging in repose those limbs which had been tossed from pole to pole, he would be placed in another ship where the same fatigues, nocturnal watches and unwholesome food would still fall to his share; or though he were allowed to solace himself for a few days after a long series of hardships he must expect to be seized in the midst of his enjoyments and to be dragged, an unwilling champion, to the defence of his country; to be cut off in the flower of his age, or to remain miserably crippled, with only half his limbs, might be the alternatives to which he would be reduced. But supposing he should escape these misfortunes, still he must earn his subsistence in England at the expense of labour and in the sweat of his brow when this eldest curse of mankind is scarcely felt at Taheitee.'

Likeable scalliwag John Marra

John Marra ran through Cook's expeditions like a colourful thread. Cook picked him up originally in Batavia, along with over twenty other seamen, to strengthen the *Endeavour*'s decimated crew. A young Irishman from Cork, Marra deserted a Danish ship to join the now famous navigator. He subsequently joined the *Resolution* as gunner's mate in 1772, although he suffered from cold feet and tried to desert before the voyage began. Now, as the *Resolution* prepared to leave Tahiti, Marra was found deserting again. Sea life and the enticement of freedom held him in conflicting thrall. Cook clearly had a soft spot for the man; when Marra once more departed without leave at Tory Channel, New Zealand, Cook had him pursued, certain that if he didn't, the wild Irishman 'would be killed and eaten before morning'. Yet Marra stole a march on Cook. Six weeks after the *Resolution* docked in England, he had an account of the voyage in press (doubtless assisted by other hands) under the arresting title, *Journal of the Resolution's Voyage . . . by which the non-existence of an undiscovered Continent, between the Equator and the 50th degree of Southern Latitude, is demonstrably proved* (1776). The book was translated into both German and French. A likeable scalliwag himself, Marra had some acute observations to make on the noble savage of Tahiti. 'Perhaps their propensity for theft,' he summed up, 'may yet be found upon examination to be less criminal in them than it is generally esteemed. Is it not very natural, when a people see a company of strangers come among them, and without ceremony cut down their trees, gather their fruit and in short take what they want, that such a people should use as little ceremony with strangers as the strangers do with them. If so, against whom is the criminality to be charged, the Christians or the savage?' Marra finally fetched up after 1800 in Port Jackson, Australia.

William Hodges's 'War Galleys at Tahiti'. This spectacle left a strong impression on the artist and the presentation of detail of the war canoes, the warriors and their spears, and the rolling mountains of the island indicate that it was a compositive painting carefully blended when Hodges returned home.

This was putting things in too dismal a light. Yet there was food for the philosophers in all this. Was the European sailor's lot so hateful and physical love on this beautiful island so strong that men were willing to give up all prospect of seeing their homes and families again? Despite the opposing evidence of Wales there was something infinitely appealing to most men about the Tahitian girl, something gentle as well as ardent, the embodiment of femininity in the smiling eyes and mouth, the bright hibiscus flower in the black hair, the bare feet and the smooth brown skin. For the sailor she had the important attribute of being available and she was affectionate as well.

On the other hand, if Tahiti was so paradisical a place, why had so many of the natives been so eager to sail with Cook, even though they were warned that they could never be brought back? Could it be that the *dolce far niente* existence could also become a decline into intolerable boredom, and that man, in addition to a fundamental sense of guilt, suffers also from a fundamental discontent? Or was it simply that human curiosity, the desire for change and adventure, was stronger than a sense of security, and that all these men were young and did not stop to think that the breaking of their traditional ties would probably be for ever?

At all events, Cook now sailed away without allowing any Tahitian to embark for England, and in July 1775 – three years after setting out – we find him back in Plymouth. This time he had lost not a single man through sickness. Again there was the excitement at his return: 'A glorious voyage,' cries Solander in a letter to Banks. The *Resolution* had brought back 'curiosities' galore: a shrivelled human head, three live Tahitian dogs, maps and charts for King George delineating his new possessions in the Pacific, casks filled with bird skins and other specimens for Banks, innumerable sketches by Hodges, and a mass of scientific observations.

Now finally at the age of forty-six the Yorkshire labourer's son had arrived, and there could be no question whatever about where the credit for the voyage lay: it was Cook whom everyone wanted to meet. A sinecure was found for him, a jump in rank and an appointment as a captain at Greenwich Hospital with a salary of £200 a year. Yet soon he was remarking ruefully,

'a few months ago the whole Southern Hemisphere was hardly big enough for me, and now I am going to be confined within the limits of Greenwich Hospital, which are far too small for an active mind like mine. I must, however, confess that it is a fine retreat and a pretty income, but whether I can bring myself to like ease and retirement, time will show.'

It took less than twelve months. There never could have been any likelihood of his hanging on at Greenwich; he was far gone with the discoverer's disease, he had the habit of risk and he could not give it up. Omai, the Tahitian whom Furneaux had brought to England, had to be returned to his home, and the Admiralty decided that this mission should be extended to an exploration of the north Pacific – a voyage which might also reveal whether or not a north-west passage existed across the north polar seas. Cook was the obvious commander, and on 12 July 1776, only twelve months after his return, he set out once more.

He carried with him in the *Resolution* as first lieutenant his old shipmate, John Gore, and the master was a promising young navigator, William Bligh. Charles Clerke was advanced to the command of the sister ship, the *Discovery*, and the artist was John Webber, the son of a Swiss sculptor. The ships took with them a rather troublesome cargo of English livestock which George III – Farmer George – wished to present to Tu.

Then there was Omai. He had had an extraordinary time in England, and he is worth considering here for a moment since he was to be the first Tahitian to return from the civilized world to his native land. He was not a very impressive young man, nor was he, as it was pretended, of noble birth. But he was

Greenwich Hospital

The idea of a royal hospital for seamen at Greenwich had been conceived by Queen Mary in 1692. It was designed as the last great architectural masterpiece of Christopher Wren, but was not completed until after his death in 1723. In addition to its paternal service to seamen, Greenwich Hospital formed part of the institutional hierarchy of the Royal Navy for high-ranking officers with commendable service behind them. Cook had been promoted post-captain on his return on the *Resolution* and immediately appointed to a 74-gun ship, the *Kent*. But within a day of this appointment, his commission was cancelled and the ship laid up at Plymouth. Cook was subsequently appointed to the sinecure as Fourth Captain on the naval establishment at Greenwich Hospital where free quarters and one shilling and twopence a day 'table money' were added to his salary of over £200 a year. 'I must confess,' he noted dejectedly, 'that it is a fine retreat and a pretty income.' But Cook was saved from such inaction by the pressing need to oversee the publication of his journal of the second voyage, a task he carried out with Mrs Cook from his home at Mile End. With this complete, his third journey to look for a north-west passage began taking shape.

fairly bright, he was biddable, and he had been a wonderful rarity in London. Furneaux's first act on his return had been to hand him over to Banks, who could speak Tahitian and who had been very ready to display this prime specimen of South Sea island life. He had dressed him up in a frogged coat and sword, had taught him a few words of English, and had launched him into the social round; he had dined with Dr Johnson (who found his behaviour elegant), had been to the theatre to see Garrick, had visited the House of Lords and at Christmas had spent several weeks at Hinchinbroke with Lord Sandwich. He had even been introduced to George III (when he came out with, 'How do, King Tosh?'). Reynolds had painted him nobly swathed in turban and robes, Nathaniel Dance had sketched him with equal grandeur (though clutching a wooden stool), and William Parry had depicted him in a formally posed group with Banks and Solander. The latter wrote:

'We dined with him at the Duke of Gloucester's. At going away the Duchess gave him her pocket-handkerchief, which he properly received with thanks, and observing her name marked upon it, he took an opportunity, when she looked at him, to kiss it.'

Fanny Burney had been entranced with this 'lyon of lyons'; he had been irresistible the way he was forever jumping up and bending over the ladies' hands. He had seemed, she had written,

'to shame education, for his manners are so extremely graceful, and he is so polite, attentive and easy that you would have thought he came from some foreign court . . . I think this shows how much more Nature can do without art than art, with all her refining, unassisted by Nature.'

Decidedly Miss Burney was on the side of the noble-savage school.

There had been a break in these enjoyments; the young man had been inoculated against smallpox and had only recovered after a long and serious con-

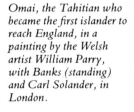

Omai, the Tahitian who became the first islander to reach England, in a painting by the Welsh artist William Parry, with Banks (standing) and Carl Solander, in London.

Omai created a stir in London

Omai, or more correctly 'Mae', had been involved with the British from the first landfall in Tahiti when he was wounded during Wallis's initial skirmish with the Tahitians. Cook's second-in-command, Furneaux, took him on the *Adventure* after the expedition landed at Matavai Bay in 1773, and at length took him with him to England. In one sense Omai was the British equivalent of Bougainville's Aotourou though he came from a different island and his status was lower. He exhibited a 'cheerful imitativeness and good-will' and created a mild stir in London. When at first, bemused by the city, he got lost, he called out loudly to be led to Mr Banks! He learnt to skate, an amazing feat for a Pacific islander, and was generally taken about and entertained by Banks as a substitute for the dead Tupia. There were cultural problems. Given a sporting gun on one estate, Omai cheerfully destroyed the barnyard fowls along with the game birds with equal display of enthusiasm.

When, after two years in England, Cook returned him to Tahiti on his third expedition, Omai clung to his English mentor and did not want to go ashore. His difficulties in readjusting to his native land were great and he died some two years later. Of Omai, the elder Dr Forster wisely remarked that he should have been taught a trade conducive to the advancement of his island when he returned: 'He should have been presented with tools, not trinkets.'

valescence in the country. But then he had gone off again with his fashionable protectors: up to Yorkshire to shoot grouse with Banks, back to London for lunch with the Burneys, down the channel in the Admiralty yacht. George III had given him a pension, and he had become so accustomed to English ways that he had been able to set up on his own in lodgings in Warwick Street. It was hoped that when Cook returned him to Tahiti he would regale his countrymen with all the wonders he had seen, and gifts were showered upon him from every side: a wardrobe of fine clothes, a portable organ, an electrical machine, a suit of armour, and a battery of pots, pans and cutlery.

All this was very well in its way, but it rather overstrained Omai's capacities as an *entrepreneur* of western culture in the Pacific. However, for the moment he was happy enough in his berth in the *Resolution*, and a fairly uneventful voyage brought the ship back to Tahiti in August 1777.

In many ways Cook's last visit to the island is the most interesting of all, since we now begin to see its future taking shape. The first thing that he heard when he got ashore on the north-eastern coast was that the Spaniards had been back. They had arrived in two vessels, the *Aguila* and another, and had landed a party of priests and their attendants who had remained for ten months before they were taken off. This was a distinct jump forward in the European intrusion, for while the Spaniards had been very correct in their dealing with the Tahitians – none of their sailors was allowed to have any contact with the women – they had attempted to convert the people to Christianity, and they had claimed the island for Spain. Cook went to see the house they had built, the first European house (if you except Fort Venus) to be erected on Tahiti. It was made of prefabricated timber and consisted of just two bare rooms in which a bedstead, a table and one or two other pieces of furniture had been abandoned. A cross was planted on the ground outside, and on it had been carved the words

CHRISTUS VINCIT

CAROLUS III IMPERAT. 1774

This was not very alarming. For one reason or another – one suspects the massive indolence of the Tahitians had something to do with it – the venture had obviously failed. Still, one can understand Cook being piqued, especially when he heard that the Spaniards had warned the Tahitians against the British, and had told them that any British ship that came to this part of the coast should be sent away as it was Spanish property. To make it quite clear that the British had prior rights Cook added his own inscription to the cross:

GEORGIUS TERTIUS REX

ANNIS 1767

(the year of Wallis's arrival); and then the dates of his own visits:

1769, 1773, 1774 & 1777

This was, perhaps, a primitive piece of claim-staking, but Spain and England were on the verge of war at this time, and it was quite possible that the *Aguila* would return to Tahiti.

Moving around to Matavai Bay with his two ships, Cook found that Obarea was dead, but Tu was still there and the island more prosperous than ever. Their expedition against Moorea of three years before had not succeeded, but they were preparing to try again, and they overwhelmed Cook with compliments and provisions in the hope that he would join them in the enterprise: a thing he absolutely refused to do. Red feathers were still the rage, and little or nothing could be bought with nails, beads and other European trinkets – indeed, the principal men had acquired so many of these articles that what they really wanted were wooden chests to keep them in. Cook got his carpenter to run up a particularly solid box for Tu; it was big enough for two men to sleep on top of at night, the only really effective guard against thieves. Furneaux's goats were thriving, and although we hear nothing of Cook's cats, a gander given to Obarea by Wallis ten years earlier was still surviving, and the Spaniards had left a bull behind. To these Cook now added a bull of his own, three cows, a horse and a mare, a number of sheep and European pigs, two turkeys, a gander and three geese, a drake and four ducks. A fruit and vegetable garden was also planted. The horses, the first seen on Tahiti, were a great wonder, and Cook and Clerke were followed by crowds as they rode round Matavai beach.

There were no thefts or disagreements on this occasion (mainly because Tu planted his own guards around the British encampment), and Cook, who could now speak enough Tahitian to make himself understood, settled down amongst them, dining in their huts and entertaining them on board the *Resolution*, almost as if he were at home in England. When he had a rheumatic pain in his legs twelve Tahitian women massaged him in the great cabin until he was comfortable again. The chiefs, too, were much franker than they had been before. Where formerly they had been very reluctant to admit that they practised human sacrifice they now invited Cook to see the ceremony for himself. It was a strange and horrifying scene, and the drawing of it by John Webber, the *Resolution*'s artist, was to become the most celebrated of all the pictures brought home from the Pacific. Cook stands to one side with Tu and a group of notables. He has removed his hat (at Tu's request) but he is wearing his full uniform of stockings, breeches, long waistcoat and top-coat and must have been uncomfortably hot, since two boys are flaying a pig on a fire before him. To the left of the picture we see two standing men beating on tall drums, and a group of priests or *arioi* seated on the ground. In front of them is the sacrifice – a middle-aged man of the lowest class who had been clubbed to death the day before. The body is trussed to a pole and lies prone on the earth. Behind this are the men digging his grave, a raised platform laden with dead sacrificial pigs, and an assortment of wooden images and the skulls of earlier victims – some forty-nine in all, by Cook's estimate, and most of them but recently placed there. In the background coconut palms and the rank vegetation of the island rise up against a cloudy sky.

The arresting thing, of course, is that Cook should have been there at all, evidently giving his countenance to the proceedings, but he makes no bones about his interest and he has left a very full description of how the ceremony continued for two days: of the drumming and the chanting, of the disembowelling of the pigs, of the burial of the unfortunate man, and of the boy who, in moments of eerie silence, screamed aloud, supposedly in imitation of the voice of God.

Cook says it was by no means a reverent or awed crowd which stood and watched; from time to time they turned their backs and talked of other things.

'A Human Sacrifice at Otaheite' by John Webber, artist to the second voyage of the Resolution. Cook was present at this ceremony performed in a Tahitian marae in 1777. The stark horror of the event was somewhat reduced by the fact that the unlucky victim – a man from the lowest caste – had been despatched by a blow on the head the previous day and his body was ceremoniously offered to the gods in the presence of King Tu, the priests and the visiting British captain. Webber's painting was to become the most celebrated of all the pictures brought home from the Pacific. It gave rather a different impression to the world of what Banks had so enthusiastically described as 'the truest picture of an Arcadia of which we were going to be kings'.

But he does convey a feeling of supernatural tenseness that was in the air, a kind of bated and trance-like communion with an invisible power that was being invoked through the sacrifice. Cook was in no doubt whatever that the Tahitians believed in the efficacy of these mysteries (in this case they were sacrificing for the success of their new expedition against Moorea), and he knew it was useless to protest. Yet it was a spectacle that did no service to Diderot and other celebrants of the cult of the noble savage. It suggested that peace and goodwill were no more possible in Tahiti than they were in Europe, and that there was a death-wish, a yearning for outrage, even here in Arcady.

Then too the return of Omai was a dismal failure. The Tahitian nobles were not at all prepared to bother with a young man who had never been of any consequence amongst them before he had sailed to England. They studiously ignored him, and it was not until they discovered that he had a hoard of red feathers that they would even speak to him. Omai himself behaved very foolishly: in an attempt to draw attention to himself he dispersed his goods with reckless generosity, and not to the influential Tahitians whose protection he needed, but to his relatives and people of his own class. Cook did all he could to check him, and eventually impounded his goods, but by then it was too late: the chiefs were furious that so many rich gifts had eluded them, and it was clear that this pet of the British was going to get short shrift once the *Resolution* had sailed away.

In the end it was decided that Omai should not be left at Tahiti but transported to the neighbouring island of Huahine. Here Cook in his anxiety over the young man's future went too far: he not only got him a grant of land by the sea, he also built him a solid European hut where he could store his possessions, and added to these two horses, some pigs and a whole armoury of firearms: a musket, a fowling piece, two pair of pistols, all with a supply of ammunition, and swords and cutlasses as well. One is hard put to understand Cook's motives here, he knew better than anyone the folly of putting fire-arms into the hands of the Tahitians, and he confessed in his journal that he saw little hope of Omai being able to withstand the jealousy which now, as a rich man, inevitably surrounded him. He had no rank or authority, and riches could never give them to him. Even before Cook sailed, Omai was putting aside his ridiculous European clothes and reverting to Tahitian manners. It was evident that it would not be long before he was outmanoeuvred and robbed of everything he owned. Whoever then got possession of the firearms was certainly going to use them.

'Omai's Public Entry on his first landing at Ota-heite', from an engraving after Daniel Dodd. Among the many gifts showered upon Omai when he left London to return with Cook to Tahiti was a sword from Banks and a suit of mail from Lord Sandwich which was fashioned for him by the armourers of the Tower of London. His reception, however, was far from triumphal and there was much jealousy over the riches and status accorded to this man who had neither rank nor authority in his homeland. Cook finally settled Omai on Huahine Island where he rapidly put aside his luxurious European trappings and reverted to Tahitian manners.

Cook was clearly much loved by Pacific islanders who saw him as a god or king. Here, the King of Owyhee (Hawaii) and his tribe bring presents to Captain Cook. From a painting by John Webber.

Already there were signs that the islanders were becoming less frightened of the Europeans. When two men deserted from the *Discovery* at Raiatea, Cook, in the usual way, seized a chief and his family as hostages, but this time the islanders attempted to retaliate; instead of bringing the men back they made plans to ambush Cook and Clerke while they were bathing on shore, and would have done so had not a native girl given the plot away. In the end the deserters were brought back, but there was a clear warning here that familiarity with the European was breeding, if not contempt, then a certain confidence that could easily turn to aggression.

Perhaps Cook, after the tremendous strain of these years, was growing tired. He is less patient, he reacts more harshly when he is opposed. He had the ears cut off a particularly persistent thief at Huahine, and we hear of instances when his temper flares up, not always with good reason. Yet he was still loved. Omai broke down when he left, and the Tahitian chiefs and their families were in tears. Cook wrote in his journal: 'It is to no purpose to tell them that you will not return. They think you must.' Then again he went back to his favourite theme, his nagging sense of responsibility to the island 'I own'. He went on:

'I cannot avoid expressing it as my real opinion that it would have been far better for these poor people never to have known our superiority in the accommodations and arts that make life comfortable, than after once knowing it, so be again left and abandoned in their original incapacity of improvement. Indeed they cannot be restored to that happy

86

mediocrity in which they lived before we discovered them, if the intercourse between us should be discontinued. It seems to me that it has become, in a manner, incumbent on the Europeans to visit them once in three or four years, in order to supply them with those conveniences which we have introduced among them, and have given them a predilection for. The want of such occasional supplies will, probably, be felt very heavily by them, when it may be too late to go back to their old, less perfect, contrivances, which they now despise, and have discontinued since the introduction of ours. For, by the time that the iron tools, of which they are now possessed, are worn out, they will have almost lost the knowledge of their own. A stone hatchet is, at present, as rare a thing amongst them, as an iron one was eight years ago, and a chisel of bone or stone is not to be seen.'

In other words, once having entered into the coil of civilization you cannot go back; you must go on whatever the dangers may be.

These were Cook's last words on Tahiti. Having spent six weeks in Tahiti itself and several more in the nearby islands, dropping off seeds and more livestock wherever he landed, he sailed to America and the arctic north, and to Kealakekua Bay, in the Hawaiian Islands, where, on his second visit, the familiar pattern was repeated: one of the *Discovery*'s boats was stolen by the natives and Cook intended to take their king as a hostage. But this was once too often. The greatest sailor of his day, the man who, in Charles Darwin's phrase, had added a hemisphere to the civilized world, was as vulnerable as other men. In a scuffle on the shore he turned his back on the enraged islanders and was stabbed from behind; this was followed by other mortal blows and he fell face downwards into the warm Pacific water. He was just fifty years of age.

Other scenes of islanders' fervour were depicted on the second voyage of the artist William Hodges. Here, Cook is shown landing on Middleburgh Island (Eua) in Tonga, being greeted by the inhabitants with gifts of fruit. A native in the pinnace holds up a leaf as a sign of goodwill. Hodges was somewhat carried away in this neoclassical depiction of the Friendly Islands.

Cook's tragic death

Cook's biographer, Beaglehole, has deeply pondered the matter of Cook's death, killed by Polynesians who revered him well. It was, he concludes, the tragic death of a tired man. Cook and his crew had been hard at it on the north American coast and in the Bering and Arctic seas when he put in at Kealakekua Bay to overhaul the *Resolution* and *Discovery*. With the theft of the *Discovery*'s cutter he went ashore, uncharacteristically, with a body of marines, to take a chief as hostage. He had, in fact, in Beaglehole's words, 'got not merely New Zealand and Australia but most of the Pacific in [geographic] order, and a good part of the south Atlantic as well.' He had repeatedly taken hostages on his voyages. But, on this occasion, he lost his temper and shot a man at a most unfavourable time. The natives's tempers flared and the great navigator, beloved of his own men and the Hawaiians, was struck down. His action, says his biographer, was evidence of a mind blunted that had 'through weariness lost its finest edge'. 'Dear Sir,' Lord Sandwich, Lord of the Admiralty conveyed the dreadful news to Joseph Banks in London in January 1780, '. . . poor Captain Cook is no more.'

5

Arcady reformed

BY THE TIME of Cook's death the Pacific had become a fashionable as well as a scientific vogue in Europe. Any sort of bric-a-brac from the islands – native carvings, pieces of coral, wooden idols, exotic sea-shells – became collectors' items, and the sailor who could produce from his locker a Polynesian head-dress or a length of cloth was sure to get a handsome price for it. Imitations of Tahitian dancing to the beating of drums fascinated London audiences no less than the hornpipe and the bagpipes had fascinated the Tahitians, and the islanders themselves were the subject of endless speculation. ★

The explorers' books, huge quarto volumes costing five guineas or more, were valuable properties, and the Admiralty tried to block unofficial publications by forcing the crews to hand over their logs and journals at their journey's end. This was not always successful. John Marra, the man who attempted to desert at Tahiti, got out an account of the *Resolution*'s second voyage within six months of his return, and George Forster, with two stout volumes, managed to precede Cook's official publication by six weeks. For a young man of twenty-two Forster wrote remarkably well, and he did not altogether deserve Dr Johnson's blunt judgement that there was a great affectation of fine writing in his book. Boswell protested, 'But he carries you along with him.' Johnson: 'No, Sir; he does not carry *me* along with him: he leaves me behind . . .'

It was Cook whom everyone really wanted to read, and his accounts of his last two voyages were substantially his own. In France Louis XVI had a special translation made for the Dauphin, and was himself so moved by the *Resolution*'s adventures that he sent out La Pérouse in 1785 to follow in Cook's wake – a tragic enterprise, for the French navigator vanished into the Pacific, never to be seen again.

Cook's own death struck a note of high emotional tragedy which was hardly to recur in England until the loss of Nelson at Trafalgar twenty-five years later. Six artists in addition to Zoffany depicted the scene at Kealakekua Bay – the dying hero falling back into the sea and the frantic savages brandishing their spears above him – and it was a theme that made a strong appeal to the Georgian poets as well. This, for them, was death in Arcady, tragedy in surroundings of extreme natural beauty, and the ignorant natives were not so much assassins as the implacable instruments of fate. Painters as well as poets were still seeing the Pacific with European eyes. William Hodges, the artist on Cook's second voyage, managed to convey an idea of strange southern light, but his Tahitians are classical figures in a landscape, their arms uplifted in a graceful pose, and his war canoes remind one of a Venetian carnival. (Inciden-

★ For an admirable exposition of this subject see *European Vision and the South Pacific* by Bernard Smith.

tally, it is odd that so gifted a man should have abandoned painting in favour of banking in later life, and that, overwhelmed with debts, he should have died by his own hand.) John Webber, who sailed with Cook on his last voyage, was a very able illustrator with a particular flair for representing vegetation and such details as a native ornament or the costume of a Tahitian dancing girl; but when he comes to paint the girl herself the Tahitian naturalness flies away, and she is a lush and voluptuous Italianate debutante who has bared her body to the waist.

In the same way Cook's voyages released a flood of imaginative travel writing, in which the European nostalgia and the European predicament linger on. The literary uses of explorers' adventures and of remote tropical islands had already been exploited in England – Defoe's *Robinson Crusoe* had been published in 1719 and Swift's *Gulliver's Travels* a year or two later – but Cook's discoveries gave a more romantic and mystical form to the movement. Coleridge's *Ancient Mariner*, published in 1798, contained descriptions that were clearly inspired by Cook's voyages, and from Coleridge the way led to Byron (whose grandfather, Commodore John Byron, had sailed in the *Dolphin* in the Pacific), and many other lesser poets who were soon to launch themselves on the luminous wastes of the southern ocean.

In 1785 the Theatre Royal in Covent Garden produced a new Christmas pantomime: *Omai, or a Trip around the World*, by John O'Keefe. Briefly the plot was as follows: Omai, heir to the Tahitian throne, is warned by a prophet that he must go to England and win the hand of an English girl, Londina, which he does. No problems of miscegenation here; Londina loves her dusky chieftain as Desdemona loved Othello. The couple return to Tahiti where Omai outwits the sorceress, Obarea, and is installed on his throne in Matavai Bay. The performance ends with a finale in which a chorus of British sailors sings a tribute to Captain Cook while a huge portrait of the navigator is lowered to the stage.

An enormous amount of money was spent on this piece. Philip de Loutherbourg, an Alsatian painter who was Garrick's stage designer, introduced many novel and spectacular effects: a storm at sea and showers of hail, a red tropical moon in eclipse (inspired by the transit of Venus perhaps), an iceberg and glimpses of Matavai Bay and other glamorous places visited by Cook on his voyages. For his costumes Loutherbourg went to the drawings and paintings of Hodges and Webber: Obarea was hung about with exotic tassels and beads, the prophet was an immense bearded figure with a necklet of red feathers and a 1.5 m (5 ft) headdress sprouting like a tree-fern from his head, and the Tahitian dancing girls were got up in billowing crinolines of red and gold. It was an entertainment that well might have had its appeal in the twentieth century, for the formula was much the same as that used in spectacular films: the romanticizing of an historical incident, the attempt at reality in the exotic decor, the white hero facing the frenzied crowd of natives, and the same bogusness over all. Nothing like it had been seen on the London stage before, and it had an immediate success. Reynolds, who went to the opening night, approved of the costumes and the scenery, and the critics were enthusiastic. The production ran for fifty performances and was repeated in the following two seasons at Covent Garden.

La Morte du Capitaine Cook, a French pantomime in four acts by a M. Arnould, had an even greater *réclame*. It followed roughly the pattern of Omai,

Cook's death and his re-
markable journeys led to a
spate of books, poems and
theatrical productions
commemorating the col-
ourful scenes at Tahiti.
The pantomine Omai,
or a Trip around the
World by John O'Keefe
was perhaps the most
romantic and extravagant
and was put on at the
Theatre Royal, Covent
Garden, in 1785. This
watercolour, by P. J. de
Loutherbourg, Garrick's
stage designer, depicts the
costume of the 'Enchant-
ress' Oberea, Queen of
Tahiti, used in the pro-
duction. The pantomine
ran for fifty performances
and was repeated in two
subsequent seasons.

the scene being set in O-Why-e, presumably Hawaii, and Cook was made to
meet his death as a consequence of having involved himself in the tragedy of
two South Sea island lovers. A volcano erupted on the stage during the performance. It was first produced in Paris in 1788 and the following year was
brought over to Covent Garden where it was described as 'a grand Serious-
Pantomime-Ballet, In Three Parts, As now exhibiting in Paris with uncommon Applause, with French Music, New Scenery, Machinery and other
Decorations'.

And so the romantic, exotic dream of the Pacific went steadily on its way. It
had not been really shaken by the sophisticated indifference of the Walpoles
and the Johnsons or by the derision of the satirists. It was too exciting for that
and, after all, there existed the good steady figure of Cook to prove – or at any
rate to seem to prove – that it was real. Above all, the Pacific was new. Here
was a whole new world to investigate, and it appeared possible that the Pacific
peoples, by remaining in a primitive state, had much to reveal about the
origins of the human race. Dr John Douglas, the Canon at Windsor, who
edited Cook's last journals, wrote in his introduction:

*'The expense of his three voyages did not, perhaps, far exceed that of digging out the
buried contents of Herculaneum. And we may add, that the novelties of the Society or
Sandwich Islands, seem better calculated to engage the attention of the studious in our
times, than the antiquities, which exhibit proofs of Roman magnificence.'*

There was indeed a great deal for the scientists to ruminate upon. Thomas Robert Malthus, for example, found support for his theories in 'the checks to population in the islands of the South Sea'. Could it be, he wondered, that the *arioi*, in practising infanticide, were deliberately ensuring that the inhabitants of Tahiti should never become too numerous for the available food supply?

Other unknown areas of the world were also being opened up at this time. We have Walpole writing in July 1774:

> *'There is just returned a Mr Bruce who has lived for three years in the court of Abyssinia, and breakfasted every morning with the Maids of Honour on live oxen. Otaheite and Mr Banks are quite forgotten.'*

Bruce had been to the source of the Blue Nile, but he was no more than a nine-days' wonder in London: it was he, not Banks, who was forgotten. Banks was still there in Soho Square, presiding at his celebrated Thursday breakfasts, expanding his collections and giving his money and his patronage to scientific enterprises of every kind. A few weeks before Cook's death in the Pacific he got married in London to a girl who was sixteen years his junior. In 1778 he was made president of the Royal Society, and from that influential post he was able to promote new expeditions to the South Seas. It was Banks who suggested that Bligh should be sent to Tahiti in the *Bounty* to collect

John Webber's painting of a Tahitian dancing girl, 'Poedooa, daughter of Orea, Chief of Ulietea'.

The controversial Captain William Bligh

Captain William Bligh transplanting bread-fruit trees from Tahiti in early 1789, from a painting by T. Gosse.

Sir Joseph Banks's abiding interest in the Pacific and in science lay behind the expedition of HMS *Bounty*. Under the command of Captain William Bligh, its aim was to collect breadfruit specimens from Tahiti and transplant them to the West Indies where, it was judged, they would provide healthy fare for the Negro slaves. Bligh was a natural appointment. He had served as master on the *Resolution* on Cook's third voyage, knew Tahiti, and had served in the West Indian trade between 1783–7. With personal instructions from Banks, he sailed from England in November 1787 and reached Tahiti eleven months later. Unluckily, Bligh was forced to wait for nearly five months on the island while the seedlings matured sufficiently to be transplanted in pots for the sea journey; and the wait proved his undoing. When the *Bounty* reached the Friendly Islands the crew, led by Fletcher Christian, mutinied, determined to return to their Tahitian attachments formed over the previous idyllic months.

Fortunately, Bligh's navigational skills had been fortified under Cook and this, with his capacity for charting, helped him navigate the 5,789 km (3,618 miles) from Tonga to Timor in a small open boat in company with eighteen 'loyalists'. Bligh not only managed to execute this perilous feat, but he charted part of north-east New Holland as he went. In 1791 he made a second attempt in command of HMS *Providence* to carry through 'operation bread-fruit', and again conducted important charting of south-east Tasmania, Fiji and Torres Straits as he carried his mission successfully west. He received the gold medal of the Royal Society of Arts on his return to England. Under Banks's patronage, Bligh became governor of New South Wales from 1806–8. As Moorehead sums up: 'It is strange that so much sentimentality about the whole *Bounty* incident has fixed itself not, as one would have supposed, on the sirenian allurements of the Tahitian women, but upon the irascible temper of this unfortunate man.'

breadfruit seedlings and then transport them to the West Indies, where, it was hoped, they would provide a staple diet for the Negro slaves.

The story of the *Bounty* mutiny has become so addled by popular myth that it is generally forgotten that it was caused, not so much by the authoritarian character of Captain Bligh, as by the undermining of his men's discipline during their long stay on Tahiti. Bligh arrived at the island towards the end of 1788, and had to wait there for five months until the seedlings were sufficiently mature to be planted in pots and stowed away in his great cabin. No large group of Europeans had remained so long on the island before, and the attachments formed by the *Bounty*'s crew with the Tahitian women were something more than those of a sailor's spree. Every man had his girl, and when they came to sail away many of them found the loss of their companions quite unendurable. That is why Fletcher Christian and his followers so treacherously rebelled when the *Bounty* reached the Friendly Islands: they wanted to return to their Tahitian girls and the easy life. Bligh's high-handedness no doubt precipitated the crisis, but it is a reasonable supposition that had they never been to Tahiti they would never have mutinied. And in fact, when the mutineers had abandoned Bligh and seized the ship, they did return to Tahiti, some of them to settle down there, others to go off with Tahitian women to Pitcairn Island.

Bligh in the meantime had performed his astonishing feat of crossing the Pacific in an open boat, had got himself back to England, and had set out for Tahiti once more with two vessels. This time he succeeded in transporting the breadfruit seedlings to the West Indies. Whatever else he may have been he was thorough, he carried out instructions, he was almost as good a navigator as Cook, and it is strange that so much sentimentality about the whole *Bounty* incident has fixed itself not, as one would have supposed, on the sirenian allurements of the Tahitian women, but upon the irascible temper of this unfortunate man.

In any case, the real importance of Bligh's two visits to Tahiti was that they greatly expanded European knowledge of South Sea island life. After his second trip in 1792 Bligh reported that a remarkable and disastrous change had overtaken Tahiti since Cook's last visit fifteen years earlier. Whaling ships had begun to call there, and the corruption of the natives had outstripped anything that even Diderot had imagined. Many of them were now addicted to drink and had discarded their own elegant clothes in favour of the dirty shirts and waistcoats given them by the sailors. They no longer washed as they had formerly done, and it was 'difficult to get them to speak their own language without mixing a jargon of English with it'. Just as Cook had feared they had become more and more dependent on European implements, and no one now bothered to make an axe or manufacture cloth, when these things could be so easily obtained from the ships.

With his usual thoroughness Bligh had attempted to prevent the spread of venereal disease. On his first trip to Tahiti he wrote in his log:

'As there was a great probability that we should remain a considerable time at Otaheite it could not be expected that the intercourse of my people should be of a very reserved nature. I therefore ordered that every person should be examined by the surgeon, and had the satisfaction to learn from his report that they were all perfectly free from the venereal complaint.'

And in fact at that time the disease seemed to be diminishing on the island; it had reverted to a milder form and the Tahitians claimed that they could cure it. But on Bligh's second visit he found that it was steadily gaining ground again – the result no doubt of the whaling ships calling at the island.

Now too the local tribal wars were much more drastic. Some fifty muskets had found their way into the natives' hands, and a chieftain's power was reckoned by the number of his European weapons. All this in fifteen years. From the pages of his journal Cook's voice might have been heard repeating, 'It would have been far better for these poor people never to have known us.'

Bligh's account was fully confirmed by the captain of the *Pandora*, which had come out to arrest the *Bounty* mutineers in 1791, and by the news of other vessels that called at Tahiti about this time. These reports did a great deal of damage to the South Sea island myth in Europe. Where now was the noble savage? His demoralization may have been the fault of the Europeans, but if he succumbed to his worst instincts as quickly as this could one really hold him up as an example to civilization, especially when one remembered that he already practised infanticide and human sacrifices (not to speak of his licentiousness) long before the Europeans arrived in the Pacific? Cook's death had been a shocking thing, and it was now recalled that he was not the only victim of the islanders' barbarity: Furneaux, on the second voyage, had lost ten men in New Zealand; they had been killed and eaten by cannibals at Queen Charlotte's Sound. Marion du Fresne, the French navigator, had also met his death in New Zealand, and fourteen of his men had been slaughtered with him. And now apparently the Tahitians too were turning on the white man; when one of the whaling ships was wrecked near the island the survivors were set upon in their boats and stripped of their clothing.

In France as well as England there were second thoughts about the docile Pacific. Marion's lieutenant, Julien Crozet, wrote on his return to Europe:

'I contend that among all created animals there is nothing more savage and dangerous than the natural and savage peoples themselves. . . . I endeavoured to stimulate their curiosity, to learn the emotions that could be awakened in their souls, but found nothing but vicious tendencies among the children of nature; and they are all the more dangerous in that they greatly surpass Europeans in physical strength. Within the same quarter of an hour I have found them to change from childish delight to deepest gloom, from complete calmness to the greatest heights of rage, and then burst into immoderate laughter the moment afterwards. I have noticed them change towards each other, one moment caressing, and menacing the next; but they were never long in the same mood, and always struck me as having dangerous and deceitful tendencies.'

We are a long way here from Rousseau and even further from Fanny Burney's talk of nature being superior to art.

Then there was La Pérouse who, before he vanished with his two ships in 1788, sent back a report from the Pacific: 'The most daring rascals of Europe are less hypocritical than the natives of these islands. All their caresses were false.' In general he found the Pacific inhabitants 'more malignant than the wildest beasts'. One wonders if wild beasts can be accurately described as malignant; still it was remarkable that La Pérouse, an intelligent and balanced man, should be so indignant.

Seen in this new light a drastically different picture of the South Sea islander

It is hardly surprising that La Pérouse should pass savage comment on the islanders of the Pacific. Members of his company were attacked at Tutuila in the eastern Samoas on 11 December 1787 as they prepared to leave, and twelve of the sixty-one men present, including the Astrolabe's *captain Commandant Fleuriot de Langle, were massacred. The ship's cleric died later on the journey from his wounds. Lithograph after N. Ozanne.*

was emerging: not a gentle or a noble savage, but, at his best, a poor benighted black, and at his worst a treacherous potential murderer who had been debased by luxury and self-indulgence. One had only to shift the evidence a little and one saw in place of idyllic love and natural goodness a world of thieves, voluptuaries, cannibals and idolaters – anarchy instead of Arcady, Sodom and Gomorrah rather then New Cythera. Civilization, it seems, had a clear duty to save these unfortunate people from themselves.

It was a point of view that was hardly less false than the original romantic dream of Tahiti, but it made its appeal to all those people who abhor a vacuum, whether geographical, commercial, political or religious. The scientists like Banks wanted to expand their investigations in the Pacific, the merchants wanted trade, the politicians wanted empire and the missionaries wanted to reclaim the pagans for Christianity.

The missionaries were first in the field. In 1795 a group of evangelists formed the London Missionary Society, and they lost no time in turning their attention to the Pacific. Thomas Haweis, one of the founders, preached the opening sermon on 'the innumerable islands which spot the bosom of the Pacific ocean'; where 'savage nature still feasts on the flesh of its prisoners – appeases its gods with human sacrifices – whole societies of men and women live promiscuously, and murder every infant born among them'. It was shocking, he went on, that the 'foolish Omai' should have been sent back to his home without any religious instruction. The money spent upon him and his futile gadgets might have maintained a mission in Tahiti. So now, Haweis proposed, the Society ought to do what the Government had failed to do – send out its own people and, with Tahiti as their headquarters, spread the gospel through the South Seas.

Within a year the money was raised, volunteers were obtained, and a ship, the *Duff*, was chartered to make the voyage. Now the London Missionary Society had nothing to do with the fashionable or scientific world of Walpole and Joseph Banks. It was essentially a lower-middle-class organization made up of dissenting clergymen, of lay preachers and of respectable artisans and tradesmen who were Protestant to the core and who believed utterly in the Bible. Their faith and their proselytizing zeal were admirable but they were not perhaps absolutely suited to undertake the conversion of the South Sea islanders. As C. Hartley Grattan says:

Voyage of La Pérouse

Comte Jean-François de Galaup La Pérouse was despatched by the French Government in command of *La Boussole* and *L'Astrolabe* in 1785 to complete Captain Cook's unfinished work in the Pacific and in particular to explore the elusive passages of the Bering Sea. The French navigator conducted an extensive reconnaissance via Cape Horn to Chile, the Sandwich Islands, Alaska and south to explore the north American coast. He then sailed across the Pacific, discovered a number of uncharted islands and visited Macao and Manila. He sailed up the coast of Tartary and from Kamchatka despatched an officer overland to report on his discoveries. From the disastrous Samoas, where he lost his second-in-command and eleven of his crew, La Pérouse sailed through the Pacific to Norfolk Island and on to Botany Bay, entering Port Jackson on 26 January, the very day that Governor Phillip and his First Fleet were making their first settlement. La Pérouse and his party stayed for six weeks on the northern shore which now bears his name and, planning to reconnoitre New Caledonia, the Santa Cruz Island, the Solomons and the Louisades, he sailed out of Botany Bay on 10 March 1788, never to be seen again. The wrecks of his vessels were eventually found forty years later in the Santa Cruz Islands.

'They hated nudity, dancing, sex (except within monogamous marriage), drunkenness, anything savouring of dolce far niente, *self-induced penury, war (except in God's name), heathenism in all its protean manifestations, and Roman Catholicism.'*

They had little interest in anthropology or in Tahitian rites and customs – indeed, they were out to suppress them. They were not collectors like Banks, nor were they concerned with scientific discoveries of any kind, nor had they any of Cook's tolerance and gift for compromise. They were practical workers in the cause of the Lord, and they were determined to recreate the island in the image of lower-middle-class Protestant England.

It was a strange boat-load that drew up to the black sand beaches of Matavai Bay in March 1797 after sailing nearly 22,400 km (14,000 miles) without sighting land, perhaps the longest ocean journey ever known. The company of thirty-nine included only four ordained clergymen, the rest being made up of butchers, carpenters, weavers, tailors, harness-makers, bricklayers, shopkeepers and domestic servants. There were also six wives and three children. All these were dumped on shore together with their baggage, their Bibles and their tracts, and after a short stay the *Duff* sailed away.

The missionaries – zealous and inflexible

The coming of the missionaries marked a new phase in the history of Pacific contact. The *Duff* carried a total of thirty missionaries, re-cruited by the London Missionary Society since its establishment in 1795, whom they prepared to re-lease on various islands throughout the Pacific. They represented, in the words of one historian, 'the most primitive, inflexible end of the range of eighteenth–century Calvinism'. Their rigid belief in their own cer-tainties was at once curiously exem-plified on their arrival in Tahiti. Coming round the world their calen-dar took no account of the date line and was a day wrong. They never put it right and fifty years later were still observing the Sabbath (one of their strictest rules) on the Saturday. Their first service at Matavai Bay was held the day they dropped anchor, their Sunday (Sat-urday, 5 March). It was attended by the *arioi*, Tahitian priests, who talked and laughed at the hymns. The missionaries themselves led an arduous life on the island, not unlike the life of a medieval monastry. A bell summoned them to prayers at 6 a.m.; in the morning they laboured at their various callings; the afternoon was spent in religious improvement, and a bell rang for prayers again at 7 p.m. But unlike the seamen who had opened up the Pacific to contact, these lower-middle-class Englishmen were not resourceful: they proved 'incompe-tent Robinson Crusoes' and the Tahitians, far from admiring their skills, pitied their clumsiness. For some, the life proved too demand-ing and eleven of the company of thirty-nine first landed at Matavai Bay (not all of whom were trained missionaries), took passage to Bot-any Bay, while another (much against his fellow missionaries' wishes) married a Tahitian and was later murdered. Nonetheless, their persistence secured some headway. Their first assault concentrated on the three deadly sins of the Tahi-tians: infanticide, human sacrifice and 'onanism' (any kind of homo-sexual activity). Even so, the London Missionary Society had to admit that the Tahitians showed up well in many examples of the Ten Com-mandments, except of course in the first, 'Thou should have no other Gods but me'. And this the missionaries set out strenuously to change.

They found the island every bit as bad as they had been led to expect. More whalers had arrived and three sailors who had taken up residence were adding to the general atmosphere of dissolution. Tu – Cook's Tu, now known as Pomare – was still there, and with the aid of some muskets given him by the *Bounty* mutineers had set up a ramshackle little kingdom in which nothing was done to discourage either the old pagan customs or the new western vices. However, he was friendly at first, and although he was impervious to the missionaries' teaching he allowed them to settle as Matavai Bay. Here they built their church and established their little colony.

It is, of course, all too easy to ridicule the early missionaries, their narrowness, their absurd and often harmful rigidities, the sheer incongruity of their ever being on Tahiti at all. Yet there were some remarkable men among them, they meant the Tahitians nothing but good, and when all their righteous follies have been noted, one is still left with a sense of astonishment at their success. Nothing dismayed them. Nothing turned them away from their purpose. Resolutely and persistently they kept hammering away at the Tahitian way of life until it crumbled before them, and within two decades they had achieved precisely what they set out to do.

One searches for reasons for this extraordinary accomplishment. Tahiti, of

'A Missionary House at Matavai, Tahiti' by James Wilson, 1799. 'Nothing dismayed them (the missionaries). Nothing turned them away from their purpose. Resolutely and persistently they kept hammering away at the Tahitian way of life until it crumbled before them . . . within two decades they had achieved precisely what they set out to do.'

course, was a soft sort of place and wide open to evangelism. The people were lazy and unresistant, they wanted to ape the manners of the western world, and no doubt the missionaries gained a good deal of authority by their very positiveness in the midst of so much *laissez faire*. Like nurses in charge of children they always seemed to know what to do, and this was something new to the islanders, something solid in their lives. Then too, the missionaries were astute enough to realize that they could only impose their will by working through the local chiefs: once the ruling clique was nobbled the docile population was bound to submit as well. Tu remained an unrepentant pagan, but he died in 1803, and his son Pomare II saw great advantages in taking on a new state religion in place of the old. It cemented his power, it was *his* religion. By obliterating the old traditional forms of worship he obliterated his rivals as well.

Physically Pomare II was a big man with a commanding presence, but he was self-indulgent. Melville describes him thus:

'Though a sad debauchee and drunkard, and even charged with unnatural crimes, he was a great friend of the missionaries and one of their very first proselytes.'

'The Family Idols of Pomare 11', from Missionary Sketches, No 111. *Pomare the Second, unlike his father Tu (later known as Pomarel) who remained a happy pagan, became a great friend of the missionaries and 'was one of their very first proselytes'. He was baptized in 1812. When, three years later, a battle took place between Pomare and his forces from Moorea and the inhabitants of Tahiti, Pomare's triumph led to the tearing down of the* marae *and their idols and unbelievers being put to death. Tactfully, Pomare relinquished his own family idols to the missionaries, either to be burnt or sent to the Society. The Rev. Samuel Marsden loudly acclaimed 'these glorious spoils of idolatory'.*

The missionaries must have blenched at using such a doubtful character as this, but no doubt they hoped to reform him and his enthusiasm for Christianity appeared sound enough; he was baptized in 1812 and although his rivals more than once drove him out to the neighbouring island of Moorea he managed to get the better of them in the end. A pitched battle took place in 1815, and in the *auto-da-fé* that followed the *marae* and the ancient idols were torn down, unbelievers were put to death, and congregations were hunted to church by warriors armed with bamboo sticks. In place of the *marae* Pomare built himself a vast cathedral, 210 m (700 ft) long, with a mountain stream running through it, and at its consecration three separate sermons were given simultaneously from three separate pulpits. Just how far Pomare made the running in all this for the purpose of extending his authority, and how far the missionaries guided him, it is difficult to say, but at all events at the time of his death in 1821 the old reprobate was firmly in control.

At home, meanwhile, the London Missionary Society was actively backing its workers in the field by raising contributions and by stirring up a conscience about the Pacific. The end, as they felt, justifying the means, a not too nice distinction was made between scientific fact and moral principle in the Society's propaganda. Passages from the explorers' books which tended to reveal the brutality and benightedness of the islanders were emphasized in their speeches and pamphlets, and even Cook's artists were enlisted in the cause: new engravings, for example, were made of Webber's sacrifice, and all feeling of dignity and grace was deleted from the Tahitian figures. They now became crude and superstitious barbarians and much stress was laid on the skulls in the background. On the other hand, we see in another celebrated picture – 'The Cession of Matavai' – what a change can be made by the gentle hand of religion. The picture was commissioned as a gift to Captain Wilson who sailed the *Duff* out, and the artist, Robert Smirke, was paid 300 guineas for his work. It shows a touching scene, the missionaries in their frock coats and their wives in

'The Destruction of the Idols of Otaheite', from a woodcut in Missionary Sketches, *1819. Pulling down a pagan altar and building a Christian church.*

'The Cessation of Mata-vaiia', by Robert Smirke, 1829. Here, too, the picture tells a chosen story. The painting, commissioned as a special gift to Captain Wilson, skipper of the Duff, shows missionaries in frock coats and their wives gracefully attired, receiving the obeisance of the carefully clothed Tahitians on their arrival at Matavai Bay. A decade or so after the missionaries' arrival, most Tahitians, it was true to say, did wear European clothes.

bonnets receiving the homage of the natives, who are now not only docile but respectably clothed as well, the women demurely holding their arms over their breasts and the men draped in togas.

And there was much truth in this. We have what is obviously a detached and accurate description of the island by Baron Thaddeus Bellingshausen, the Russian navigator who visited Tahiti in 1820. He found the natives, though still gay and ebullient, were changed beyond belief. All those who could wore European clothes, and both men and women had their heads shaved – that lovely gleaming black hair which once fell to the girls' waists was apparently regarded by the missionaries as both sinful and unsanitary.* Tattooing had been discouraged, liquor was banned, and no one danced any more or played Tahitian music. Even the weaving of garlands of flowers was forbidden. Of prostitution there was not a sign; only men came to barter on the Russian ships, and instead of thieving they begged incessantly for trifles. The ruling clique no longer lived in huts open on all sides to the breeze, but in enclosed houses made of timber, and they slept in beds rather than on the ground. Human sacrifice with all other manifestations of the Tahitian religion had long since been swept away, and the *arioi*, those votaries of free love, were married. Morality police roamed the countryside by night pouncing on illicit lovers.

On Sunday all activity ceased, and the people attended church, the women with hats on their shaven heads. By now a printing press had been set up and the Bible had been translated into Tahitian.

The diet was much the same but the Tahitians now had oranges and lemons as well as European vegetables, and on ceremonial occasions the nobles ate

*Though there is some evidence that the Tahitians of their own accord had taken to depilation.

with plates, knives and forks. The *marae* had collapsed into heaps of stones, and were overrun with rats.

Perhaps the most remarkable thing of all was that the natives had been induced to work; under the guidance of the missionaries they had established an export trade in coconut oil. When the Russians were preparing to sail away a party of well-dressed girls came aboard and sang hymns and psalms on the quarter-deck. (Banks's comments on this would have been interesting, but it so happened that he had died, full of honours, the same year in London.)

Bellingshausen made only a short stay on the island and was conducted everywhere by Henry Nott, the senior missionary, who had come out in the *Duff*. Thus it is possible that there were many things that he did not see, and that his trips ashore, limited as they were to Matavai Bay and the settlement of Papeete close by, gave him no inkling of what went on in other parts of the island. Yet his report is confirmed by other visitors to Tahiti around this time: the islanders really had turned this patch of the Pacific into a respectable English suburb, and, according to the missionaries, willingly so. Two observers sent out by the London Missionary Society were much moved by the way the Sabbath was observed:

'Not a fire is lighted, neither flesh nor fruit is baked, not a tree is climbed, nor a canoe seen on the water, nor a journey by land performed, on God's holy day; religion – religion alone – is the business and delight of these simple-minded people on the Sabbath.'

King Pomare himself unfortunately had not quite reformed as yet. Bellingshausen related that one day when he and Nott were visiting the royal palace, a large structure of wood and thatch 15 m (50 ft) long, Pomare drew him aside into a small private room:

'I noticed that the presence of Mr Nott was unwelcome to the King, and that he hastened to close the door. He then showed me his clock, his map, his copy-book, and the elementary principles of geometry, which he was studying with the help of an English book, which he understood, transcribing it into the copy-book in the Otahitian tongue. From the box he took an inkstand, a pen and a few scraps of paper, which he gave to

Under the influence of the London Missionary Society, new engravings of John Webber's famous painting, 'A Human Sacrifice in Otaheite', rendered the scene more brutal and hideous and 'much stress was laid on the skulls in the background'. The dignity and mystery of the original work portrayed by the artist present at the scene (see page 84) had been removed.

The adventurous Bellingshausen

In 1819, Emperor Alexander I of Russia sent Bellingshausen in command of the *Vostok* to carry out the first Russian exploration of the Pacific and the Antarctic. Bellingshausen was a great admirer of Cook; his reports were always sensible and illuminating, and bring to a conclusion the work of discovery which Cook began half a century before. In 1819, the map of Antarctica was exactly as Cook had left it in the 1770s i.e. blank. The Russians crossed the Antarctic Circle early in 1820 and two weeks later they almost certainly caught sight of the Antarctic mainland – probably the first ever to do so. Bellingshausen and his crew visited Sydney in 1820, and set out from there to Tahiti. In the same year he discovered Raratonga (Cook Islands) and Vostok Island in the Carolines, naming it after his sturdy vessel.

me, asking me to write in Russian that the bearer of the note should be given a bottle of rum. I wrote to the effect that he should be given three bottles of rum and six bottles of Teneriffe wine. At this moment Mr Nott and Mr Lazarev [the commander of one of the Russian ships] came in. The King looked confused, hid the note and changed the conversation to his ink, paper and geometry book.'

Then, on another day,

'the Queen, seizing the opportunity of being alone with Mr Lazarev, begged that he would give her a bottle of rum, and when he assured her that it would be sent to the King, she replied: "He always drinks the whole bottle and never leaves a drop for me." On that he ordered two bottles of rum to be sent to her.'

This perhaps was a small thing, but Pomare was to die of drink in the following year, and it was evident that the missionaries had to be constantly on the watch that there should be no back-sliding from the code they had imposed with so much diligence on the island.

Yet it had been an extraordinary thing, this little crusade in the remote Pacific. Tahiti was still Arcady perhaps – the climate had not changed nor the marvellous beauty of the mountain valleys running down to the coral sea – but it was Arcady reformed and evangelized, and naked Venus had been supplanted by Mary Magdalen. Where there had once been unashamed free love there now existed Christian guilt. It was just a question of how long the Tahitians could stand the strain.

6

Nevermore

'. . . Otaheite, that fallen Paradise.'
CHARLES DARWIN

ALL THROUGH these years the Pacific had remained a no-man's sea. Spain's vague and general claims to the entire ocean had long since become meaningless, and as yet no other power had taken possession of Tahiti or any of the hundreds of other islands that had been discovered. The explorers, it is true, went through the business of running up their national flags on any new piece of land they happened upon, but it was quite impossible for them to occupy these places or to oust the native governments.

Now, however, with the ending of the Napoleonic wars in Europe and the improvements in navigation, things were changing. Government expeditions and private traders began to appear more and more frequently, and the Pacific islands were coming to be regarded as valuable possessions. Whales and fur seals, sandalwood and *bêches-de-mer*, pearls and perhaps gold as well – all these were available to the enterprising adventurer who came in on the heels of the explorers and the missionaries. Little settlements of white men began to appear in the islands, mostly ports where the ships could refit and provision themselves, and it soon became necessary for governments to send out consuls to look after the interests of their nationals. What was happening, in short, was that the huge sea was being brought into the politics of the west, and the scramble for colonies was beginning.

Thus there was never the ghost of a chance that the missionaries would be left in quiet possession of Tahiti. By the 1830s it was a famous place, and it was merely a question of time before one or other of the European nations moved in. Yet even if the missionaries had not been disturbed by the outside world it is doubtful if they could have kept control. Their imported system of taboos put an impossible strain on the Tahitians; if the island was going to achieve a synthesis with the West it was not in this uncompromising, artificial way. After the first wave of evangelism had spent itself the reaction was bound to set in.

Otto von Kotzebue, the leader of a second Russian expedition that followed Bellingshausen into the Pacific in 1823, felt strongly about this matter. He wrote:

'A religion like this, which forbids every innocent pleasure and cramps or annihilates every mental power, is a libel on the divine founder of Christianity. It is true that the religion of the missionaries has, with a great deal of evil, affected some good. It has restrained the vices of theft and incontinence, but it has given birth to ignorance, hypocrisy and a hatred of all other modes of faith, which was once foreign to the open and benevolent character of the Tahitians.'

The deterioration of life in Tahiti is marked by the pantomine appearance of three of the king's guards sketched in the early 1830s. 'King Pomare III's guard was made up of handsome men,' observed the 'French Commander Louis Duperrey in 1823, 'but I would rather they had been clothed in their attractive national costume than in a few old striped black jackets, no doubt the cast-offs of some dead missionaries.' Original wash by L. F. Lejeune.

The islanders of course found ways to break the new rules – a thing, incidentally, they seldom did with their old system of taboos. Charles Darwin, who arrived in the *Beagle* in 1835, records a revealing little incident that occurred when he went up into the mountains with two Tahitian guides:

'I took with me a flask of spirits which they could not resolve to refuse; but as often as they drank a little, they put their fingers before their mouths and uttered the word, "Missionary".'

The chief trouble was that there was now nothing for the Tahitians to do. Before the Europeans arrived they had their own occupations and had enlivened their days with their own rituals and entertainments, but now all these had been taken away from them, and the singing of Christian hymns was really not enough to compensate. In that soft soporific climate it was impossible to make the people work for long. They would try hard but things always went wrong in the end. The missionaries imported a weaving machine, and for a month or two the girls worked it with great enthusiasm. Then the novelty wore off and the machine was left to rust away in its palm-leaf hut. It was the same with the attempts to start cotton and sugar-cane growing; after the first season or two the workers drifted away. Their own arts and crafts had long since been forgotten; no one could make cloth from the bark of a tree and there no longer seemed any point in building the great double-canoes with their high carved prows: a crude boat hacked out of a tree-trunk was good enough. Even the sport of surf-riding became too burdensome and was abandoned.

And so listlessness fed on itself, and even the Quaker Daniel Wheeler, who called on the missionaries in 1834, was forced to admit, 'There is scarcely anything so striking or pitiable as their aimless, nerveless mode of spending life.' Tuberculosis, smallpox and dysentery, as well as venereal disease, were now being passed on from one generation to the next, and those perfect Tahitian teeth, which the first explorers had so much admired, were beginning to decay with the importation of European food. There were no doctors or dentists on the island. And despite all the strictures of the missionaries the people found ways of brewing their intoxicating *ava* in secret.

The high tide of the missionaries' success was probably around 1827, when Pomare's eldest daughter, Queen Pomare Vahine III, was set up on the sad little mockery of a throne. After this the decline begins and accelerates fairly rapidly. The population figures are appalling. In Cook's time there were probably around 40,000 people on the island. The missionaries in the *Duff* said that by the turn of the century not more than 15,000 or 16,000 were left, due to wars, infanticide and disease. Bellingshausen in 1820 was given a somewhat lower estimate. By the end of the 1830s the figure was down to 9,000 and it was eventually to drop to 6,000.

It was nonsense to claim, as so many of the visiting Europeans did, that the Tahitians themselves were to blame. Even if you believed that on the whole the influence of the missionaries had been good, there was still the effect of the whaling and sealing ships to be taken into account. As many as 150 of them were calling regularly at Tahiti by the 1830s, the majority of them American vessels plying out of Nantucket, and the crews were just about as tough a lot as you could find. When they came ashore they wanted girls, and the Quaker owners of the ships, though often teetotallers themselves, were not averse to paying for fresh provisions with hard liquor. Conditions aboard these ships were so dreadful, the life so hard and dangerous and the food so rotten, that it

Pomare, Queen of Tahiti

A somewhat romanticized portrait by G. Baxter of Pomare II's eldest daughter, who inherited the royal title of Queen Pomare Vahine III, in 1827. Charles Darwin, who met Pomare in 1835, described her as 'a large, awkward woman without any beauty, grace or dignity. She has only one royal attribute – a perfect immovability of expression under all circumstances, and that a rather sullen one.' While Queen Pomare enjoyed an increasingly Europeanized mode of life, driving about in a carriage she received as a present from Queen Victoria, she ruled over a decade that saw the decline in the population of Tahiti from about 12,000 to 9,000.

was a common thing for the sailors to desert whenever they had the chance. On the smaller islands around Tahiti just one deserter with a brace of pistols or a musket could set himself up as a chief and behave exactly as he liked.

Then in addition there were the convicts who managed to escape to Tahiti on the whaling ships that called at the penal settlements in Australia. As early as 1806 (a period when the missionaries were temporarily in eclipse) alarming stories about these men were reaching England. We have Banks writing:

'*Otaheite is said to be at present in the hands of about one hundred white men, chiefly English convicts who lend their assistance as warriors to the chief, whoever he may be, who offers them the most acceptable wages, payable in women, hogs etc.; and we are told that these banditti have by the introduction of diseases, by devastation, murther, and all kinds of European barbarism, reduced the population of that one interesting island to less than one-tenth of what it was when the* Endeavour *visited it in 1769. Surely these people will, if not otherwise provided for, soon become buccaneers and pirates.*'

Thus a new man was entering the Pacific – the beachcomber, the throw-out of the West. Sometimes he turned himself into a small trader or a planter, but more usually he simply hung about the native settlements in a daze of drunkenness and soft sensual living until his money or his credit gave out. Despite all the missionaries' efforts there were still at least 100 of these men living on Tahiti at the end of the 1830s and nothing could be done about them. In their sermons the missionaries repeatedly warned the Tahitians against the ungodly sailors, but they had no power to turn them out of the island and there were no police to control the nightly brawls along the watefront.

Frederick Debell Bennett, a surgeon on one of the whaling ships, writes,

'. . . *the abundance and indiscriminate sale of ardent spirits, as well as the laxity of the laws which permitted the sensuality of a seaport to be carried to a boundless extent, caused scenes of riot and debauchery to be nightly exhibited at Papeete that would have disgraced the most profligate purlieus of London. By partaking in these the natives had degraded their physical no less than their moral state, and in the slovenly, haggard and diseased inhabitants of the port it was vain to attempt to recognize the prepossessing figure of the Tahitian as pictured by Cook.*'

Perhaps this was making out too black a picture. Darwin did not think things were quite as bad as this, especially in the country districts where life went quietly on. Wandering inland he was much struck by the handsomeness of the men:

'*There is a mildness in the expression of their countenances which at once banishes the idea of a savage; and an intelligence which shows that they are advancing in civilization. The common people, when working, keep the upper part of their bodies quite naked; and it is then that the Tahitians are seen to advantage. They are very tall, broad-shouldered, athletic and well-proportioned. It has been remarked that it requires little habit to make a dark skin more pleasing and natural to the eye of a European than his own colour. A white man bathing by the side of a Tahitian was like a plant bleached by the gardener's art compared with a fine dark green one growing vigorously in the open fields. Most of the men are tattooed, and the ornaments follow the curvature of the body so gracefully, that they have a very elegant effect. One common pattern, varying in its details, is somewhat like the crown of a palm-tree. It springs from the central line of the back, and gracefully curls round both sides. The simile may be a fanciful one, but I thought the body of a man thus ornamented was like the trunk of a noble tree embraced by a delicate creeper.'*

The new port of Papeete, some 14 km (9 miles) to the west of Matavai Bay, was a very pretty place and had taken on the appearance of an established port. On approaching from the sea one descried the house of the British consul; it had a wide verandah, glazed windows, and a lawn in front with the Union Jack flying overhead. The American and French consuls also had their houses on the shore, and a lovely boulevard, the Broom Road, led away through the palms and the flowering creepers into the jungle. The wreck of an American whaler, its bows pointing up into the sky, lay near the reef and nearly always there were sailing ships anchored in the harbour. Money in the form of dollars was replacing barter, and some of the Tahitians were wealthy enough to offer 100 dollars for a horse – that same animal which they had fled from in Cook's day, calling it a 'man-carrying pig'. Everyone of consequence now rode, the chiefs as well as missionaries, and Queen Pomare sometimes went about in a coach she had received as a present from Queen Victoria. A gaol known as the Calabooza Beretanee had been established about 1.6 km (1 mile) from Papeete, and it was a rustic sort of place with a stream running beside it. The prisoners were given a good deal of liberty except at night, when they were confined in stocks with leaves for a bed and a coconut trunk for a pillow. Oranges and other imported fruit and vegetables were to be had in abundance, and if the standard of living was low no one was actually starving. Nearly all the Tahitians about the port spoke a few words of English and among the elderly men it was a social distinction to be able to claim that they had once known Captain Cook.

It is the fragility of the island through these years that strikes one. With the protection of its isolation gone and its whole way of life turned upside down, it was at the mercy of any intruder. The missionaries themselves saw all too clearly that they would have to get political backing from Europe if they were going to carry on. Naturally they would have preferred that this backing should have come from Britain, and with Queen Pomare's consent they actually proposed annexation. But the British were already exploiting Cook's discoveries in Australia, and were about to set up a government in New Zealand; for the moment they wanted no more commitments in the Pacific. Spain had dropped out of the colonizing race, and America and Russia were interested only to the extent of sending out scientific expeditions. Thus it was left to the French to pounce, and paradoxically it was the missionaries themselves who provided them with the opportunity. They would allow no Roman Catholics on the island, and two French priests of the Picusian order who attempted to settle there were quickly bundled out again. This happened twice, in 1835 and again in 1836, and it was enough to enable the French to treat the matter as a national insult.

We need not go too deeply into the ensuing events, since they are a repetition of what happened everywhere in the nineteenth century when a colonizing nation believed its honour involved and felt obliged to pacify the natives for their own good. Admiral Dupetit-Thouars was cruising with a squadron in the Pacific and was able to take the matter in hand. He turned up in his flagship, *La Reine Blanche*, trained his sixty guns on Papeete and threatened to bombard the town unless he was paid an indemnity and the rights of French nationals were respected. The missionaries were quite unable to prop up the faltering little queen. She was forced to pay up and ask for French protection. Priests and a garrison were landed, and in 1843 Tahiti was formally annexed. Affronted by her conquerors the Queen fled to Moorea, and the French soldiers with their firearms made short work of the 'rebels' in Tahiti who tried to support her.

It was the brutal end of what you might call the entrée of Tahiti into the

Tahiti's annexation by France, 1843

The extraordinary turning-point in Tahitian affairs: annexation by France. After their long association with Cook's expeditions and the incursions of the English missionaries, it seemed logical to suppose that Tahiti would become a British possession in the Pacific. Not so. Britain, preoccupied by commitments in Australia and about to set up a government in New Zealand, declined a proposal for annexation made by the missionaries with Pomare's backing. When, however, the English missionaries refused to allow French Roman Catholic priests on the island in the mid-1830s, the matter fell into French hands. Admiral Dupetit-Thouars arrived off Papeete on his flagship (ironically named *La Reine Blanche*, the white queen) in 1842, with clear indications that he intended to protect the rights of French nationals, and Queen Pomare ultimately asked for French protection. Tahiti was formally annexed to France in 1843.

Herman Melville and the noble savage

Melville, whaler turned writer, strenuously deplored the fate that overtook the Tahitian people with colonization. His two autobiographical books, *Typee* and *Omoo* are a sustained tirade against the sullying of natural beauty and natural manners in the Pacific. Portrait by Joseph Eaton.

western world. Just over seventy years had elapsed since the first shock of contact, and if ever Diderot's warning against the Europeans should have been remembered it was now: 'One day they will come, the crucifix in one hand and the dagger in the other, to cut your throats or to force you to accept their customs and opinions.' But the rest of his prophecy – 'under their rule you will be almost as unhappy as they are' – was that also true?

Herman Melville was in no doubt whatever about this question; and since he was the first writer of genius to enter the Pacific and was himself a witness of these closing scenes, his opinion is worth having. He thought that an outrageous crime had been committed, and he saw no happiness for the islanders any more. Melville, in short, was right back with Rousseau. He was anti-missionary, anti-colonialism and absolutely in favour of the noble savage.

His two autobiographical books, *Typee* and *Omoo*, are a sustained tirade against the sullying of natural beauty and natural manners in the Pacific. It is the French who are the barbarians, the missionaries who are the real purveyors of cant and superstition. 'The voluptuous Indian,' he cries (these were still the days when all coloured people were indiscriminately called Indians), 'with every desire supplied, whom Providence had bountifully provided with all the sources of pure and natural enjoyment, and from whom are removed many of the ills and pains of life – what has he to desire from the hands of civilization . . . ?' Why should the Tahitians be forced to attend an alien church, to submit to an alien government, to adopt alien and harmful ways of living? Why not leave them alone?

'Distracted with their sufferings, they brought forth their sick before the missionaries, when they were preaching, and cried out, "Lies, lies! You tell us of salvation; and behold, we are dying. We want no other salvation than to live in this world. Where are there any saved through your speech? Pomaree (sic) is dead; and we are all dying with your cursed diseases. When will you give over?"'

Now Melville was a wild character, a sailor who had deserted his ship and who had promoted a mutiny. In Tahiti they had marched him to the Calabooza Beretanee and had put him in the stocks – 'a clumsy machine,' he remarks, 'for keeping people in one place.' It was hardly likely that such an obstreperous young man could attract much attention. Yet he had lived among the Polynesians in the Marquesas Islands which were still unspoilt, he had seen

Gauguin's famous painting 'Nevermore', inspired by Edgar Allan Poe's poem 'The Raven'. 'In Gauguin's paintings no man or woman ever smiles; supine, defeated, despairing and beautiful, his people gaze in a reverie

what was happening at Tahiti, and his protest rings across a century of time with more force and clarity than all the self-justification of the politicians and the churchmen.

He was possibly libellous and certainly scandalous in much that he wrote, but his account of the sleaziness and inertia that had overtaken life in Papeete in 1842 is remarkably vivid. It almost seemed that the heart had gone out of the people, and that they had lost the will to survive. Pulled one way by the mis-

sionaries, another by the whalers, and now another by the French officials, they subsided with a sigh. The effort to adjust themselves to the outside world had been too much. Why bother to struggle any more? Even the very animals of the island were dying: the little vegetarian dog, so much relished by Cook, had been bred out by the larger European species and was now extinct. Only the flowering jungle seemed to be as virile as ever. Melville quotes an old Tahitian song:

into the lost past.' In 'Nevermore', Gauguin has painted his Tahitian beauty waiting for nothing . . . a dark conspiratorial couple in the background, and all around them the shapes and symbols of the tropics.

113

Disenchanted, subjected to a regime that was austere and puritanical, the islanders, writes one French source commenting on this unhappy group, 'lost their taste for life', and there were certain fears for the survival of these people. From La Grande Luxe du Pacifique.

The palm-tree shall grow,
The coral shall spread,
But man shall cease.

The French administration was certainly no worse than that of any other colonizing nation in the Pacific; indeed, the French policy of tight government control combined with a *laissez-faire* attitude to the Tahitians' morals was an improvement on the English rigidities. But Melville, like Diderot, was not concerned with fairness in the Christian sense; he thought the original crime of the European intrusion had put all subsequent talk of fairness out of court.

After he was released from gaol he had one last glimpse of the lost world of the islands he so yearned for. He crossed to Moorea and visited a remote village called Tamai, where 'Tahitian life was seen as formerly existing in the days of young Otoo (Tu), the boy-king, in Cook's time.' He persuaded the local chief to allow a performance of a forbidden dance known as the 'Lory-Lory'. Cook's description of it, seventy-five years previously, had been:

'Among other amusements they have a dance called Timorodee, which is generally performed by ten or a dozen young females, who put themselves into the most wanton attitudes, keeping time during the performance with the greatest nicety and exactness.'

Melville was more lyrical. He describes how the girls, wearing short skirts of native cloth and with flowers in their long black hair, form a ring with two leaders in the centre.

'The ring begins to circle slowly, the dancers moving sideways, with their arms a little drooping. Soon they quicken their pace, and at last fly round and round; bosoms heaving, hair streaming, flowers dropping and every sparkling eye circling in what seemed a line of light.'

This was the first movement and it was followed by a pause:

'. . . the girls, deeply breathing, stand perfectly still. They pant hard and fast for a moment or two; and then, just as the deep flush is dying away from their faces, slowly recede, all round; thus enlarging the ring. Again the two leaders wave their hands, when the rest pause; and now, far apart, stand in the still moonlight like a circle of fairies. Presently, raising a strange chant, they softly sway themselves, gradually quickening the movement, until at length, for a few passionate moments, with throbbing bosoms, and glowing cheeks, they abandon themselves to all the spirit of the dance, apparently lost to everything around. But soon subsiding again into the same languid measure as before, the eyes swimming in their heads, join in one wild chorus, and sink into each other's arms.

Such is the Lory-Lory, I think they call it; the dance of the back-sliding girls of Tamai.'

Gauguin, arriving on the island fifty years later, found nothing so gay as this. Tahiti was now tamed, compartmentalized, and finally civilized. One could hardly expect Gauguin to approve; like Melville he was a mighty inveigher against petty white officialdom, and he had come to paint the Tahitians in their natural state: 'These nymphs, I want to perpetuate them, with their golden skins, their searching animal odour, their tropical savours.' He was appalled by the desecration of the islands, by the deadly hand of the white man:

'The natives, having nothing, nothing at all to do, think of one thing only, drinking . . . Many things that are strange and picturesque existed here once, but there are no traces of them left today; everything has vanished. Day by day the race vanishes, decimated by the European diseases . . . There is so much prostitution that it does not exist . . . one only knows a thing by its contrary, and its contrary does not exist.'

In Gauguin's Tahitian paintings no man or woman ever smiles; supine, defeated, despairing and beautiful, his people gaze in a reverie into the lost past. They have no hope at all. They see nothing but the broken stones of their *marae*, their fallen idols, the great legendary war-canoes with their tattooed warriors in their elaborate robes, the forgotten dances and rituals of the *arioi*. They ask, *'D'où venons-nous? Qui sommes-nous? Où allons-nous?'* and the answer is silence. The overwhelming physical beauty of the girl remains, but she does not dance. Instead she lies inert and naked on her bed, and Gauguin painted her waiting for nothing, hoping for nothing, the petals of the tiare tahiti scattered about her, a dark, conspiratorial couple in the background and all around them the mystical shapes and symbols of the tropics. On this canvas the painter has written in English the one word 'Nevermore'.

PART TWO
AUSTRALIA

Aborigines dancing at Brighton, Tasmania, a fine painting by John Glover. Most dancing and performing were theatrical displays communicating a tribal cult.

I

Botany Bay

AFTER HIS FIRST VISIT to Tahiti in 1769 Cook sailed south to New Zealand and spent six months charting the coastline on the two islands. More than a year and a half had now elapsed since he had left England, and it was time to think of returning home. The obvious route to take was the one across the south Pacific to Cape Horn, since that would have enabled him to continue his search for a southern continent, but the winter was coming on, barely six months' rations remained, and the *Endeavour*'s sails and rigging, now badly in need of repair, were hardly likely to stand up to the Antarctic gales in that vast stretch of ocean. Consequently another and more promising plan was decided upon: they would strike westward until they reached the eastern seaboard of the country of New Holland and then follow it to the north or wherever it took them until they reached its extremity. Then they would turn west and sail to the Dutch outpost of civilization at Batavia, where they could refit and revictual the ship.

It was a hazardous proposition. The west coast of New Holland (it was not to be called Australia until half a century later), was known in rough outline, but the east coast was entirely unexplored; no white man had ever been there and the existing maps were merely guesswork. But the *Endeavour*'s crew had been restored to health by their six months' stay in New Zealand, and the officers, on being consulted, were all eager for new discoveries; and so on 1 April 1770, they set sail for the unknown. It was a fair voyage; the weather was

'The Heads of Six Men, Natives of New Zealand', engraved by T. Chambers from the original studies by Sydney Parkinson (now lost) in Queen Charlotte Sound, c. April 1770. These formidable people were to prove extremely dangerous to Furneaux on his second voyage. Ten of his company were eaten by cannibals at Queen Charlotte Sound.

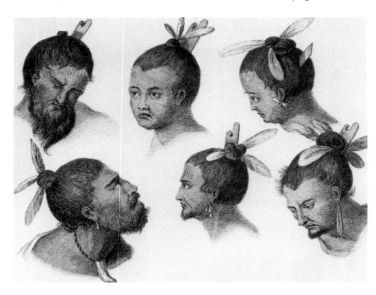

The hostile Maoris

Sketch by Sydney Parkinson of a New Zealand war canoe bidding defiance to the Endeavour.

Cook had spent a much less conducive time charting the New Zealand coastline than in Tahiti. The Maoris were hostile, Tupia constantly warned against them, and the evidence of cannibalism necessitated utmost caution. In the above sketch by Parkinson, a New Zealand war canoe offers a formalized defiance to the *Endeavour* which Banks gives a detailed description of in his journal: 'During this time they brandish their spears, hack the air with their patoo patoos and shake their darts as if they meant every movement to begin the attack, singing all the time in a wild but not disagreeable manner and ending every strain with a loud and deep fetched sigh in which they all join in concert. The whole is accompanied by strokes struck against the sides of the Boats & with their feet, Paddles and arms, the whole in such excellent time that tho the crews of several Canoes join in concert you rarely or never hear a single stroke wrongly placed.'

warm, dolphins leapt about the ship 'like salmons', and *Diomedea exulans*, the wandering albatross, that largest and strongest of all sea birds, came circling trustingly around the rigging, a wonderful and easy target for Banks's gun. He must have bagged twenty or more of them before the *Endeavour* reached home.

Herman Melville described very well what it was like to sail in these seemingly endless seas:

'The Trades were blowing with a mild, steady strain upon the canvas, and the ship heading right out into the immense blank of the Western Pacific. . . . Forever advancing we seemed forever in the same place, and every day was the former lived over again. . . . We saw no ships, expected to see none . . . porpoises and other fish sporting under the bows like pups ashore . . . at intervals the grey albatross, peculiar in these seas, came flapping his immense wings over us.'

Melville arrived in the Pacific seventy years later than Cook and knew where he was headed for; Cook did not. Day after day the dawn disclosed nothing but the empty ocean, and no one knew when he would see land again. Thus it was an event when on the sixteenth day the officer on watch thought –

he was not quite certain – that he saw a butterfly, and a little later a small land bird like a sparrow came on board. This was followed by the appearance of a gannet holding a steady course for the west – the *Endeavour*'s course – as though it knew that there was land in that direction. Squally weather set in. Then on 19 April Lieutenant Zachary Hicks cried out at first light that land lay ahead. Cook stood towards it for two hours, and at 8 a.m., when he was 24 km (15 miles) from the coast, altered course so that he could run beside it. He had sighted the extreme south-eastern corner of the continent of Australia, and he named it Point Hicks – a timely gesture since the lieutenant, like so many other unfortunate young men in the ship, was to die before the next year was out.

Rain and gales continued through the day – this part of the Tasman Sea is notorious for rough weather – and at one time the grey sky joined the sea between them and the shore in three transparent wavering waterspouts. Next day they had a clear view of the land and Banks thought it looked very promising:

'The country this morn rose in gentle sloping hills which had the appearance of the highest fertility, every hill seemed clothed with trees of no mean size; at noon a smoke was seen a little way inland, and in the evening several more.'

Smoke meant inhabitants, and sure enough on 22 April they saw through their glasses five black men standing on the shore. It was impossible, however, to make a landing; heavy waves were beating on the rocks, and a fresh breeze drove them steadily northwards. Soon they came up with chalky cliffs that reminded them of England, and more natives were seen, two of them carrying a canoe. Cook put out a boat, but heavy surf prevented him from landing and they went on again. At last, on 28 April – nine days after they had first sighted the coast – they saw an opening in the cliffs and the *Endeavour* put in for the shore. There were natives about, some of them spearing fish from canoes,

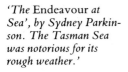

'The Endeavour *at Sea', by Sydney Parkinson. The Tasman Sea was notorious for its rough weather.'

others watching from the rocks and along the cliffs.

Now the Australian Aborigines were no graceful South Sea islanders with golden skins such as the *Endeavour*'s crew had encountered at Tahiti. Already they had been given an unflattering reputation. The Dutch who touched on the north-west of the continent in 1606 had described them as 'wild, cruel, black savages . . . poor and abject wretches'. William Dampier, who had also been on the north-west coast in 1688, had written his famous and extremely uncomplimentary account:

'The inhabitants of this country are the miserablest people in the world. The Hodmadods (Hottentots) of Monomatapa, though a nasty people, yet for wealth are gentlemen to these; who have no houses and skin garments, sheep, poultry and fruits of the earth, ostrich eggs etc. as the Hodmadods have; and setting aside their human shape, they differ but little from brutes. Their eyelids are always half-closed to keep the flies out of their eyes. . . . They have great bottle noses, pretty full lips, and wide mouths. The two foreteeth of their upper jaw are wanting in all of them, men and women, old and young; whether they draw them out I know not; neither have they any beards. They are long-visaged, and of a very unpleasing aspect, having no one graceful feature in their faces. Their hair is black, short and curled like that of the Negroes; and not long and lank like the common Indians. The colour of their skins, both of their faces and the rest of their*

'Aborigines Spearing Fish', by Joseph Lycett. Such was the sight that greeted the Endeavour company as they sailed up the south coast of New South Wales. For their part, the indigenous inhabitants hardly stopped to gaze upon the newcomers although it has been suggested that some of their fires were warning fires to alert coastal tribesmen to the presence of strangers along the shore.

The Australian Aborigines were no graceful South Sea islanders with golden skins such as the Endeavour's crew had encountered in Tahiti. The contact British voyagers were now making was entirely new. 'Two men with different kinds of weapons came out and made towards us,' wrote Parkinson. Engraving by Thomas Chambers after Parkinson.

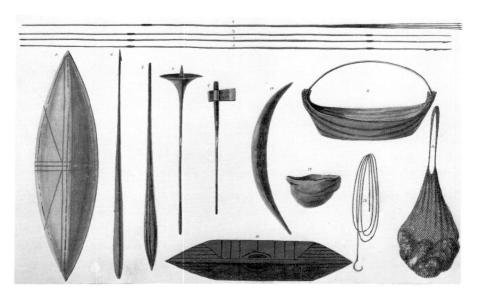

Some of the Aboriginal weapons seen by Cook and his companions at Botany Bay, April 1770. 1. Mooting or fish gig; 2–4. Comoy or spears; 5. Hylliman or shield; 6. Wamia or throwing spear; 7. Waddy or battle club; 8. Cadgawang or battle club; 9. Ilybo or hatchet; 10. Wamering – thrown to disperse a crowd; 11. Tundi or basket; 12. Coonoonang or calabash for carrying water; 13. Heringung and wallingan or fishing line and hook; 14. Genojang or net; 15. Murribi for warding off blows of the battle club.

body, is coal black like that of the Negroes of Guinea. They have no sort of clothes, but a piece of rind of a tree like a girdle about their waists and a handful of long grass or 3 or 4 small green boughs full of leaves thrust under their girdle to cover their nakedness.

They have no houses, but lie in the open air, without any covering, the earth being *their bed and the heaven their canopy. Whether they cohabit one man to one woman, or promiscuously, I know not but they do live in companies, 20 or 30 men, women and children together. Their only food is a small sort of fish . . .for the earth affords them no food at all. There is neither herb, root, pulse nor any sort of grain for them to eat that we saw; nor any sort of bird or beast that they can catch, having no instruments where-withal to do so. I did not perceive that they did worship anything . . .'*

In short, the lowest of the low.

The bay the *Endeavour* was now entering was divided by 3,200 km (2,000 miles) or more from the north-west coast of Australia, but it was presumed by Cook and Banks (who had both read Dampier) that the inhabitants, if not the landscape, would be pretty much the same all over the continent – if it was a continent. But this was not at all so. The natives they were now observing in a setting of gently rising, wooded hills were a lithe and nimble people, their hair was straight, not woolly like a Negro's, the men were bearded and their skins were dark brown rather than black. Moreover they had weapons, spears, shields and throwing sticks, they built canoes, they lived in crude huts made of branches, and there was every evidence that they hunted, not only animals of some strange sort, but also the marvellously coloured birds that were flying through the trees.

In other words, this contact they were making was something entirely new, and one can imagine the excitement with which Cook and his men gazed through their glasses as the *Endeavour*, with one of her boats sounding the way ahead, came quietly through the entrance of the bay and soon after midday found an anchorage on the southern side, abreast of a group of huts.

There is a strange quality in the Australian landscape. To a European and especially an English eye it is, at first, lacking in freshness and greenness; the

Sketches made by Sydney Parkinson at Botany Bay including the famous 'Crucifix' painting. This depiction has caused much comment. The men of the Botany Bay tribe, now extinct, wore a character-istic body paint design. Triangular in form, it stretched from both shoul-ders to the centre of the chest, then down the cen-tre of the body to the waist. In making his drawing, Parkinson per-ceived it in the form of a crucifix. All other Par-kinson drawings are exact and precise representa-tions. As he was a devout Quaker, it has been sug-gested that this striking body painting impressed itself upon his Christian perception. It has, hence, been viewed by some as evidence that, at the first moment of European con-tact on eastern Australia, one conscience at least was troubled.

light is too harsh, the trees too thin and sparse, the ground too hard and there are no soft outlines anywhere. Desiccation seems to be the theme, a pitiless drying-out of all sap and moisture, and monotonous is the favourite adjective for the bush: monotonous and therefore worthless. It is a country for the ants. But then on closer acquaintance one begins to perceive that, very silently and slowly, life is going on here at another level: the embattled young sapling that looks so gnarled and old is full of strength, its tiny flowers are a gay miniature of larger flowers, and its leaves, when burnt or crushed, release a smell as pungent as a lemon's. Dead fallen trees, it is true, give a graveyard appearance to the ground and the prevailing colour of the scrub is greenish grey. But then unexpectedly a flock of pink galahs will perch on the bare branches, or one catches sight of the wattle in flower and it is more gold than gold can ever be, a clear leaping colour in a field of grey. The bell-bird's single note is a small bell sounding against utter silence, and the fungus, pushing up through the cracked brown clay, is a dome of bright scarlet. These things, however, have to be discovered. Nothing is at once revealed. You must walk some way alone and gradually the feel of the bush begins to seep into the mind, its immense stillness and quietness; and out of that austerity it is a wonderful thing to see a wild animal start up and bound away, or to come on a group of herons fishing in a waterhole. There is nothing menacing in the bush – even the snakes will avoid you if they can – and nearly always overhead there is the pale blue sky. Like the bush itself it has a kind of implacable indifference but it is not oppressive. One feels very well in this dry air.

RIGHT
The lonely, quiet continent of Australia with its prevailing colours of green and grey. Here, clearly, was an ancient land whose people seemed to the travellers as inscrutable as their countryside.

The part of the coast on which Cook was now making his first landing is not quite typical of all this dryness. The bush here comes down to the shore and the transparent sea water froths and sparkles like champagne as it tumbles in long rollers on to beaches of yellow sand. In the estuaries one escapes from the restlessness of the sea into backwaters full of reeds where ducks and wading birds abound, and beyond these the hills, thickly covered with bush, rise up from the sea plain. One glimpses here and there a rocky precipice. It is not a grand or dramatic spectacle, but it is very beautiful and it has that kind of rugged expansiveness that makes the traveller feel alive and free. In Cook's time it must have seemed excessively remote.

Some odd things were happening on the shore as the *Endeavour* approached. One group of natives, about twelve in all, went up on to a rise to watch, and when the vessel's boat came near they beckoned the sailors to come ashore. On the other hand, no notice at all seemed to be taken of the *Endeavour* herself. There she was 31.8 m (106 ft) long, with her high masts and her great sails, and when she passed within 330 m (360 yds) of some fishermen in four canoes they did not even bother to look up. Then when she had anchored close to the shore a naked woman carrying wood appeared with three children. Banks tells us:

'*She often looked at the ship but expressed neither surprise nor concern. Soon after this she lighted a fire and the four canoes came in from the fishing: the people landed, hauled up their boats and began to dress their dinner, to all appearance totally unmoved by us . . .*'

The Englishmen ate their midday meal on board and then in two boats set out for the shore, thinking that these strange quiescent people would allow

them to make a peaceful landing. They were wrong. Two natives menaced them from the rocks with long spears, and they were not deterred by the fact that there were at least thirty men in the *Endeavour*'s boats. No amount of pleading with them by signs had any effect, so Cook took a musket and fired it over their heads. Still they held their ground, and Cook fired a second shot at their legs knowing that he could do them little harm, the distance being 36 m (40 yds). The only result of this was to make one of the natives run off to his hut for a shield and then, as the sailors came ashore, both men threw their spears. Two more shots had to be fired before they were driven off. Cook and Banks went up to the huts, where they found six children who showed no interest of any kind when they were given presents of beads and ribbons; they left them lying on the ground.

There were some interesting aspects in all this. The sight of the *Endeavour* had apparently meant nothing to these primitives because it was too strange, too monstrous, to be comprehended. It had appeared out of nowhere like some menacing phenomenon of nature, a waterspout or a roll of thunder, and by ignoring it or pretending to ignore it no doubt they had hoped that it would go away. As Sydney Parkinson wrote, the natives 'were so abashed at first they took little notice of us'. But when the small boats had put out from the ship it had been another thing: the English sailors had been instantly recognized as human, a palpable evil, and despite their clothes and pale faces, despite even their roaring incomprehensible shooting-sticks, they had been courageously opposed.

And so it went on for the next few days while the *Endeavour*'s crew came ashore to gather wood and to fill their water-casks. Little groups of blacks would appear through the trees and stand for a moment to shout and throw a spear or two. Then they would vanish again into the bush. Every attempt to parley with them or to offer them presents came to nothing. Had they been wild animals they could not have been more difficult to deal with. 'All they seemed to want,' Cook wrote, 'was for us to be gone.'

An early depiction of the wombat.

WOMBACH.

Emu?

The Peppermint Tree.

(Dampier, on his second voyage to north-west Australia in 1699, had had similar experiences, but had been more drastic. When one of his sailors was speared he fired his gun, he says, and 'frighted them (the blacks) at first, yet they soon learnt to despise it, tossing up their hands, and crying Pooh, Pooh, Pooh; and, coming on afresh with great noise, I thought it high time to charge again, and shoot one of them, which I did.')

For the rest it was an excellent landfall. The crew netted enormous quantities of fish in the bay, and there were giant oysters and other shellfish to be found on the rocks as well. The botanists, wandering ashore, came upon trees and plants that had never been described before; the eucalypt, for example, with its long thin scented leaves, and a shrub with large furry nuts which was eventually to become known as the banksia. The birds were wonderful – great flocks of brightly coloured cockatoos and lorikeets that were entirely strange to European ornithology – and since they had never been shot at before Banks brought down as many as he wished. The skins he preserved, and with the meat the *Endeavour*'s cook made an excellent parrot pie. Sometimes the foraging parties caught glimpses of queer elusive animals: a quadruped about the size of a rabbit, a much larger beast that fed on grass and resembled a stag, another that looked like a wolf, and still another that seemed to be some sort of a polecat or a weasel. But none of these creatures lingered in sight long enough to be described or drawn.

A week went by very pleasantly, and it was marred only by the death of a consumptive seaman named Forby Sutherland, the first white man to be buried on this distant coast.

There was a ceremony on shore before they sailed. The Union Jack was flown, the ship's name and the date were carved on a tree, and the hospitable

ABOVE, RIGHT
The peppermint tree with its leaves curving upward, a characteristic that British visitors were to find so strangely distinctive of Australian foliage.

ABOVE, LEFT
The emu, Australia's flightless bird. Cook and his party saw hints of strange fauna at Botany Bay; footfalls, dung and scratchings. They never saw an emu, but their journals reflect a feeling for the unseen secrets of the new landscape.

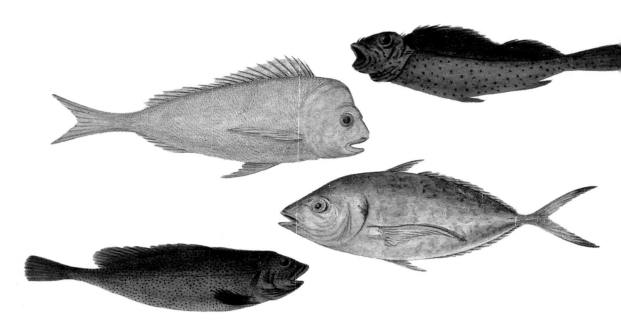

Fish, new to science, found in Australian waters. Watercolour by T. R. Browne.

harbour which had supplied Banks and Solander with so many new plants was named Botany Bay. It seems ironic that so innocent a name was to become a synonym for all that was heartless and cruel, not only in this new country, but in Georgian civilization as well.

So now on 6 May 1770 they sailed on to the north, noting from the sea, but not entering, Port Jackson, which was later to be the site of Sydney, one of the largest cities in the Southern Hemisphere; past Cape Byron which was named after Byron's grandfather, the *Dolphin*'s first captain; past the site of Brisbane and on into the tropics.

The black and white cockatoos of New Holland. 'All things in this land seemed quaint and opposite. Parrots and Paraqueets most beautiful,' wrote the eager young Banks. Watercolour by T. R. Browne.

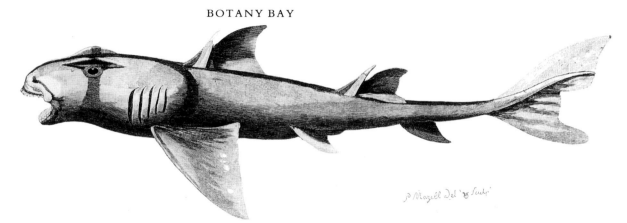

Cook was now forcing the pace, his men were growing weary and were eager to reach civilization again. After so many months on those confined decks, irritations and enmities were beginning to fester; just how much so is revealed by one particularly horrible incident. A clerk named Richard Orton went to bed drunk and someone attacked him and cut off his ears. Life on a British sailing ship in the eighteenth century was tough enough – even brutal by our standards – but this was criminal and Cook was enraged. Yet even the offer of fifteen guineas and 68 litres (15 gallons) of arrack – a huge reward – could not induce the crew to reveal the name of the culprit. Suspicion fell on Patrick Saunders, one of the midshipmen, but nothing was proved against him. It was significant however that Saunders deserted when the ship eventually reached Batavia.

A month after leaving Botany Bay they were still toiling slowly northward, nearly always in sight of the coast but seldom landing, and on 6 June they arrived at Magnetic Island, so called because it affected the *Endeavour*'s compass. Many tropical islands and coral reefs now began to close round the ship, and Cook sprinkled them liberally with the names of the British aristocracy – Halifax, Sandwich and so on – as he went along. It was a world of watersnakes and turtles, of oysters growing in mangrove swamps, of dolphins and huge sharks, of pandanus palms and pelicans. They shot a wild turkey weighing 6.8 kg (15 lb) and it was the finest meal they had eaten since leaving England nearly two years before.

At times the sea was so full of fish that the nets they let down were torn to pieces. Parkinson, the artist, was kept hard at work drawing the plants they collected while they were still fresh and green; he actually drew ninety-four of them in fourteen days, and still more specimens came in whenever they made a landfall.

Sometimes when they sailed close inshore they saw groups of natives, but the same curious indifference persisted; both men and women would gaze for a moment at the ship and then apparently dismiss it from their minds. If a boat was put ashore they quietly disappeared leaving uneaten shellfish around their camp fires.

Neither Cook nor anyone knew about coral reefs then, so when the ship grounded on those sharp and beautifully coloured coral antlers at 11 p.m. on the night of 11 June, it was a more fearful thing than any of them could have imagined. They were sailing gently along in the moonlight in a calm sea under double-reefed top-sails, and with a man continually sounding the depth. Cook

Port Jackson shark, one of the formidable inhabitants of New Holland's harbour. The Endeavour *crew, however, saw and caught so many stingrays during their first landfall that Cook originally named Botany Bay Stingray Bay. As work proceeded on the botany of that landfall, he renamed the spot Botany Bay.*

as usual had given his instructions for the night and had just undressed and gone to sleep. He was awakened by a horrible scraping in the bows and the ship rocked so violently he could scarcely stand upright. Coming on deck in his underclothes he found the vessel stuck fast on the coral, and immediately ordered the boats and the anchors to be got out. But no amount of heaving would bring her off, and it became clear that she was badly holed; at midnight the false keel came away and they could see pieces of sheathing boards floating about them in the moonlight. Mercifully it was a calm night, but when the tide began to ebb the ship settled more firmly than ever on the coral and there was every danger of her breaking up. The coast was 38 km (24 miles) away and there was no possible hope of the *Endeavour*'s boats getting them all off. Banks tells us that he packed up his most valuable possessions and prepared to abandon ship.

Meanwhile what could be done to save her was being done; six guns were thrown overboard together with their cannon balls, a quantity of stone ballast, the fresh water and all those casks that contained decayed stores – some 41–51 tonnes (40–50 tons) in all. Dawn found them still afloat and they waited all morning for the rising tide. When it came the ship began to rock again on the coral and to take in water fast. One of their four pumps was out of action, but every man, Cook himself included, now got to work on the other three. There seemed to be only one hope: that they could get the *Endeavour* off before she broke up and then keep her afloat just long enough to beach her on the mainland. With luck, they then might be able to build a smaller vessel out of the wreck and sail her to Batavia or some other civilized port in the East Indies.

At nightfall the water was still gaining on them, and no amount of hauling on the anchors with the capstan could get them off the reef. They could only continue what they were already doing and since they expected to die, the men worked very quietly, efficiently and willingly. There was no panic anywhere on the ship. Then at 10 p.m., twenty-three hours after they had first struck, the hull began to move and within a few minutes they had hauled her into the clear sea. There was nearly 1.2 m (4 ft) of water in the hold and the carpenter reported that it was gaining so fast that there was little hope of the pumps keeping pace with it. Later he went down to the hold again and discovered he had made a miscalculation – the water was not coming in so rapidly as he had thought; and when this news reached the exhausted men on the pumps it acted, Cook says, 'like a charm'. When the second dawn broke they were even gaining a little on the leak, and the sails were set for the mainland.

Jonathan Monkhouse, the younger brother of the *Endeavour*'s surgeon, now came forward with a suggestion that they should 'fother' the ship – a thing he had seen done in similar circumstances before – and Cook agreed. A sail was filled with oakum, earth, odd rags and bits of sheep's wool, and then dragged with ropes under the hull until it covered the hole. The pumps instantly began to gain at a faster rate, and by the night of 13 June, the third day after the disaster, they had the ship almost dry. Cook anchored offshore for the night, and in the morning the pinnace was sent off to reconnoitre the coast. It returned at night with the good news that there was a harbour in the estuary of a river a little way to the north.

But now a gale with rain blew up, such a gale as would have destroyed them utterly had they still been on the reef, and they waited all through 15 June and

again through 16 June for the wind to drop. Cook himself took the pinnace out and buoyed a channel through the coral into harbour, and at last on 17 June they got in, bumping twice on the passage. They moored within 6 m (20 ft) of the shore, and the next day they shifted to a steep beach where the ship could be run aground at high water. Immediately they made a ramp to the shore and began taking everything out of her. At least they were all alive; it now remained to see what damage had been done and to estimate what the chances were of repairing her on this primitive coast.

There were natives about – one could see their signal fires – and Cook mounted four of his remaining guns on the quarter-deck in case of attack. Through the next few days a smithy and a sailmaker's workshop were set up on shore, together with tents for the sick and the storage of provisions, and on 22 June they had the vessel empty enough to run up her bows on the beach at high tide, her stern being left afloat. They could now inspect the damage. It was almost as bad as they had imagined. The bottom had been scored by the reef as though someone had attacked it savagely with an axe, but by a miracle of luck a chunk of coral had become wedged in the largest hole and had prevented them from foundering at once. The carpenter believed that within a few weeks he could make provisional repairs, enough at any rate to get them to Batavia. So now, among the mangroves in a tropical river, absolutely isolated from the outside world on an unexplored coast, and with the rain falling upon them, they set about eking out a Robinson Crusoe-like existence until the day they could escape.

The Endeavour, *safe on the beach at the river's mouth in North Queensland, which would bear its name. Here, extensive repairs were carried out over six weeks, from 17 June until early August 1770, to make the ship seaworthy. The enforced wait gave Banks and Solander a rich opportunity to collect and study the flora and fauna of the region, from which much of their remarkable Australian collection was made.*

2

Australia observed

SIX WEEKS ELAPSED before the *Endeavour* was ready to sail, and in that time Cook and his companions were able to study the Australian scene much more closely than they had done before. It was true that they were confined to a tiny corner of the continent, but they had already traversed almost all of the 3,200 km (2,000 miles) or so of the eastern seaboard, they had come up from the temperate south to the northern tropics, and their experiences at Botany Bay had given them a basis for comparison. Moreover they were diligent and enthusiastic observers and they soon became aware that they were confronted here with something infinitely strange: an utter primitivism, wild creatures that had not developed beyond the marsupial stage, plants that did not appear to fit into the Linnean or indeed any other system of classification, and a nomadic people who lived more like animals than men. It was as though they were looking straight back into the beginnings of creation.

Thus it is hardly surprising that there is a wonderful freshness in Banks's and Cook's descriptions. Each day, while the ship was being repaired, they walked out into the surrounding bush and at every step of the way they came on something new. The part of the coast on which they found themselves was not particularly hospitable. They were surrounded by mangroves, dismal trees growing out of the tidal mudflats of the estuary, and inland there was little else but sandy and barren hills covered with thin scrub. Yet life pullulated here. The warm sea was boiling with fish, birds in thousands made bright splashes of colour in the sky, and where else in the world could you see anthills rising to a height of 1.8m (6 ft) or more, and looking like 'Druidical monuments'?

Banks was out with his gun shooting pigeons when he caught another glimpse of the stag-like animal he had seen further south at Botany Bay. It was 'of a mouse-colour and very swift'. A day or two later both he and Cook had a clearer sight. It seemed, Cook noted, to have a large tail and it appeared to jump like a hare or a deer. 'What to liken him to I cannot tell,' Banks wrote. 'Nothing, certainly, that I have seen at all resembles him.' A little later his greyhound put up two more of the animals, and although they made off rapidly through the long grass, Banks had time enough to see, quite definitely, that they did not run – they hopped. Then at last, more than three weeks after their landfall, Gore, the third lieutenant, managed to shoot one. It was a young beast weighing only 17 kg (38 lb) and they found it excellent meat. It was probably this skin which Banks preserved and brought back with him to England where it was stuffed and given to Stubbs to paint. Sydney Parkinson also executed several lively pencil sketches of the animal on the spot. Later again Gore got in a shot at a larger animal weighing 38 kg (84 lb) but it did not eat so well as the first one. Thus, the Kangaru or Kongouro or Kangaroo – Banks got the word phonetically from the blacks – made its first appearance in Europe.

Now too they had a closer view of many of the other animals that had so puzzled them before: the dingo or wild dog (which they thought was a wolf), the smaller varieties of the kangaroo, the wallaby and the kangaroo-rat, the opossum and an extraordinary creature described by the sailor who first saw it as being 'about as large as a one-gallon [4.5 litre] keg, as black as the devil and with wings and two horns on its head' – in other words, a flying fox.

All these creatures were excessively shy, and Banks had the greatest difficulty in collecting specimens. But the birds were plentiful, and he lists dozens of them: 'Parrots and Paraqueets most beautiful: white and black cockatoos', cranes, pigeons with odd topknots on their heads, pelicans in many thousands, crows, sea birds of every kind, bustards, doves, and whistling geese that flew by night. (Strangely they never saw an emu, the huge walking bird that resembles an ostrich.)

The butterflies were incredible. On one of the Barrier Reef islands Banks says that,

'the air was for the space of 3 or 4 acres [1.2 or 1.6 ha] crowded with them to a wonderful degree; the eye could not be turned in any direction without seeing millions, and yet every branch and twig was almost covered with those that sat still. Of these we took as many as we chose, knocking them down with our caps or anything that came to hand. On the leaves of a gum tree we found a pupa or chrysalis which shone almost all over as bright as if it had been silvered over with the most burnished silver, and perfectly resembled silver. It was brought on board and the next day came out into a butterfly of a

Sydney Parkinson's sketch of the young kangaroo shot at the Endeavour River. It was a small animal which made good eating for the company, and its skin, taken to England and stuffed, was to provide the first representation in England of this distinctive marsupial. In addition to the skin, which was given to Stubbs to paint, the company took a skull back to London and presented it to William Hunter, the physiologist. It remained in the Royal College of Surgeons until it was demolished by German bombs in World War II.

'The air for a space of 3 or 4 acres [1.2 or 1.6 ha] (was) crowded with butterflies to a wonderful degree,' wrote Banks of one landing on the New Holland coastline. 'The eye could not be turned in any direction without seeing millions, and yet every branch and twig was almost covered with those that sat still. Of these we took as many as we chose.' Watercolour by T. R. Browne.

The Endeavour's exploring parties caught glimpses of extraordinary animals such as the wallaby which never lingered in sight long enough to be described or drawn.

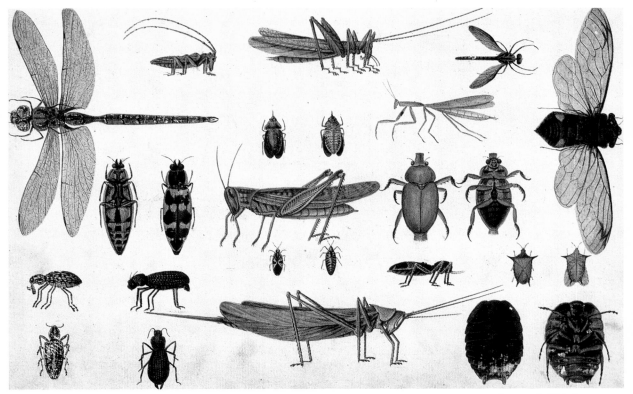

Insects of all kinds abounded. The mosquitoes particularly plagued the company. Banks gave a sharp account of these 'indefatigable insects'. 'At night,' he noted in his journal, 'we took up our lodgings close to the banks of the river and made a fire, but the Mosquitoes, whose peace-full dominions it seems we had invaded, spared no pains to molest as much as was in their Power: they followed us into the very smoak, nay almost into the fire, which hot as the Climate was we could better bear the heat of than their intolerable stings.' Watercolour by T. R. Browne.

The botanists on the En-deavour came upon trees and plants that had never been described before: the waratah, with its unique red crown, attracted the eyes of the early botanists.

velvet black changeable to blue, his wings both upper and under marked near the edges with many light brimstone spots . . .'

Stinging ants or termites were everywhere, both those that constructed the huge anthills and those that lived in trees and made nests as big as a man's head by glueing the edges of the leaves together. Then on the mudflats there was an astonishing fish about the size of an English minnow that jumped about from stone to stone and was even capable of climbing trees: the mud-skipper, as it came to be known. Large animals that hopped, foxes that flew, fish that climbed – this was the world of Edward Lear and his *Book of Nonsense*.

The vegetation was disappointing. The trees did not grow close together as they did in England, but far apart, and the wood was so hard that it damaged the crew's axes. There was the universal eucalyptus or gum tree that yielded a blood-red resin, a few cabbage palms and not much else except mangroves around the *Endeavour*'s anchorage. Had they made their landing a little further south they would have been among the great rainforests with their trailing lianas and might have ascended to the wooded valleys of the Atherton Table-land; but knowing nothing of these Banks was forced to conclude that the eastern coastline was a dry and arid place, capable of supporting shipwrecked sailors perhaps, but not much more: 'Barren it must be called and in a very high degree . . .' Apart from yams and a kind of cherry with bitter berries they found no fruit or vegetables worth eating, and were forced to rely on what they could get with the gun and the fishing net. Here they did well. Every day something between 23 and 91 kg (50 and 200 lb) of fish were caught, and the topknot pigeons were knocked down by the dozen. Best of all they liked the meat of the great green turtle; just one of them would provide for the whole of the ship's company, and it abounded in this warm sea. The poor helpless creatures were speared or lassoed and then laid out on their backs on the *Endeavour*'s decks so that they would stay alive until they were wanted; had they been the right way up they would have been suffocated by the heavy weight of their carapaces pressing on their lungs.

Often the men went out in boats and explored the Great Barrier Reef, the marvellous labyrinth of coral that runs for 1,600 km (1,000 miles) or more down the east Australian coast. Not even in the Pacific islands had the *Endeavour*'s men seen such a teeming abundance of sea birds and of fantastic tropical fish; and in the depths of the coral pools there lurked monstrosities like the giant clam which looked as if it might seize a man in its scarlet lips and hold him until he drowned. Banks described the reef as,

'a wall of coral rock rising almost perpendicularly out of the unfathomable ocean, always overflown at high water commonly 7 or 8 ft [2.1–2.4 m], and generally bare at low water. The large waves of the ocean meeting with so sudden a resistance make here a most terrible surf, breaking mountains high . . .'

The sailors feared the reef, as well they might, for they still had to thread their way out through it once the *Endeavour* was fit to sail again. The sea was full of menace; crocodiles lurking round the ship, sharks swimming along the outer edge of the reef, and almost every day a gale coming up.

Compared to these natural hazards the blacks they encountered were next to harmless. They first made contact with them about a fortnight after they got ashore. Four men appeared in an outrigger canoe and when the sailors called to them and threw them presents of beads and cloth and other trinkets they were gradually induced to approach and disembark. They became very nervous when the sailors passed between them and their spears which, as a sign of friendship, they had laid on the ground, and showed very little interest when further presents were offered them. However, they were delighted with a gift of fish, and they stayed for a while on the shore jabbering in a language which bore no relationship at all to the Polynesian which the sailors had heard in the islands. They repeated often the word 'Tut', but what it meant no one knew.

After this first uneasy meeting the natives came back on successive days, adding to their numbers, and Cook and Banks were able to make very full notes about them – indeed, theirs is the first authentic account we have of the Australian Aborigines. They were completely naked, but they tended to keep one hand over their private parts and were excessively dirty – so dirty, in fact, that Banks had to wet his finger and rub it on a man's skin before he discovered that its natural colour was chocolate brown. Yet they were not ugly or uncouth: the majority were small, slender men, around 1.68 m (5 ft 6 in) in height, with good teeth, lively eyes and bushy beards. Each man had a bone about 15 cm (6 in) long stuck through a hole in the cartilage of his nose, and most of them wore necklaces of shells, and belts and armlets made of twisted palm-fibre or of human or kangaroo hair. Some of them also had suspended by a cord from their heads a little net bag in which they kept such things as fish-hooks and lines, spear points and crude shell ornaments. They did not oil themselves like the South Sea islanders and instead of tattooing, painted their faces and bodies red and white with ochre and pipeclay in lines and large irregular patches. In addition, the fleshy parts of the arms and thighs were scored with self-inflicted scars which had apparently been made with a seashell or a sharp stone. Ashes or clay had been rubbed into the wounds while they were fresh so as to make these scars stand up boldly on the skin. Banks

The Aborigines' attitude to clothes fascinated the British visitors. They tore up and discarded any of the cloth the Endeavour's officers left for them. There was uncompromising nudity. 'Of clothes they had not the least part,' Banks wrote in one of his philosophical ruminations, 'but naked as ever our general father was before his fall, they seemed no more conscious of their nakedness than if they had not been the children of Parents who eat the fruit of the tree of knowledge.' 'A Group on the North Shore of Port Jackson', by Thomas Watling.

Two men fishing in a canoe. The Aborigines of the Endeavour River were, the company recorded, small, slender men, with good teeth and lively eyes. Banks observed that they were 'exceedingly black . . . blacker than any we have seen in the Voyage tho by no means Negroes . . . the hair of their heads was bushy and thick . . . they were lean and seemed active and nimble; their voices were coarse and strong . . . they seemed to have a redundancy of hair upon those parts of the body where it commonly grows.' Such an account was one of the first authentic records on the natives of New Holland. Painting by A. Browne.

fancied (erroneously) that the blacks had mutilated themselves in this way as a form of lamentation for their dead. Some of the men chewed the leaf of a tobacco-like plant called pitjuri which had narcotic properties, but they seemed to know nothing of any other drugs or intoxicants.

Their weapons were spears, three or four to each man, and these were from 2.4–4.2 m (8–14 ft) long, and were pointed with the stings of stingrays and barbed with bits of shells or sharp pieces of wood that were stuck to the shafts with resin. To launch a spear they used a woomera – a short throwing stick with a notch into which the haft was fitted – and they were incredibly swift and accurate in their aim. Over a distance of 45 m (50 yds) the weapon would never be more than 1.2 m (4 ft) from the ground. Their sea-shell fish-hooks and lines were well made, and they possessed another sort of spear with a cord attached for the harpooning of turtles and fish. Sharp stones and wooden mallets seemed to be their only tools, and apart from water-buckets made of bark they possessed no household utensils of any kind. Their canoes were tree-trunks hollowed out with fire and with a crude outrigger of wood attached. Their huts were as primitive as they could well have been: shelters made of branches and just big enough for four or five people at the most to huddle in at night. One end of the hut was kept open, and here a fire usually smouldered to keep the mosquitoes at bay, though whether or not a mosquito could have bitten through all that dirt and pipeclay it was difficult to say.

Fire they made by taking a pointed stick and twirling it rapidly round with the palms of their hands on a base of soft wood, a thing they could do in the space of two minutes. Food was either roasted on an open fire or baked on hot stones, but for the most part it was eaten raw and it was a hotch-potch of fish, shellfish, the meat of the kangaroo or any small marsupial, roots, lizards, snakes, grubs – indeed, almost anything that moved. Honey they got, as well as grubs, opossums and birds, by cutting notches into the tree-trunks and climbing to the upper branches. Sometimes they set fire to the dry grass to drive out kangaroos and other animals, and they usually carried fire in a small heap of seaweed in their boats – apparently for the purpose of cooking the fish as soon as they caught them. When they wanted to shorten their beards they singed them.

After encountering such hordes of Polynesians in the Pacific islands Banks was struck by the small numbers of Aborigines:

'This immense tract of land, the largest known which does not bear the name of a continent, as it is considerably larger than Europe, is thinly inhabited even to admiration, at least that part of it that we saw; we never but once saw so many as thirty indians together . . .'

On the Endeavour River – the name given by Cook to the estuary where they were stranded – the entire tribe consisted of twenty-one people: twelve men, seven women and a boy and a girl.

Why were there so few? Because of the barren soil? Because of tribal wars? Or had the very primitiveness of these people prevented their increasing? After all, they were, Banks thought, 'but one degree removed from the brutes'. Cook was a little more indulgent. He found them 'far from being disagreeable, the voices soft and tuneable . . . a timorous and inoffensive race, no ways

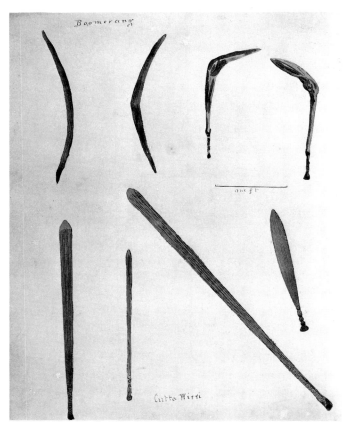

Aboriginal boomerangs and implements named 'Cutta Wirri'. Banks completed a short list of Aboriginal words while at the Endeavour River. Watercolour by W. A. Cawthorne.

The nimble Aborigine, hunting lizards and other small fauna in the trees. 'Honey they got, as well as grubs, opossums and birds, by cutting notches into the tree-trunks and climbing to the upper branches.'

inclinable to cruelty . . .' Yet 'they seem to have no fixed inhabitation but move about from place to place like wild beasts in search of food . . . we never saw one inch of cultivated land . . .'

It was a delicate business making contact with these limited minds, rather like trying to gain the confidence of backward or mentally deficient children. An instinctive, basic wariness governed all their actions, and there was always the danger of their suddenly taking fright or of some misunderstanding arising, and then all headway would be lost. Never would they go more than 18 m (20 yds) from their canoes and they were extremely jealous of their 'sooty wives'. Just once a woman appeared in the distance but nothing would induce her to approach.

Yet as the weeks went by the familiarity ripened. By pointing to things a simple vocabulary of native words was built up and the tribesmen were skilful mimics of the English voices. Then, suddenly, around the middle of July an incident occurred. A small group had been persuaded to come on board the *Endeavour* one day. They looked about with uncomprehending eyes at the rigging and the guns, but it was the turtles lying stranded on the deck that really caught their eyes. Turtles were meat, and meat was a communal thing to be shared. They grabbed one of the animals and were about to make off with it to the shore when Cook intervened; after all, his own men were living on hard rations and he wanted the turtles for the voyage through the unknown waters that lay ahead. But the blacks could not understand. They kept grabbing at the animals and were furious when the sailors drove them away. Finally they leapt into their canoes and paddled for the shore. Here they ran to the 1.2 m (4 ft) high dry grass on the bank and set it on fire with the obvious intention of burning down one of the ship's tents and some clothes and nets that were hanging out to dry. A tremendous blaze developed and would have demolished all the *Endeavour*'s stores on shore had not Cook twice fired his musket and driven the natives off.

Next day like children they came to ask for forgiveness, and an old man indicated by signs that they would light no more fires about the ship.

It was an adumbration of the tragic future: the white man and the blacks competing for possession of the natural resources of the country. Now it was the turtles that were in dispute, soon it would be the land, and there was not much doubt about what the outcome would be. The blacks were weak and had to lose. Yet for the moment Cook was inclined to envy them. He wrote:

The Aboriginal way of life

The *Endeavour* party could form no real conception of the Aborigines' culture which, in the British way, they were disposed to consider backward and 'childlike'. Yet these people, who set so little store by material possession, held traditions that for them were old, continuous and true. Unlike the visitors, they were not concerned with the idea of man's perfection. For them, as for all cultures, there had been an Age of Heroes, but it was not idealized and they did not look back on it with nostalgia. Nor did they worship any gods: they had none. Rather, they linked their lives, both contemporary and past, with the 'dreaming' which was their narrative of things past, a charter of things that still happen and a kind of principle of order embracing everything significant for Aboriginal man. There was a natural unity between their waking daily life and the 'dreamtime'. With their soft dignity they tended to hold themselves aloof from the visitors. Their sense of the person was deep and kept them from casual contact of the kind the Polynesians had exhibited. To the Aborigine, his name, his shadow, his spirit and his totem (that linked the individual with a non-human entity) were all essential parts of 'him' and he did not allow others lightly to learn them. In this sense the Australian Aborigines were the most distinctive and intact of all the peoples encountered on the *Endeavour* voyage. It was an attitude of mind and a detachment that would puzzle the British settlers in future years.

'They may appear to some to be the most wretched people on earth but in reality they are far happier than we Europeans; being wholly unacquainted not only with the super-fluous but with the necessary conveniences so much sought after in Europe, they are happy in not knowing the use of them. They live in a tranquillity which is not disturbed by the inequality of condition: the earth and the sea of their own accord furnish them with all things necessary for life . . . they live in a warm and fine climate and enjoy a very wholesome air so that they have very little need of clothing . . . they seem to set no value upon anything we gave them, nor would they ever part with anything of their own . . .'

Banks was inclined to agree. He went wandering inland and found that all the clothes that had been given to the tribe had been abandoned as useless in a bush. He wrote, 'Thus live these I had almost said, happy people, content with little, nay, almost nothing.' And he went on to moralize about how luxuries had become necessities in civilized societies and how riches increase responsibilities.

There was some confusion of thought here, and Cook and Banks were not the only ones to be enmeshed in it. Where was the happy life? The natives they had met on Tahiti had every natural luxury and seemed to be happy. The Australian Aborigines with the barest subsistence were apparently happy too. But the Europeans with their complicated civilization were unhappy. That was the dilemma: civilization had failed because it had abandoned nature. And yet you could not turn your back on civilization; once it was known there was no choice but to continue with it.

Needless to say none of these speculations prevented the *Endeavour*'s crew from being eager to set out on their return journey. They were all, as Banks said, 'far gone with longing for home'. By 7 July the major damage to the ship had been repaired, and with the aid of barrels lashed to her side and the high spring tides she was floated again. The reloading began and by the end of the month they were ready to get away. Foul weather delayed them for another week, and then at last, on 4 August, they set sail for the north.

There followed during the next two weeks Cook's brilliant manoeuvring through the coral, and it was a frightful experience. More than once it seemed that nothing could save them from drifting on to the reef, and Cook himself almost reached the end of his endurance. In a rare outburst of exasperation he wrote in his journal:

'Was it not for the pleasure which naturally results to a man from being the first discoverer, even was it nothing more than sands and shoals, this service would be in-supportable.'

However, on 21 August they were round Cape York (which Cook named after the royal duke), and after enduring the coral for 1,600 km (1,000 miles) were out in the open sea. They paused then at a little island which they named Possession to make a formal declaration of their discoveries. Cook had himself rowed ashore and on a piece of land from which he could see the mainland he hoisted the Union Jack. He then claimed all the eastern seaboard of the conti-nent for King George III, and he called it New South Wales. Three volleys were fired, and they were answered from the ship. This was at sunset on 22 August 1770. The country's history had begun.

3

The Aborigines

THE IMPORTANT THING about the Australian Aborigines was not that they were so very different from these first white men who came among them, but that they were so very similar. Cook and Banks in fact were observing a primitive manifestation of themselves, and Dampier was absolutely wrong. The Aborigine was not a woolly-headed Negro or a copper-skinned Polynesian; he was a Caucasian who had probably migrated from the Euro-Asian land mass when it was joined to the Australian continent, and he may once have been just as white as the white man was. As he came south into hotter climates the pigmentation in his skin had increased, but in most other aspects he appeared to have remained a European stone-age man, a living fossil of ourselves as we were in the beginning.★ In Australia there had been no need for him to develop; the climate was warm enough for him to do without clothes or houses, there was sufficient food to be had without forcing himself to the hard labour of tilling the ground, no wild animals threatened him, and he was so few in number (probably a good deal less than half a million), that he was not often obliged to resort to drastic tribal wars to defend his hunting grounds. Cook and Banks saw him as he had ever been, in a state of balance with nature, not entirely freed from want – a prolonged drought could be very hard upon him – but able to survive without extreme neurosis or fear, and his codes of behaviour were, on the whole, very sensible.

The women gave birth quickly and easily, squatting on their heels, and the child, whose skin was sometimes pink for the first few weeks, was dried in ashes and placed in a bark cradle. It was not weaned until it was three or four years old, and all through this period it was carefully nurtured, the mother carrying it on her shoulders or pinned with her arms across the small of her back. As they grew older the children played as white children play: they loved to swim and to climb trees, they skidded stones on the water-holes and made mud-pies, they employed a stick as a bat and a seed-pod as a ball, they played hide and seek and used stones as dolls; they also had clay spinning tops and skipping ropes made of vines. Their parents taught them songs and dances, they learned the calls and notes of the animals and birds, and with drawings made with a pointed stick in the dust they were instructed in the art of track-

★According to the Australian anthropologist, Hebert Basedow, 'the Aboriginal is no more black than the average modern European is white . . . under normal conditions the Australian is a velvety chocolate brown.' He also asserts that the children of successive marriages between Aborigines and whites become white and do not revert to black. The complex subject of the origin of the Aborigines is debated by Ronald M. Berndt and Catherine Berndt in *The World of the First Australians*. They emphasize that the Aborigines were not really a survival of the Stone Age but were as much 'modern men' as the white races are.

RIGHT
'A Young Aboriginal Woman', by Nicholas-Martin Petit.

Aboriginal women

Aboriginal women were first thought by the early observers and anthropologists to be the second players in a male-dominated society. Many remarked on the brutality with which the men treated their women. But, as more women anthropologists entered the field, more information has been elicited on the key roles played by women. Certainly in many parts of the country, women left their clans to marry. Marriages were most often arranged on a basis of extended kinships or interclan relationships. A man often married the daughter of his 'promised mother-in-law' in what was known as 'mother-in-law bestowal'. Here, two men would agree that the daughter of one would marry the son of the other. 'Sister and mother bestowal' could operate for women's later unions. Normally a man would be forbidden to marry most of his kinswomen and this meant that women of a certain category, and no others, were isolated as potential wives for the man. In this way, women, as wives, bridged the gaps between clans. They played their most important roles as nurturers and the maintainers of harmonious relations in a nomadic society. But they were also important upholders and transmitters of the religious heritage. Their roles were complementary to their menfolk. Various formal rituals involving the pattern of women's lives were certainly decreed by men in response to economic circumstances. These included the segregation of the sexes, the late sexual maturing of girls, a tolerance of infant mortality and infanticide and the broad belief that large families were undesirable. Yet women set the moral tone and the older Aboriginal women became the moral watchdogs of the whole camp. In marked distinction to 'civilized' societies, the older woman was not judged by her own people to be an 'old hag'; younger men and women looked to her for a sense of purpose, strength and knowledge.

ing. They kept pets, young wallabies, possums that learned to ride in the girls' hair, and cockatoos which had had their flight-feathers pulled and which learned to repeat a few Aboriginal words. Their dogs were very much cherished: when ill they were placed near the fire and covered up to keep warm. As they grew older the boys were given instruction in the making and use of weapons, and the girls were taught how to gather roots and grubs and to cook. Both sexes were entirely naked.

The moment of reaching puberty was the first great incident in their lives, and they did not disguise it, or pretend to ignore it, or regard it with secret shame, as sophisticated people do; they celebrated it with a public ceremony. Invitations would be sent to the neighbouring tribes to attend, and preparations would be made for weeks or months in advance. While the ceremonial grounds were being laid out and the costumes being prepared, sometimes great feathered headdresses, the boys who were to be initiated would be taken aside by the old men and given instruction on the importance of the occasion and on the adult duties that lay before them. Great emphasis was placed on the ability of the novices to endure physical pain, and from infancy they were prepared for it by such trials as the placing of a red-hot ember on their arms.

The actual initiation ceremonies were of several kinds, and all were concerned with pain. In some tribes the first step was the adorning of the young boy with a nose ornament; a hole was made through the cartilage and a short stick or bone was passed through it to be worn thenceforth as a mark of matur-

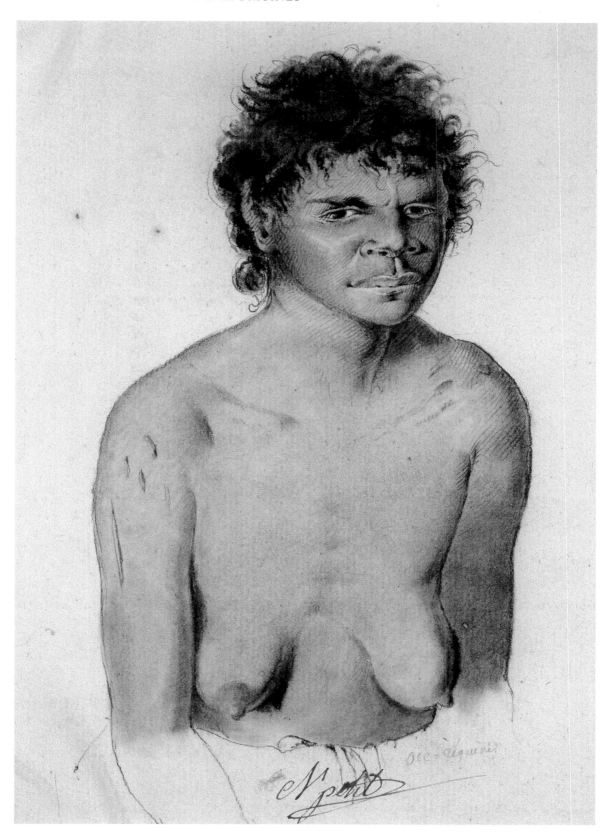

*Aboriginal male, orna-
mented and decked for a
ceremonial occasion.*

ity. Then one or more of the front teeth would be taken out, the teeth first being loosened from the gums with a pointed stick or a bone and then being finally knocked out with a stone. Most tribes practised scarification: the gashing of the bodies with primitive knives of shell or bone. These scars were tribal marks, usually dots or lines, and were regarded as decorative, but the underlying reason for them was to innure the child to pain. When the operation took place, and it was often protracted, the boy was expected not to whimper or to cry out.

All this was leading up to the all-important ceremony of circumcision. For some time previously the novice would be separated from his mother and sisters, and no woman was allowed to watch the operation. As the time of the ceremony drew near the elders of the tribe deliberately induced an atmosphere of high excitement, and sometimes the dancing and singing would continue for days on end, to the accompaniment of the bull-roarers – pieces of wood which, on being whirled around at the end of a string, would emit a fluttering, fateful noise, something between a groan and a shriek. At the climax of the proceedings the novice would be gagged to prevent him crying out, and then either flung to the ground or made to lie across the back of a kneeling man who served as a crude kind of operating table. There was much blood, and the scene no doubt was barbaric: the dancers in the smoking glow of the campfires, the hullabaloo of the bull-roarers and the grunting cries, the old men, their bodies painted in red and white stripes, gathered round the prone and bloody figure of the boy. Yet probably the victim was anaesthetized to some extent by the greatness of the occasion, and the frenzy all around him, and he had his reward: after the operation he was given a spear and a tassel of fur or grass or a

Sketches of rites and dances performed by the Aborigines. The top sketch is a battle dance, watched by two European observers. The middle sketch depicts a hunting rite where men fish with spears and a small figure climbs the tree in search of an opossum. The bushes tied around the legs of the dancers denote the area from which the group comes. In both the middle and lower sketches the women beat time for the dancing.

Aboriginal dances had many purposes. Some were concerned with initiation; some were used as a means of communicating with dead ancestors: sometimes dances represented wars and action; sometimes the participants danced out of pure delight in dancing and performing. Yet mostly they were theatrical displays communicating a tribal cult. For the important fertility rite, dancing and chanting could be carried out over several weeks or even months. Painting by John Glover.

sea-shell which was suspended from a string about his waist and which, in the manner of a statuary figleaf, covered his pubes. He was now a man.

There was a further and more drastic operation performed among some tribes: the splitting of the urethra. It was believed that this mutilation increased a man's carnal powers – and indeed older men sometimes submitted to it more than once, the split each time being enlarged until it was 2.5 cm (1 in) or more in length – but it seems not impossible that it might have been a form of birth control among tribes where there was not enough food to go round; by allowing his sperm to spill on to the ground at intercourse, the man would prevent the woman from conceiving. This view seems open to question but at all events, once the operation was performed, the novice, who, prior to the operation was separated from the women, was again permitted to consort with them.

There was less commotion over the initiation ceremonies of the girls but these were almost as drastic. When a virgin's breasts began to develop they would be anointed and sung to by the older women in order to make them grow. At her first menstruation she too would submit to the gashing of her skin for tribal scars, and often a joint of one or more fingers would be taken off by tightening a ligature until it stopped the flow of blood. All this was done to the accompaniment of dancing and singing, and among sea-tribes it was the custom of the women to wade out up to their hips in the sea and to cavort about in the moonlight. Then a fire would be made on the beach and covered with wet seaweed upon which the virgin was perched until she was thoroughly smoked. It was the men, the elders of the tribe, who took the girl's virginity away either by the insertion of their fingers or with a smooth stone.

Marriage was a loosely organized affair. As a rule a girl would be allotted to a grown man at birth, and he would superintend her education until around the age of twelve, when she would be ready for sexual intercourse. There was much promiscuity. An elder of the tribe might have several wives whom he would obtain by bartering away his own daughters, and generally young girls were reserved for the older men; the younger warriors had to wait until they were twenty or so before they could afford a wife. Women were the absolute property of the men and could be disposed of at will, the brother giving away his sister and the husband his wife. Sometimes wives were exchanged, and during certain ceremonies women slept promiscuously with 'tribal husbands'. Male visitors from another tribe would sometimes be offered one or more young married women for the duration of their stay, and there were tribes which supported prostitutes. In the main, however, husbands and wives tended to remain together, at any rate until their children had grown up.

To European eyes the treatment of the women was very harsh, and we have Sir George Grey, one of the most accurate of early observers, declaring:

'The early life of a young woman at all celebrated for beauty is generally one continued series of captivity to different masters, of ghastly wounds, of wanderings in strange families, of rapid flights, of bad treatment from other females amongst whom she is brought a stranger by her captor; and rarely do you see a form of unusual grace and elegance but it is marked by the furrows of old wounds; and many a female thus wanders several hundred miles from the home of her infancy, being carried off successively to distant and more distant points.'

It was true that the women were savagely beaten, usually about the head, that theirs was the never-ending duty of bearing, feeding and carrying the children, of collecting firewood and cooking food, and of shouldering the heavy burdens on the march. Yet one should not too easily gauge a primitive society by our own standards. There is no evidence that the women lived shorter lives than the men, or were less healthy, and it is certain that the men were quite ready to meet death in a war with a hostile tribe to protect their families. Childbearing was the preoccupation of the whole tribe, and elaborate taboos were set up to prevent inbreeding between close relatives. The young mother had very definite rights, and if on a journey the women were forced to carry the water and firewood there was a reason for it: the men had to march ahead unencumbered by any burdens except their weapons, so that they could be in instant readiness to hunt for game or to deal with enemies. It was not always the men who engaged in domestic quarrels; often the women would fight amongst themselves over some such matter as a petty theft. There would be an exchange of abuse and then the opponents would snatch up heavy sticks and beat one another about the head until one of them was badly wounded or fell unconscious to the ground. When this happened the men of the tribe would sit a little distance apart and look uneasily away.

They were an emotional people, quickly moved to anger but equally ready

'A Group of Tasmanian Aborigines', by Nicholas-Martin Petit. The Tasmanian Aboriginals were a different race of people from Aborigines on the Australian mainland. Their hair was woolly and sometimes reddish in colour. Some of the men had shorn heads like a monk's tonsure. They wore capes and belts made of kangaroo skin. To Cook and his company they appeared to be a mild and cheerful race. They became the subject of serious study when the commander of the French expedition of science and discovery under Nicholas Baudin called at Tasmania and neighbouring Maria Island, in 1802. This portrait by the expedition artist has been 'Europeanized' by the hand of the engraver.

to laugh or to cry. A man returning to his tribe after a long absence would be met with tears of joy, and it was a common thing for both men as well as women to walk hand in hand with one another through the bush. If a man broke his spear in a duel his opponent did not take advantage of him but waited until he had picked up another. There were no unnatural vices among them, nothing like torture was practised against captured enemies, and they certainly had no customs as vicious as the human sacrifices of the South Sea islanders. In hunting – and they never hunted or destroyed any creature merely for sport – they had perfect concentration and great endurance. For hours at a time a man would stand poised with his fishing spear beside a water-hole, and when he struck he very rarely missed. In the bush he saw and heard and smelt a thousand things that would have escaped the white man, and one glance at a footprint in the dust was enough to inform him just what man or animal had gone that way and how long ago. A woman gathering firewood did not stoop, she picked up the sticks with her toes, and a man could climb straight up the smooth bole of a tree using his feet like hands. They were not ugly to an unprejudiced eye, indeed in the early photographs the bearded older men look very handsome, and the younger people, who seem always to be smiling, have a certain boyish charm. They had much less fat on them than Europeans, a smaller posterior, a straighter backbone, much narrower hips, and longer, thinner legs. The mouth was large with full lips, the nose broad and the eyes were deep-sunken to protect them from the sun. They ate hard foods and used toothpicks made of twigs, and as a result their teeth were perfect, as ours are not.

Aborigines stalking emus. Watercolour by W. F. E. Liardet.

A word must be interpolated here about the inhabitants of Tasmania, for they were quite different from the Australians, so different in fact as to constitute a separate race. These people, and there were only about 5,000 of them, are an enigma. They bear some resemblance to the Papuans, but no one knows how they reached their remote fastness off the southern coast of Australia. Possibly they crossed from the mainland before Tasmania was cut off by the subsidence of Bass Strait, possibly they came down from Papua by sea – though this seems hardly likely since they possessed no boats. Their hair instead of being straight was woolly and sometimes reddish in colour, their skins very black, and they were so primitive they did not even have the boomerang, let alone the bow and arrow. Cook landed on the island on his third voyage and noted that they were a good-looking, slightly built people, who despite the heavy rainfall and the cold climate wore nothing but capes and belts made of kangaroo skin. Among one group of twenty there was a hunchback who acted as a kind of tribal jester, and some of the men had their heads shorn in the manner of a monk's tonsure. They showed less timidity than the Australian blacks; even when Omai fired a musket over their heads they soon came back and accepted presents of beads and medals from the white men. They appeared to be a mild and cheerful race.

One must take note of this cheerfulness of the Aborigines, for it seems to have struck all the more perceptive of the travellers who followed Cook to Australia. Charles Darwin, arriving in 1836, wrote that the Aborigines were 'good-humoured and pleasant, and they appeared far from being such utterly degraded beings as they have usually been represented'. Charles Pickering, the American naturalist, also saw the Aborigines in a wild state in the 1830s and he wrote:

'The finest model of human proportions I have ever met; in muscular development combining perfect symmetry, activity and strength, while his head might have been compared with the antique bust of a philosopher.' So wrote the American naturalist Dr Charles Pickering, from the American Museum of Natural History, who visited Australia in 1839–40 as one of the corps of civilian scientists attached to the United States Exploring Expedition to the Pacific and Antarctic.

'Strange as it may appear, I would refer to an Australian as the finest model of the human proportions I have ever met; in muscular development combining perfect symmetry, activity and strength, while his head might have been compared with the antique bust of a philosopher.'

In death the Aborigines' skin turned white, and thus they had a great fear and veneration of the first Europeans; they thought they were their dead ancestors returned to earth. A party of Europeans travelling in the remote bush would hear a shrill melodious call, something like the word *coy* with the *y* drawn out (it was the origin of the word *coo-ee* which is still used as a bushman's call at the present time), and then the dark figures of naked men would be seen gliding from tree to tree and from rock to rock. As they came nearer they kept constantly calling but they would not actually approach; if the white men stopped they stopped, if the white men went towards them they vanished, and then when the march was resumed they followed on. So it might go on all day and only in the evening, when camp was made, would they come forward bearing in their hands the universal symbol of peace – a bunch of leaves. Sometimes a young boy would be pushed forward as a hostage, and if he came to no harm the older men at last would gather round the fire. It was noticed that they took great care of their spears; they were not laid on the ground lest they should warp or be trodden on; they were propped against a tree.

On their journeys, and they were forever on the move, they carried a firestick, a dead branch with a burning end that was waved about to keep it alight, and on making camp their first thought was to start a cooking fire. The cooking was hardly more than a scorching off of an animal's hair, and they had no cooking utensils; nevertheless, nearly everything they ate, whether fish or birds, kangaroos or lizards, birds' eggs or the witchetty grub (the larva of the big Cossus moth), was either grilled in embers or covered with ashes and roasted on hot stones. Their delicacies were such things as the rare little berry fruits of the bush, the eggs of the larger birds, the black swan, the native goose and the emu, snails that were picked up by the women (with their toes) after a fall of rain, and honey which was easily gathered as the wild bee had no sting. They were adept at rounding up their prey. A line of men advancing through the mud of a water-hole would drive the fish into the shallows where they could be snatched up and thrown to the women on the bank, and often they would set fire to the grass so that they could catch the reptiles and small animals as they ran before the flames. They made pitfalls in the ground and the kangaroos, sometimes as many as 100, would be driven upon them, the does bounding in front and the males coming on behind. They knew the migratory movements of the birds, and a young man, perched motionless high on a tree, would grab them as they came in to roost on the branches at night. Never knowing where the next meal would come from they gorged themselves when they could.

In the colder weather they lived in caves, shelters of overhanging rock and in hollowed-out trees, but more usually they built crude huts and windbreaks and slept in beds scooped out of the sand. Sometimes they actually covered themselves with sand to keep the mosquitoes off, and occasionally they used rugs of kangaroo or opossum skins. In the hotter regions they rubbed themselves with emu grease as a protection against the sun and wind.

It was a democratic and highly conservative society. Each tribe had its council of elders who saw to it that the ancient laws were observed. They arranged the social calendar, the dates and places of initiation ceremonies and of the dancing corroborees, and they also settled family disputes and decided upon peace or war. Often too there was a medicine man who would be required to consult his oracles in the case of some natural phenomenon such as a drought. Wars were usually caused because some tribe trespassed upon the hunting grounds of another, but there were long-standing feuds as well, traditional animosities, and perhaps too, they sometimes suffered from ennui and felt an instinctive urge for a sudden commotion. The young men no doubt wanted to

William Buckley, escaped convict

Buckley was able to capitalize on the Aboriginal belief that a white man could be one of their dead ancestors returned to life. He was transported to New South Wales in 1802 for having received a roll of stolen cloth, but when taken with a party to the new settlement at Port Phillip being established under Lieutenant-Governor Collins, he managed to escape and was befriended by the Watourong tribe who believed that the big white stranger was a reincarnation of their dead chief. Buckley lived with the tribe for thirty-two years on the southern coast of Victoria, learning their language and customs and acquiring a native wife. He gave himself up in 1835 when he overheard the Aborigines plotting to rob a visiting ship and murder the intruders. By then he had forgotten his own name and language and was identified by a useful tattoo on his arm. The surveyor J. H. Wedge, who found him, recommended a pardon and employed Buckley as an interpreter. He later became a government interpreter, but Buckley's life experiences disillusioned him. He gave up after two years, believing that neither the government nor the Aborigines could be trusted.

put their prowess to the test in war and to prove themselves before the women. Once battle was decided upon there would be an air of excitement and exhilaration in the camp, the men mending and trying out their spears and flinging themselves into impromptu warlike dances, and the women urging them on. Sometimes the enemy would be ambushed while he was asleep in the early morning, but if it was a set-piece battle both sides would draw up in the open and work themselves into a frenzy by making threatening gestures and loudly abusing one another. Then the first spear would be thrown and that would be the signal for a general assault which would continue perhaps for an hour or two. The wounded, retiring out of the fray, had clay put on their wounds by their women waiting in the rear, and it was customary, after all was over, for parts of a dead enemy's body to be eaten, not because the Aborigines were habitual cannibals, but because it was thought that some of the dead man's best qualities would be passed on through his flesh to the living. Hatreds seldom continued for very long; it was not unusual, after the first fury had spent itself in a tribal war, for peace to be made and then both sides would make camp and carouse together.

Not all their ceremonies were concerned with initiations; they danced sometimes as a means of communing with the spirits of their dead ancestors, sometimes out of nothing more than pure delight in dancing and performing. Their forte was mimicry, especially of the sounds and movements of animals and birds, and for these pantomimes they would paint their bodies with pipeclay and red ochre and put on costumes and headdresses made of leaves and skins and feathers. Some of the tribes had a drone-pipe, a *didjeridoo* which was a piece of bamboo, 1.2–1.5 m (4–5 ft) long, that emitted a dull funereal note, but otherwise they had no instruments except the bull-roarer, and they possessed no drums. The women kept time by striking their thighs and buttocks with their hands, or by clapping boomerangs together, or by rustling leaves tied to their ankles. Experienced singers led the choruses, and although the tunes they sang were simple and monotonous, degenerating at times of high excitement into mere animal grunts, the sense of timing and rhythm had an African exuberance. Among some tribes, those on Cooper's Creek in the centre of the continent for example, additional effects were added by fixing embers into the anal apertures of beetles which flew among the performers as they danced.

Charles Darwin witnessed a corroborree of the White Cockatoo men and local natives at King George Sound in Western Australia, and it is as good a description of the dancing as has been written:

'As soon as it grew dark, small fires were lighted and the men commenced their toilet, which consisted in painting themselves white in spots and lines. As soon as all was ready, large fires were kept blazing, round which the women and children were collected as spectators; the Cockatoo and King George's men formed two distinct parties, and generally danced in answer to each other. The dancing consisted in their running either sideways or in Indian file into an open space, and stamping the ground with great force as they marched together. Their heavy footsteps were accompanied by a kind of grunt, by beating their clubs and spears together, and by various other gesticulations, such as extending their arms and wriggling their bodies. It was a most rude, barbarous scene, and, to our ideas, without any sort of meaning; but we observed that the black women

and children watched it with the greatest pleasure. Perhaps these dances originally rep-
resented actions, such as wars and victories; there was one called the Emu dance, in
which each man extended his arm in a bent manner, like the neck of that bird. In
another dance, one man imitated the movements of a kangaroo grazing in the woods,
whilst a second crawled up, and pretended to spear him. When both tribes mingled in the
dance, the ground trembled with the heaviness of their steps, and the air resounded with
their wild cries. Everyone appeared in high spirits, and the group of nearly naked
figures, viewed by the light of the blazing fires, all moving in hideous harmony, formed
a perfect display of a festival amongst the lowest barbarians. In Tierra del Fuego, we
have beheld many curious scenes in savage life, but never, I think, one where the
natives were in such high spirits, and so perfectly at their ease. After the dancing was
over, the whole party formed a great circle on the ground, and the boiled rice and sugar
were distributed, to the delight of all.'

John Edward Eyre, one of the earliest explorers to make a thorough study of
the Aborigines, did not altogether agree with this description. He found the
dances very moving and beautiful and some of their more elaborate numbers
he thought 'would have drawn down thunders of applause in any theatre in
Europe'. He says:

'The dances usually commence an hour or two after dark, and are frequently kept up the
greater part of the night, the performers becoming so much excited that, notwithstanding
the violent exercise required to sustain all their evolutions, they are unwilling to leave
off. It is sometimes difficult to induce them to commence a dance; but if they once begin,
and enter into the spirit of it, it is still more difficult to induce them to break up.'

Eyre had a theory that the Aborigines had originally migrated southwards
from the northern coast of Australia, in three waves, one coming down from
the west coast, another down the east, and a third through the centre, and he
believed that the tribes, constantly passing back and forth along these routes,
took their dances with them. A tribe with a particularly skilful dance would
become celebrated and the choreography would be imitated by other tribes
and would pass, as it were, into their repertoire. Thus new themes and movements were constantly being introduced, and from time to time as many as six
tribes would gather to contend with one another. A specially effective number
would draw from the audience, sitting in a circle round the fires, 'a rapturous
exclamation of delight'.

The three basic themes of the dances were fighting, hunting and making
love, sometimes the men performing alone, sometimes the women, and sometimes both sexes intermingling together. Eyre goes on:

'The women have occasionally another mode of dancing, by joining the hands together
over the head, closing the feet, and bringing the knees into contact. The legs are then
thrown outward from the knee, whilst the feet and hands are kept in their original
position, and being quickly drawn in again a sharp sound is produced by the collision.
This is either practised alone by young girls, or by several together for their own amuse-
ment. It is adopted also when a single woman is placed in front of a row of male dancers
to excite their passions; for many of the native dances are of a grossly licentious char-
acter.'

This was written in the 1840s when the definition of licentiousness was perhaps somewhat narrower than it is now. The natives themselves, in any case, were not much concerned with our kind of moral values. Fighting, hunting and sex were the bases of their lives, it was only natural that these matters should have been celebrated at their festivals; and now that these dances have been lost forever one fancies that it is not something 'barbaric' that has gone so much as a valuable and lively link in the development of human culture.

It was the same with their other expressions of the artistic impulse. All through the nineteenth century and a great part of the twentieth Aboriginal drawings were regarded as 'crude', 'debased' and 'childish'; as anything but works of art, which is what they really were. With charcoal, red ochre and primitive chisels they made drawings and carvings of kangaroos, emus and

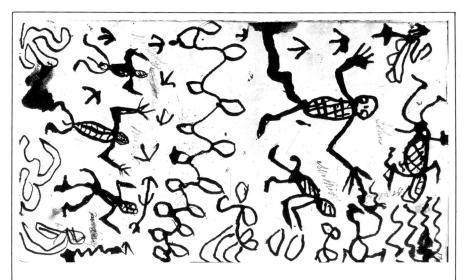

Aboriginal art

Like their customs, Aboriginal art shows considerable diversity across the tribes of Australia. The artists use several media. They paint on the walls of caves, on the bodies of performers in the ceremonial dances; they draw on the sand or soft earth using this means to instruct the initiates into the rules of the tribe; and they engrave complex patterns on sacred stones and wooden objects. The equipment used to make their designs is simple and consists of narrow strips of bark lightly chewed at one end, or the top of a forefinger. The pigments that provide the rich colours are red and yellow ochre, white pipe-clay and crushed charcoal or the black of one of the iron ores which are ground on a rough stone to a soft liquid consistency. Sometimes the depictions are repre-

This Aboriginal drawing was bound into the notebook of George Augustus Robinson, protector of Aborigines in Tasmania and Port Phillip in the 1830s and 1840s. The drawing clearly illustrates the uniqueness of Aboriginal design and imagination.

sentational; sometimes abstract; often the figures painted are mythical figures, full of meaning to a particular tribe whose presentation helps keep alive age-old beliefs, passing these on from generation to generation. These mythical figures are linked to 'the dreaming'. The artist who paints them performs a crucial role. He is the 'recreator' responsible for 're-activating' the spiritual powers of 'dreaming' spirits and, in this sense, becomes the living representative of the beings he draws. Aboriginal art is essentially land–based, every cave painting being related to ownership of certain tracts of country.

lizards, and of the human figure in all its activities, hunting, fighting and danc-ing. Their canvases were the boles of trees and strips of bark, but more usually the walls of a cave or the inner surface of an overhanging shelf of rock. They loved also to make stencils of their hands and feet by blowing over them from the mouth on to the rock a solution of ochre. Some of the drawings are very ancient, and they depict huge serpents as much as 9 m (30 ft) in length and giant prehistoric kangaroos. In order to make what he was depicting absolute-ly clear the native artist would sometimes put in details which he could not see; thus, in the manner of Picasso, we have portraits which combine the full face with a profile. Others, like the early Egyptians, placed the heads of animals and birds upon human forms, and others again produced ideographs, stylized picture-patterns that bear a certain resemblance to Chinese writing.

Herbert Basedow, the best of the anthropologists who were still able to observe the Aborigine in his native state at the beginning of the present cen-tury, puts the matter very well when he says,

'an Aboriginal's design may be crude, but his imagination is, nevertheless, wonderful; we see the line, but he sees the life; we behold the image, he the form.'

Basedow reveals how their ideographs and abstract drawings were de-veloped from natural objects. Thus in the following sketches we see the normal conventional frog and the tortoise becoming emblematic patterns:

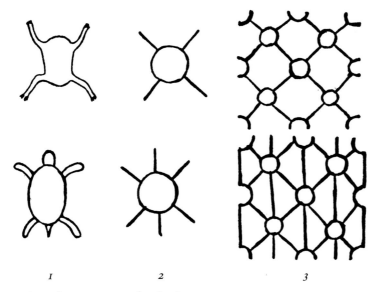

1   *2*   *3*

Even a written language was beginning to emerge:

Crossed boomerangs   *Symbol for a fight*

There were many totally different dialects but the Aborigines usually man-aged to make themselves understood through gestures which were known everywhere. Thus the slapping of the right hand against the buttocks meant

'Follow me'; the placing of the hands over the breasts meant a woman, and the stroking of the chin, a man. Animals and birds were easily described by imitating their calls and through motions of the hand. They counted by using the fingers and the toes, and the passage of time was indicated by the number of 'sleeps' and of moons. A rendezvous would be fixed by a man pointing to the anticipated position of the sun. Anyone who has stayed long enough among primitive people for a routine of habits to be established will know how quickly and completely a sign language of this kind can be built up; it becomes a kind of second nature and is infinitely preferable to the hideous pidgin-English which was forced upon the Aborigine when the white man arrived.

Few idols existed, but there was a community of religious feeling among the tribes and a veneration of their ancestors. The fear of evil spirits was also fairly general, and certain tribes worshipped the sun, others fire, while others again possessed stone phalluses which were regarded as sacred. The snake also played an important part in Aboriginal mythology. Every tribe had its *kobong* – its totem – which might be an animal like the dingo or a bird like the white cockatoo, and every man had his secret name, and took his part in the secret rites of his tribe. Indeed, there seems to have been a continual preoccupation with the mystery of life and death, and all that was unknown or not physically present at any given moment was referred to as being 'in the dreaming'. This

Aboriginal treatment of the dead

The body was laid out on a platform and left to dry for a long period. A bone might in time be removed as a sacred relic for a close kinsperson. Later the remains would be cremated and the burial place left strictly alone for a longer period to keep the spirit site free from contact. Attitudes to death relied heavily on sorcery as an explanation. Aborigines generally ascribed the death of a young or middle-aged person to sorcery to account for why one individual should be struck down instead of another. Bone pointing was a highly effective means of ridding the tribe of someone who had transgressed against tribal laws. Alternatively, the transgressor could be 'sung to death' by poison songs. In such cases the body was left where it fell and not given burial because it was considered too poisonous to handle.

An Aboriginal woman in mourning. Her face is covered in whiting and grease; the remainder of her body is smeared over with yellow clay found in the river. These elaborate decorations are designed to fend off the spirit of the dead person. The design is intended to conceal or alter the appearance of the mourners so that the spirit of the dead, who are watching, will not recognize them and steal their spirits as companions, thereby causing their death.

world of dreams was very real and could become nightmarish for a man outlawed by his tribe. The ritual pointing of a bone or stick at a man was enough to condemn him to death. Unless the witchdoctor could produce counter-spells to save him, he really did die. Basedow has described how a 'boned' man he once saw stood aghast and terrified as though he felt the lethal magic pouring into him. He tried to shriek, then fell to the ground and crawled away, refusing to eat or drink until at last death relieved him from his misery.

The dead were carefully buried, for it was believed that the spirit of man was eternal and could take possession of his bones at some future day. Relatively little ceremony took place at the death of the old, since it was thought that to some extent their spirit had already departed from their bodies. But the death of a young person was the occasion of great burial honours. Amid loud and continuous wailing his fellow tribesmen would mutilate their bodies and scalps with sharp bones, often inflicting terrible wounds; and for a long period of mourning a widow would separate herself from the tribe.

These, then, were the tough, vigorous, gentle, superstitious and conservative people whom Banks found but one degree removed from the brutes, and whom Dampier described as the miserablest on earth. Yet they were neither brutal nor miserable before the white men came. In a harsh and barren country they had established a perfectly valid way of life, they had kept the race alive through unknown centuries of time, they threatened no one, and coveted nothing except the barest minimum of food. They had the art of living for the day, they knew how to laugh and enjoy themselves, and if they had no ambition at least they possessed the Greek quality of φιλοτίμῶ-the knowing of one's place in the world.

It remained now to see if they could still keep that place when the white men came to settle in Australia.

4

The settlement

FOR NEARLY EIGHTEEN YEARS after Cook's departure the Aborigines of New South Wales remained undisturbed, and would have continued so even longer but for the American war of independence. The British defeat in 1781 meant that the American colonies could no longer be used as a convenient dumping ground for criminals, and in order to relieve the overcrowding in the British gaols it was necessary to set up a penal settlement in some other country. As early as 1779 the matter was considered by a committee of the House of Commons. New Zealand was rejected on the grounds that the Maoris there were too ferocious, but Banks came forward with the suggestion that Botany Bay on the eastern coast of Australia might be the answer to the problem. Banks had been none too enthusiastic about the place – its soil or its water supply – when he had actually been there with Cook in the *Endeavour*, but time and distance had lent enchantment to the scene, and now he thought it might do very well if seeds and livestock were taken out from England. The committee agreed, and Lord Sydney, the Secretary of State for the Home Office, submitted the plan to the Treasury for its approval.

Botany Bay had obvious attractions. The natives were few in number, and being of a timid disposition were not likely to cause trouble. The land was there for the taking; no other European nation claimed it, and it was also commendably distant from England; once landed in New South Wales the criminals would not have much chance of getting home again.

Even when one remembers the precariousness of life in the eighteenth century, the universal poverty and the great difference between the rich and the poor, one is still hard put to understand the callousness and ruthlessness of the authorities in dealing with law-breakers. They had advanced beyond the stage of cutting off hands and feet, but not very far. Three hundred lashes, more than most men could bear, was not an uncommon punishment for the theft of a sheep, and it made no difference if the culprit was a boy of twenty or even less; he was a criminal, the curse was in the blood, and that was that. It was almost as if society was in a state of permanent civil war, the haves against the have-nots, and it hardly needed the French revolution to remind the English gentry that the mob at home could be just as menacing as any enemy they might encounter in a foreign war. Relax the criminal code, show a little humanity to the first offender or the hungry prostitute, and chaos would result.

So now it was proposed to ship the sheep-stealer and the pickpocket, the forger and the house-breaker and the other undesirables out to the uncivilized Pacific for a period of seven years or so – which was much the same thing as saying for the term of their natural lives. Speaking of the convicts who were sentenced to forced labour on one of the prison hulks at Woolwich Dr Johnson declared roundly,

'I do not see that they are punished by this; they must have worked equally had they never been guilty of stealing. They now only work; so after all they have gained; what they stole is clear gain to them; the confinement is nothing.'

Dr Johnson did not know what he was talking about.

By the middle of the 1780s these hulks were becoming very crowded, and their squalor was such that men, women and children were dying in them. At last in 1787 it was decided to get the Botany Bay scheme under way. The 'First

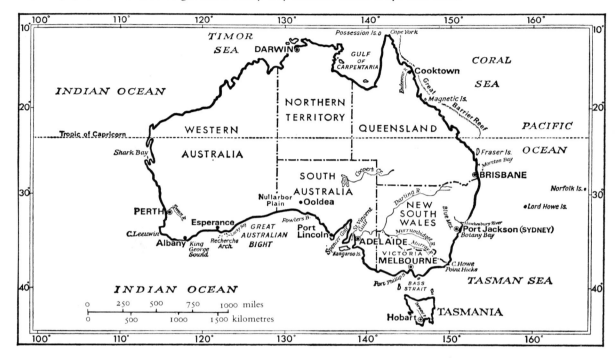

Fleet' to sail was to consist of eleven ships: HMS *Sirius*, 622 tonnes (612 tons), the sloop *Supply*, and nine transport and store-ships, all of them around 305–406 tonnes (300–400 tons). A naval officer, Captain Arthur Phillip, was to have the command, and later, when the new colony was established, the status of Governor. To control the convicts he was to be given four companies of marines, some of whom were permitted to take their wives and families with them, and there were also 443 sailors. The prisoners numbered just on 800, of whom about a third were women, the sexes being kept apart in separate ships. There was much waiting about while two years' stores were got on board, but eventually on 13 May 1787 the unhappy little squadron got away from Spit-head.

Things went unexpectedly well. The weather was good; the male convicts, though still confined below decks, had their fetters struck from their ankles, and now that the die was cast and there could be no turning back, a certain cheerfulness was generated (if we are to believe the diarists on the voyage) by the fact that they were all committed together to an extraordinary adventure. Who knew what the new land would provide? Perhaps goldmines, perhaps rich farming valleys, perhaps a chance of making a new start. Anything, at all events, was better than lying rotting in hulks in the Thames.

They called at Teneriffe, Rio de Janeiro and Capetown to pick up livestock

The First Fleet entering Port Jackson.

and fresh provisions, and towards the end of the year they were approaching the Australian coast. Phillip now went on ahead with four of the fastest ships to prepare for the landing at Botany Bay, and on 18 January 1788, with the aid of Cook's chart, they sailed into the *Endeavour*'s old anchorage. During the next few days the remainder of the fleet came in as well. They had been just over eight months on the voyage; the convicts, threatened with death if they mutinied, had given no trouble, and only twenty-three of them had died, which was regarded as no bad record in those days. Phillip, on going ashore to reconnoitre, managed to make contact with the Aborigines. They appeared to have no memory of Cook and were very curious about the white shaven faces of the British sailors. They asked by signs if they were men or women, and on being told they were men, burst into great laughter.

So far so good. But Phillip did not like the land he saw. It seemed to him to be flat, featureless and barren, and now, at the full height of the summer, there was very little water about. He did not see how his very large company could support themselves there, and it says a good deal for his resourcefulness that he at once sent his sloop to investigate Port Jackson, the other harbour a few kilometres to the north, which Cook had sighted, but not entered, eighteen years before. The *Supply* returned in a day or two with a highly favourable report; Port Jackson was an almost land-locked harbour with a deep-water estuary running inland for many kilometres and the land appeared to be fertile. Phillip decided to move the whole fleet there without delay, and they were actually putting out to sea when two strange ships were seen to be making in towards Botany Bay. This was an extraordinary event. No ships had entered

162

Governor Phillip, brave and honest

Governor Arthur Phillip had had a varied if not highly illustrious career as a naval officer and as a gentleman farmer in Hampshire when he was selected for this arduous commission across the world. He had also served for several years as a captain in the Portuguese fleet during the Spanish–Portuguese war where he won the reputation of being 'brave, honest, obedient and self-sacrificing'. He would want all these qualities in New South Wales. Fortunately, his experience had fitted him for command and authority, had injected a knowledge of farming and equipped him with liberal ideas for the future of his colony. He landed 1,030 persons, of whom 736 were convicts (including 188 women), the remainder marines and civil officers, 27 with wives, and 37 chil-

dren. Phillip's commission gave him extraordinary powers and he was formally placed in charge of the whole area of eastern Australia and adjacent Pacific islands. The Crown vested him with complete authority over the inhabitants and gave him the right to introduce regulations touching practically all aspects of their lives. During his governorship, some 3,546 male and 766 female convicts were handed over to his care, many unfit subjects for an experiment in colonization. Phillip found them lazy and anxious to avoid work by any means possible. Few had technical abilities, but the Governor's special strength was to generate optimism, encourage agriculture to feed the settlement and maintain harmony with the Aborigines. He left the colony in December 1792 to seek medical aid. Seven years later he became a Rear-Admiral of the Blue, and in the year of his death, 1814, Admiral.

these waters since Cook's day, and none were expected there now. Phillip waited for the strangers to come up and was relieved to find it was the French explorer La Pérouse with *La Boussole* and *L'Astrolabe*. They had had a momentous journey round the world since leaving Brest two and a half years before, and were now investigating whaling prospects in the Pacific. La Pérouse as a boy had been wounded and captured at sea by the British, and subsequently had fought them in various parts of the world. But he bore no grudge, and after a warm exchange of courtesies with Phillip he anchored in Botany Bay, while the convict fleet sailed on to its new landfall in Port Jackson.

Even today, after nearly 200 years of haphazard municipal planning and the activities of property developers, Port Jackson is a wonderful sight to behold. There is some truth in its claim to be the loveliest harbour in the world. Once inside the narrow heads the traveller has the sensation of being on an inland lake with long arms reaching away on every side into delightful coves and hidden bays.

Phillip's company was no fervent band of *Mayflower* pilgrims escaping persecution in a new land – the persecution was still decidedly with them – but just the same it must have been an exhilarating thing to have coasted into this sprightly bay where everything was pristine and untouched, and where no white man had ever been before. They longed to get ashore. It was not just a question of the eight months voyage they had just made; some of the convicts had been serving long sentences in the hulks on the Thames and it was years since they had put foot on land.

Having passed through the heads into the calm water of the harbour the Fleet sailed along for 6.4 km (4 miles) in a westerly direction and then reached a 'snug cove' where a small stream ran down to the shore. Here (it is the present site of Circular Quay, whence the ferry boats go out across the harbour), they dropped anchor in water so deep that they could tie up to the shore. The disembarkation immediately began and continued for the next two days. It must have been a lively scene: the tents pitched beside the little stream, the woodcutters at work, the blacksmith's forges and the camp ovens being set up, the marines parading in their red coats, and the come and go of little boats around the fleet. Indeed, it was rather more than lively. No one had quite foreseen the effect of segregating the sexes in different ships for so long a time, and now, when the convicts were brought ashore, there was a general rush for the women.

The memorialists of the voyage avert their eyes from what happened with something like a shudder, and apparently for a while things got out of hand. There had not been much delicacy or regard for privacy in the convicts' lives in England, and now all inhibitions vanished entirely, the women being no less willing than the men, and the marines as eager as the convicts. The debauch seems to have continued whenever opportunity offered for some days and nights, and Phillip, holding divine service under a great tree on the first Sunday, earnestly recommended marriage to the congregation – a course which, incidentally, many of them soon followed. Meanwhile the camp was taking shape. A boundary had been drawn round it, and the few natives who appeared were made to understand that they must not cross it. This boundary was also patrolled day and night by marines to prevent the convicts from escaping into the bush. Scurvy had broken out, and foraging parties were sent

off to seek for fresh food. They had little success; a blundering marine with a musket had not much hope of getting within range of the timid kangaroos, no eatable green plants were to be found, and even the fishing boats that trawled the harbour with nets were disappointed. As yet, however, there was no cause for alarm; they had ample provisions in the ships and the livestock they had brought with them were regaining condition ashore.

The first encounter with the native women at Port Jackson, New South Wales. Governor Phillip's instructions ordered him to 'establish contact and maintain friendly relations' with the natives. He personally interested himself in their life and customs and managed initially to live in amity with them.

Since this stock was so vital to the isolated life that lay before them it is worth listing. They had 1 stallion, 3 mares, 3 colts, 2 bulls, 5 cows, 29 sheep, 19 goats, 49 hogs, 25 pigs, 5 rabbits, 18 turkeys, 29 geese, 35 ducks, 122 fowls and 87 chickens – a pitifully small collection to maintain well over 1,000 people, but it was hoped that it would soon increase by breeding.

On 7 February, nearly two weeks after they had got ashore, Phillip held a parade for the formal taking over of the new colony. He revealed in an address to his followers that he had been given by the King virtually absolute powers, not only over the settlement (which he had named Sydney Cove), but of the entire eastern seaboard discovered by Cook. It was an immense responsibility, and there were people in England who had questioned Phillip's ability to undertake it. He was rather a delicate-looking man, and there was nothing much in his past record to inspire great confidence. He had been born forty years before in London of a German father and an English mother with naval connections, and had made his way quietly up through the ranks of the Royal Navy. It was true that he had travelled widely in the Mediterranean and in the Atlantic, and that at one stage, when he was attached to the Portuguese Navy, he had transported 400 convicts to Brazil. But it had been a mediocre career, and he had actually been living on half-pay as a gentleman-farmer in Hampshire when he was chosen to take command of this very hazardous adventure in the Pacific.

Phillip, however, seems to have been one of those quiet, competent men who are not really interested in power, but who will use it very well if it is thrust upon them. He had been firm and sensible in getting the right equipment for his ships before setting out, he had brought them through the long voyage without mishap, and now, in a practical and decisive way, he began to exhibit qualities of leadership that had been hardly suspected before. He was confident enough to be humane. We find him holding his hand at first from excessive punishment, and he gave the clearest orders that they must at all times try to befriend the blacks.

But already the deficiencies of the expedition were making themselves felt. Incredibly they had no botanist or geologist with them, and practically no one who could advise them usefully about that most difficult of things which they had set out to do: to make European plants grow in land that was utterly alien to them, a country where winter fell in summer, where there was no manure for the soil, where no one knew from one day to another what the temperature was going to be, where the wind was going to come from and at what velocity, or whether or not rain was going to fall. In principle the convicts had been chosen because they were either farmers or craftsmen, but in fact there was precious little skill amongst them, and they were not the sort of men who could easily adjust themselves to new conditions, especially conditions so entirely strange as these.

No one had envisaged the extreme toughness of the timber to be cleared, nor the aridity of a soil that was baked iron-hard by the fierce summer heat. No one had anticipated that no limestone would be found for the making of

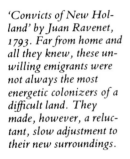

'Convicts of New Holland' by Juan Ravenet, 1793. Far from home and all they knew, these unwilling emigrants were not always the most energetic colonizers of a difficult land. They made, however, a reluctant, slow adjustment to their new surroundings.

Captain Watkin Tench, keen explorer

Tench sailed as a marine officer in the First Fleet transport *Charlotte* which arrived at Port Jackson three days after Phillip. The young Tench was a keen explorer, sympathetic to the Aborigines and instantly fascinated by the Australian landscape, its strange solitude and its informal camp fire nights. His two books on the journey to the colony and its early settlement: *A Narrative of the Expedition to Botany Bay* (1789) and *A Complete Account of the Settlement at Port Jackson in New South Wales* (1793) contained a wealth of observations on the natural productions, inhabitants and character of the infant colony and provided the most perceptive and literary account of the settlement.

mortar, or that long droughts would be followed by floods that would wash away the surface soil from their fields. They had no horses to plough with, and once their provisions were exhausted, no reserves of any kind. Crops had to be raised within the next eighteen months or they would starve. It was difficult for them to discover more about the country and its possibilities by befriending the blacks, because by the very fact of their presence they were antagonizing and frightening the tribes. They were bound to seize the Aborigines' hunting grounds for their crops and to trespass upon their fishing grounds, and the Aborigines were bound to try and defend their rights and to take reprisals. And over all, oppressive and persistent, stultifying every enterprise, was that dead, sullen atmosphere of a gaol. The man in fetters, dressed in a coarse blue and yellow prisoner's jacket and working in a chain gang, was hardly likely to throw himself into the creation of the new colony with a sense of burning enthusiasm. For him it was simply another gaol.

It was a situation that bordered on lunacy. How could they hope to survive in this arid and hostile place unless they forgot their differences, unless all of them, gaolers and prisoners alike, turned to and worked the land with their utmost energy? In this emergency every man was vital. But no, it would not do; the punishment had to continue, the artificial conditions established 24,000 km (15,000 miles) away in England had to persist here in the wilderness. And so we have the grotesque spectacle of the prisoners shackled one to another being marched off into the bush, where a warder with a loaded musket stood over them while they worked. On paper then, Phillip was defeated before he had even begun. But he did not know this, he did not really know anything about the future, and so in merciful ignorance he got to work.

The best authority for the first few years of the colony's existence is a twenty-year–old marine officer, Captain Watkin Tench. He was an educated

The settlement at Sydney Cove, 1788. Already dwellings had been erected; gangs of convicts had cleared the environs; the British flag flew gallantly over a remote and struggling colony. Some forty-eight years later, Charles Darwin, landing in Sydney in the Beagle, *would marvel at the development of a colony 'stained in crime'.*

man, he wrote well, and his diary is honest. 'In Port Jackson,' he cries at one point, 'all is quiet and stupid as could be wished.' It was the stupidity of endless, uneventful days, of incessant, repetitive physical labour, of boring and brutish companions who had nothing to say, of nostalgia for even the smallest luxuries of a civilized society – and perhaps too of a nagging recurring fear that in the end all would fail, all would be lost, and the little settlement would die without the outside world ever knowing anything about it. Nothing ever seemed to go right. The seeds they planted – and with what devastating labour of hacking away the bush and of scratching at the ground with hoes – refused to come up, or having come up, were blasted by the sun. It was so hot that bats and parakeets fell dead out of the trees. The sheep died of some strange disease. The cattle strayed and were not recovered.★

Phillip had a fine plan for a new town with a main street 60 m (200 ft) wide, but it went forward with excruciating slowness; after months of work they had only achieved two small brick-and-stone houses, an observatory and a wooden hospital. Most of the colony were still living in tents or huts made of branches and clay. Weevils and maggots had got into their stores, and still the intensive hunting and fishing yielded next to nothing. The scurvy continued and there were soon fifty dead. Presently the whole colony was facing slow starvation, and by night both convicts and marines would loot from each other's gardens the few pitiful vegetables that had managed to survive. These thefts became so bad, so threatening to the security of the whole colony, that Phillip was forced to take desperate measures: six marines were hanged for breaking into the public stores, others were given 300 lashes, and he even contemplated marooning some of the more recalcitrant pilferers among the cannibals in New Zealand. Had they been able to get inland to more fertile land things might have been better, but they had few horses, and every

★When they were eventually found in the bush seven years later the two bulls and four cows that had escaped had multiplied into a herd of sixty-one and all had gone wild. Their retreat was subsequently named The Cowpastures.

attempt to reach the mountains on foot was defeated by thirst and hunger. The blacks had become menacing. When their fishing tackle was stolen by convicts and all the wild game about the settlement had been driven away by gunfire, they fell upon any straggler they found in the bush and speared him to death.

This still did not prevent some of the convicts from trying to escape from the settlement. Until La Pérouse sailed away in March their main idea was to desert to the French ships in Botany Bay, and when this failed they became obsessed with the absurd notion that China was the place to make for; they believed it lay just 160 km (100 miles) away over the mountains. A group of Irishmen actually set out for Canton, and some came back half-dead from hunger, while others were speared or collapsed in the bush. Others again were tougher and managed to 'go native', and these were the original bushrangers; they lived by making raids into the settlement by night.

In these dismal circumstances the little colony struggled through the first summer into the autumn and winter, and because, from the Governor downwards, there was no hope for any of them unless they battled on, they did not absolutely lose heart. Tench, at all events, manages to write of these early days, not as a long catalogue of disasters, but as a chronicle of the natural setbacks of a great experiment, and through his pages one begins to note a certain slow adjustment of the colonists to their harsh surroundings, the growth of a simple expertise in forcing the land to produce. In any case, not all the news was bad. The little *Supply* went off on the 1,600 km (1,000 miles) journey to Norfolk Island* to start a subsidiary settlement, and they found there a better climate, fish in abundance and vast pines, 54 m (180 ft) high, which were infinitely superior to the Australian eucalyptus for masts and

The rugged shore of Norfolk Island. Governor Phillip had been instructed to settle this potentially useful spot to forestall occupation by any other power. He therefore early despatched his old friend and second-in-command Philip Gidley King aboard the Sirius, in February 1788, to found a subordinate settlement. King landed with a company of twenty-three, including fifteen convicts, and was formally appointed lieutenant-governor of the island in December 1789. By 1794, the Norfolk Island establishment had become self-sufficient in grain and was exporting pigs to Sydney. King subsequently became governor of New South Wales in 1800.

*First discovered by Cook in the *Resolution* in October 1774.

Rose Hill, the fertile land some 24 km (15 miles) from Sydney, which the early settlers turned into a granary for Port Jackson. Rose Hill soon reverted to its native name, Parramatta.

building timber. On her return voyage to Sydney the ship chanced upon another uninhabited island (which they named after Lord Howe), and here they discovered large green turtles and myriads of birds that were so tame they could be knocked over with a stick. Things also began to take a turn for the better in November 1789, when the colonists, despairing of the poor soil around Sydney Cove, pushed up the estuary for 19 km (12 miles) and found good ground at a place they named Rose Hill. It abounded in a species of beautiful scarlet birds which became known as 'Rose-hillers' – a term that was contracted later to Rosella, despite the fact that Rose Hill itself soon reverted to its native name, Parramatta. Still another more fruitful farming ground was found on the banks of the Hawkesbury River to the north of Sydney. It soon became famous for its oysters.

Now too, they began to discover that the bush was not absolutely barren. They made a drinkable infusion from the root of the sarsaparilla plant, red gum from the eucalyptus trees was of some help in treating scurvy, fish became more plentiful at certain seasons, and they grew more skilful in trapping the native birds. They were still very much attached to England, the homeland that had rejected them, for where else in this wilderness were their thoughts to turn? None of them thought of themselves as 'Australians'; indeed, the term had not been invented as yet, and the country was still referred to as New Holland, or, more vaguely, as just Botany Bay. June 4, 1788, was the fiftieth birthday of George III (who was then declining into his first bout of insanity), and it was celebrated with a salute of guns, the lighting of bonfires and a banquet. Phillip pardoned four men who had been condemned to death.

So by the end of the first year they were in a situation that was critical, but not absolutely desperate. Their main hopes were fixed upon the *Sirius*, which had been sent off to the Cape of Good Hope for wheat, and with their numbers down to around 900 they set themselves to weather through their second long summer as best they could. Despite its setbacks the little colony was beginning to wear a more settled air. A routine was developing. In addition to the communal farms every man had his little plot that he worked himself, and the convicts were allowed to rest through the hot hours of the day. By night the ships at anchor in the cove tolled the hours with their bells, and from the shore the sentries shouted in answer 'All's well'. The thieving continued, but at least there was no murder or suicide.

All through this time Phillip kept making efforts to come to terms with the blacks, but they rejected every approach. They were so suspicious that they even refused to give sanctuary to a Negro convict who had absconded. But Phillip was determined at least to learn their language, and in the end he sent out two boat-loads of marines on a kidnapping raid. They managed to grab a man and bring him back to Sydney Cove, where they soothed him and fed him, and after he had been bathed and shaved, they dressed him in shirt and trousers. There he was, got up like some wild animal in a circus, and after a while he learned to eat bread and drink tea. Then a disaster happened. In April 1789 black bodies were suddenly seen to be floating in the harbour and washed up in the coves. Smallpox had struck. The man they had captured was one of the first victims, and by May the disease had swept through all the harbour

'The Rosehill Parakeet' by John Gould. The beautiful scarlet birds became known as 'rosehillers', a term contracted later to 'rosella'.

171

The capture of the Aborigines, Colebe and Bennelong, by Lieutenant Bradley's crew at Manly Cove on 25 November 1789. Colebe was about thirty-five years of age and was obviously a senior of Bennelong, who treated him with deference. Colebe escaped after three weeks but subsequently brought his family to Sydney and acted as a guide to Governor Phillip on his inland journeys to the Nepean River and other places. He sometimes dined at Government House and, many years later, this 'go-between' between the two cultures was granted 12 ha (30 acres) of land by Governor Macquarie at South Creek and later still a similar grant at Bathurst.

tribes. A few of the sick who were too feeble to protest were brought to Sydney for treatment, but the majority, comprehending nothing of this mysterious enormity that had struck them down, quietly succumbed by their campfires. They had had no serious diseases before this, but it is doubtful if they guessed that the white man was the cause of their misery. This terrible, lethal thing was simply an evil that descended upon them out of the sky – out of the dreaming – and there was nothing their medicine men could do about it.

Phillip was determined to get another black protégé to replace the one who had died, and when the worst of the plague was over he succeeded in capturing a young man of twenty-six named Bennelong, who was much scarred by tribal wars but otherwise a healthy specimen. He proved more adaptable to white men's ways than his predecessor, for he soon developed a taste for European food and drink and he was kept as a sort of pet at Government House. Tench describes him as 'of good stature and stoutly made, with a bold, intrepid countenance, which bespoke defiance and revenge'. Others found him 'communicative and affable'. Poor Bennelong. He was the first guinea-pig to be used in the attempt to make a fusion between the black man and the white, and it is true that they made some headway with him; he learned to speak a little English, he adopted European clothes and began to wash, and although he was allowed to come and go as he pleased he preferred to linger on in the settlement. Sometimes he rejoined his tribe for a few days but he always came back.

The rest of his story can be conveniently and briefly related here. Like Omai, he was sent to England later on to be displayed, and was taken up by society there for a year or two. On his return to Sydney he found that his wife

Bennelong, a tragic experiment

Bennelong, captured at Manly Cove in November 1879 by order of Governor Phillip, took readily to life among the white men. He relished their food, learned to speak English and became particularly attached to Phillip in whose house he lodged. He escaped some months later and was present at Manly Cove when Phillip was speared by blacks; but he took no part in this and appeared regularly at Government House to enquire after the Governor's health. In 1791 a brick hut was built for him on the eastern point in Sydney Cove, now called Bennelong Point. 'Of good stature and stoutly made,' wrote Tench, Bennelong had 'a bold, intrepid countenance.' Taken home to England by Phillip, Bennelong was later returned to Sydney by Governor Hunter. But he was now a victim of his displacement, unable to find full acceptance or contentment with his fellow Aborigines or the whites. He died in 1813.

was pregnant by another man and she died in childbirth. The story goes (and possibly it is apocryphal) that Bennelong killed his rival with a spear and then built a pyre upon which he threw at first the dead body of his wife and then the living child. He is said to have declared that he did not wish the boy to grow up and live as unhappy a life amongst the whites as he himself had done. Soon after this he returned to the bush, where he died in a tribal fight in January 1813. The place where the pyre was built was named Bennelong Point, and that is the site of the Sydney Opera House, a splendid, grandiose building, something in the white man's dreaming.

There never was much chance that a real rapprochement could be made between the white men and the Aborigines in their wild state. The gap between them was too great. The black man may have been a better physical specimen than the white, but he had to change if he was going to adjust himself to the European way of life, and in making that change he lost his strength and his virility. The few Aborigines who now, little by little, began to come into the settlement to beg for food and tobacco – and eventually liquor – and who paraded themselves in dirty and ragged cast-off clothing, were not half the men they had been when they were living with their tribes in the bush. It seems a strange thing to say, but apartheid might have saved them. Had they been kept out of the settlement, had they been allotted hunting and fishing grounds from which the white men were excluded, they might have made the transition to civilization in their own good time. But this was a head-on conflict between the two races, both wanted the same territory in order to survive, and impatience and fear were created by hunger. The convicts, not to speak of the marines, were hardly the sort of people to make allowances for the Aborigines. They treated them like wild dogs, and when the Aborigines tried to defend themselves they shot them. Thus violence alternated with cosseting; the tame Aborigine who hung around the settlement was indulged and tolerated, the wild one was killed; and both in the end were despised. Even Watkin Tench, who had started off as a follower of Rousseau and a great supporter of the noble savage, began to change his views, and although he never became a black-hater he grew to believe that the Aborigine was pretty well a hopeless case.

It was Phillip himself who brought matters to a head. One day a dead whale was washed up on the shore on the northern side of the harbour, and the Governor went over there in his boat. He found a group of natives feasting on the flesh, and for some reason or other – perhaps because they thought that Phillip and his party were going to drive them off the carcass – they picked up their spears in a menacing way. In Cook's fashion Phillip went towards them unarmed, and making friendly gestures. It was unwise. One of the tribesmen plunged a spear into his shoulder, and Phillip, quite badly wounded, was carried off to his boat. This outburst of ferocity was followed by an immediate reaction in the tribes; like children they were sorry for what they had done and came forward asking for forgiveness. And indeed for a time there was a much

An idealized portrait, from a sketch by John Hunter, of Governor Phillip, Lieutenant-Governor David Collins, Rev. Richard Johnston, 'chaplain to the settlement' (overlooking the hedge), Captain John Hunter and First Fleet surgeon John White attending on the Aborigines.

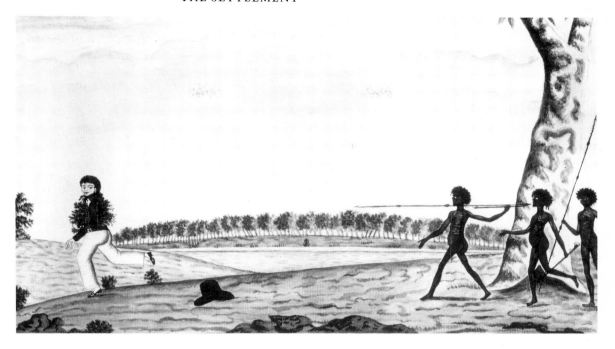

better relationship with them. But all this ended abruptly in another more serious incident. M'Entire, the Governor's gamekeeper, a man much hated by the blacks (probably with good reason – he was known to have shot at them from time to time), was out with a hunting-party beyond the confines of the settlement when a group of tribesmen fell upon his camp and speared him dead. This was too much, even for Phillip. He sent Tench out on a punitive expedition with orders to shoot six blacks as a reprisal. It was a ridiculous business; Tench made two forced marches into the bush with a company of marines and it is difficult to understand how he ever imagined that such a heavy-handed operation would have the slightest chance against such expert stalkers and huntsmen as the naked Aborigines. They must have seen the red coats a great distance off, and they vanished. Tench and his men finished up in the moonlight in a quagmire at the head of Botany Bay, and then trailed back to Sydney without so much as catching sight of a single black.

Thus the misunderstanding and mistrust went grimly on, and it was relieved only occasionally by a gesture or a moment of compassion. Once a marine, lost in the bush, was confronted by a party of blacks who offered to lead him back to the settlement if he surrendered his gun. The soldier in great fear handed it over and at once the Aborigines laid down their spears. They then conducted the man to his home and when they reached it gave him back his gun. But such incidents were rare.

In May 1789 the *Sirius* got back from Capetown, their first visitation in seventeen months from the outside world, but her cargo of wheat was only a temporary relief. By the end of that year the famine was increasing again, clothes and uniforms were wearing out, and many of the men went barefoot. Most of the ships of the First Fleet had returned to England, and when now the *Sirius* was wrecked off Norfolk Island and the sloop *Supply* was sent to Batavia for provisions, they were entirely cut off. Every day a watch was kept from

'The Hunted Rushcutter' by the Port Jackson painter. Despite good early relations, mistrust and misunderstanding developed between Aborigines and white men within the first year. Here, Aborigines pursue a bedecked rushcutter with spears.

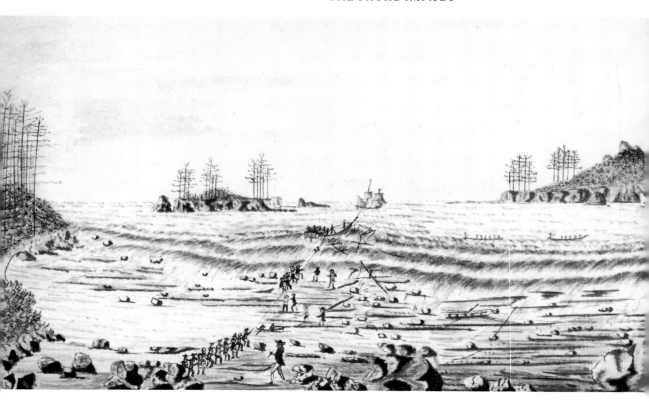

The disastrous wrecking of the supply ship Sirius, *19 March 1790, on the reef off Spring Bay, Norfolk Island. Such a loss was critical for the struggling colony at Port Jackson.*

Sydney heads for the sight of a sail from England. Six months went by before the cry went up at last – a ship approaching. It was the vanguard of the Second Fleet, the *Lady Juliana*, eleven months out from London, and during the next few weeks she was followed into port by four more ships. This was not much more than a mixed blessing. One of their storeships, the *Guardian*, laden with livestock, fruit-trees and other supplies, had struck an iceberg and had returned to Capetown, and the convicts in the other vessels were in appalling condition through malnutrition. Of the original 1,038 who had sailed from England, 273 had died on the voyage and another 486 were ill. The captains, apparently, had been profiteering by cutting down the rations. Only the slave-traders then running Negroes from Africa to America and the West Indies could have been quite so inhumane as this.

However, now, after two and a half years they had mail from home, and they heard for the first time of the outbreak of the French Revolution. One rather wonders what they made of the Terror. Were the convicts delighted that the underdog was having his day? Did any of them pause to reflect that in France, the most sophisticated country on earth, men and women could watch the guillotine at work in the public streets with sadistic indifference, while here in New Holland the Aborigine, the most primitive of all human beings, burst into tears when he saw a warder flogging a prisoner? No torture was practised among the Aborigines, and the pointing of a stick was perhaps a more subtle and successful deterrent against wrong-doing than the bloody guillotine.

Few of the colonists were reconciled to their exile as yet. The marines longed for their terms to expire so that they could return home, and not many of them elected to take up free grants of land. The convicts continued to try and escape. There was one really spectacular attempt early in 1791. Eleven men, a woman and her two children seized the Governor's cutter and, inspired apparently by Captain Bligh's exploit in an open boat, miraculously made their way to Batavia, 4,800 km (3,000 miles) away. Here they were handed over by the Dutch to a British ship, and with seven of their number dead (including the two children) were eventually taken to England. The penalty for absconding from a penal settlement was death, and it is pleasant to recall that James Boswell, in one of his storms of indignation against injustice, took up their cause. The woman, Mary Bryant, who was only twenty-eight, he took into his custody with a pension of £10 a year, and the men of the party were also released through his exertions.

The Pacific was losing some of its terrors by this time. La Pérouse, it is true, had vanished after he had sailed away from Botany Bay, and another thirty-five years were to elapse before it was discovered that his two ships had been wrecked on the reefs of Vanikoro in the New Hebrides. But Phillip was starting to send his own ships as far afield as China and Tahiti, where it was thought that native wives might be obtained for the convicts. A whaling industry had begun: large numbers of sperm whales had been sighted off the New South Wales coast, and the English captains, having dumped their passengers at Sydney, set off in pursuit of them. Then in July 1791 the Third Fleet of ten ships began to arrive, bringing in them 1,865 male convicts in addition to 144 prostitutes. One of these vessels, the *Mary Anne*, had made the voyage in record time, just over four months.

There were now more than 4,000 people in the settlement, some 3,000 of them established at Sydney and Parramatta and the rest on Norfolk Island. The colony was not really secure as yet. In the autumn of 1791 they were again on short rations, and a disastrous drought continued until August. But then with the beginning of the spring the rain fell, and out at Parramatta the threadbare crops were starting to show a small return at last and they even managed to produce a little tobacco. It was a tremendous moment when two bunches of grapes were cut from the vines in the Governor's garden. Yet it was still a

Mary Bryant, escaped convict

Mary Bryant was the first woman convict to make headlines as an escapee. She had arrived with the First Fleet on the *Charlotte*, as Mary Braund or Broad, charged with assault and robbery. On the voyage she gave birth to a daughter which, with some spirit, she named after the vessel transporting her. Soon after arriving in Botany Bay she married a fellow convict, William Bryant. But the privations of Sydney evidently held few charms and in March 1791, the Bryants and their two children escaped with ten other convicts, using the Governor's stolen cutter. Their epic voyage took them some 5,206 km (3,254 miles) up the eastern coast of Australia, through the Barrier Reef, to Timor and hence to Koepang in Batavia which they reached in sixty-nine adventurous days. There, they were handed over by the Dutch and shipped to Britain. For Mary, it proved a disastrous escapade. Her husband, four of the men, and both her children had died and she and the remainder of her party were sentenced to death. But the bold attempt to regain their homeland won public support in England, and Mary and the remaining men of the party were pardoned in 1783.

Settlers of New South Wales: An officer and his wife display their finery. Social gulfs remained large in the colony. The officer elite and their wives clung to the remembered refinements of England. The soldiers and free settlers formed a middle group. At the far bottom end was the illiterate mass of convicts whose hopes of comfort flickered dimly in those first hard years of settlement.

RIGHT, ABOVE
Government House, Sydney, Port Jackson, 1791.

RIGHT, BELOW
'View of the English Colony of Parramatta in NSW', 1792, by Fernando Brambila. Sun, rain and good soil saved the colony. Four years after settlement, Parramatta presented a thriving centre.

bizarre existence, the *élite* of the officers and their wives clinging to the refinements of Europe, the soldiers and the free settlers forming a middle group, and beneath them the unhappy mass of convicts, the illiterates from the Irish bogs and the English slums, the forgers, the footpads and the political undesirables. Some remarkable characters were beginning to emerge. Tench speaks of the counterfeiter Frazer:

'The governor had written to England for a set of locks to be sent for the security of the public stores, which were to be so constructed as to be incapable of being picked. On their arrival his excellency sent for Frazer, and bade him examine them, telling him at the same time that they could not be picked. Frazer laughed and asked for a crooked nail only, to open them all. A nail was brought, and in an instant he verified his assertion. Astonished at his dexterity, a gentleman present determined to put it to further proof. He [Frazer] was sent in a hurry some days after to the hospital, where a lock of still superior intricacy and expense to the others had been provided. He was told that the key was lost and that the lock must be immediately picked. He examined it attentively, remarked that it was the production of a workman; and demanded ten minutes to make an instrument 'to speak with it'. Without carrying the lock with him, he went directly to his shop; and at the expiration of his term returned, applied his instrument, and open flew the lock . . .'

There remained enormous social gulfs between the three layers of the little community, yet their common experiences in a land that was basically hostile to white men were beginning to bind them together. It might have been argued

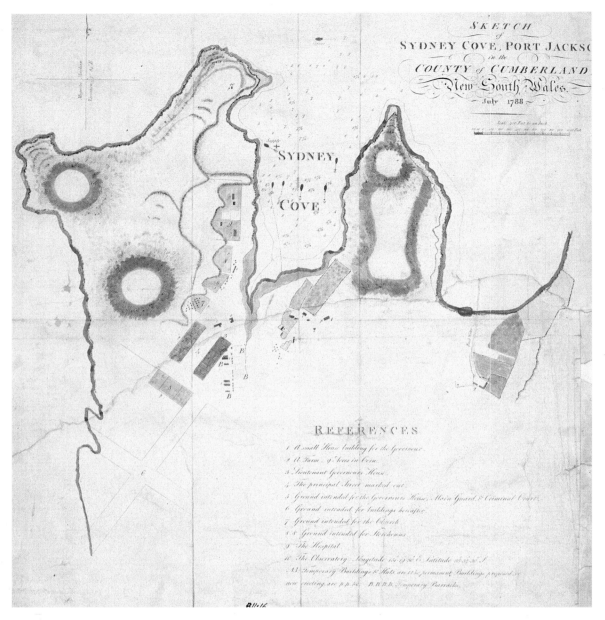

A map of Sydney Cove, Port Jackson in July 1788.

that the colonists had not been very adventurous. They still knew next to nothing of the real life of the shadowy blacks or of the resources of the country itself. In more than three years they had hardly explored for 80 km (50 miles) around Sydney, and they were fond of describing the surrounding bush as 'impassable desert', which it was not. They had not penetrated the Blue Mountains, 64 km (40 miles) away, nor had they traced the short Hawkesbury River to its source. As for the general outline of the Australian coast, it remained pretty much as Cook had left it in 1770.

Yet the first shock of contact was over, a pattern of existence, or at any rate of survival, had been established, and like a virus that suddenly proliferates in uncontaminated fields they were ready to spread out and make the continent their own.

5

The spreading out

AUSTRALIA, so far as the outside world was concerned, had no real identity of its own before 1800. It was 'Botany Bay', a penal settlement somewhere in the remote Antipodes, and the country itself had no shape. It was an amorphous and shadowy outline vaguely known as New Holland, and dotted lines were used on the maps to indicate the great stretches of the coast that were still uncharted and unexplored. Was it one vast island? Or was it slit up by straits and inland seas into an archipelago? The British had a *prima facie* claim to the eastern seaboard explored by Captain Cook, but all the rest 'belonged' to nobody as yet. The French could easily claim it. So could the Dutch. If they were going to be forestalled it was imperative for the British to explore the country on which they were so precariously perched at Port Jackson, to get its coastlines precisely charted and placed on the map, to name the bays and capes and rivers, and to investigate the country inland.

Up to this date the 'European view' had been very strong. Native names had been disregarded and had been replaced by such terms as New South Wales, New Holland and New Caledonia, even though these places bore very little resemblance to Wales, Holland or Scotland. There was a strong tendency to fit the natural phenomena into preconceived European ideas. Open bush country was described as parkland, and every green valley summoned up memories of England. The painters had not been able to grip the fact that in Australia you can actually see through the spare foliage of the trees, and so they had turned the eucalyptus into shady oaks and elms. Where the landscape simply would not conform to European standards it was described as dull and uninteresting and was ignored. The Aborigines meanwhile had been given the full noble savage treatment: sketch after sketch endowed them with heroic heads and classical torsos, and they were often depicted in the act of striking elegant poses with their spears and shields. William Blake in England produced a typical engraving of a family group, and it was even more of a caricature than the crude naturalistic drawings made by amateur artists on the spot. In short, it was the myopia of Tahiti all over again.

But now in 1801 came the first of a series of expeditions which were to open up the country, and to make people see it for the first time, not as an appendage to Europe, not as something monstrous or bizarre, but as it really was. In 1799 the French had announced that they were sending out an expedition of two ships well staffed by *savants* of the Institute de France to explore Australian waters, and this prodded the British Admiralty into setting up a voyage of exploration of its own. The command was given to a remarkable young naval officer named Matthew Flinders. Flinders was only twenty-seven, but he was a protégé of Banks and already he had had a great deal of experience in the Pacific; he had sailed with Bligh on his second voyage to Tahiti, and during the past five years he had explored the coast of New South Wales and Tasmania,

'Native Family of New South Wales', from a sketch by P. G. King, 1792. Like other sketchers of this period, the future Governor King here gives the Aborigines the idealized 'noble savage' look.

mostly in open boats. He had learned his navigation from Bligh (just as Bligh had learned it from Cook), he was a precise and able naval draughtsman, he had an interest in natural history, and exploration was the passion of his life. If he was not quite another Cook, at least he was just as steady and adventurous and he had the manner of command.

The ship they gave him, the *Investigator*, was hardly ideal as an exploring vessel. She was old and leaky and not very big – 339 tonnes (334 tons) – but Flinders would have sailed in anything. He had her refitted and copper-bottomed, and in July 1801 he set off with a crew of volunteers and an excellent scientific staff nominated by Banks.

The cruise of the *Investigator* takes its place, after Cook's original voyage and the setting up of the colony at Sydney, as the third great event in Australian history. She began her circumnavigation by charting the whole of the southern coast from King George Sound in Western Australia to Point Hicks on the east coast – the point where Cook had first sighted land. After a refit at Sydney she then continued up the New South Wales coast and gave it a more thorough investigation than Cook had been able to do. Next the Gulf of Carpentaria and the north coast of the continent were explored, and although the

charting of the west coast had to be abandoned – the *Investigator*'s planks were so rotten that she threatened to sink in every storm – they completed the circumnavigation and returned to Sydney in June 1803. It was a major achievement, far more than the French expedition was able to do, and at the end of it, Flinders and his companions were able to put together a description of the continent that was infinitely more detailed and accurate than anything that had appeared before. They may not have quite achieved a revolution of clear vision, but at least they moved towards it; they reacted to what they saw rather than to tradition, and no doubt they gave encouragement to a new group of artists in the colony – men such as John William Lewin – who were beginning at last to see the Australian landscape in a more iconoclastic way.

The political and geographical results of the voyage were very great. No one from this time onwards seriously challenged the British claim to the country, and within Australia itself – it was Flinders who suggested that the name should be changed from New Holland to Australia – the colonists now had some notion of where they could best establish new settlements round the coast. One after another the good harbours that Flinders and others had charted were occupied; at first Hobart in Tasmania, then Brisbane, then King

Wreck Reef. Here the ill-fated Matthew Flinders was wrecked aboard HMS Porpoise *in 1803 when sailing to secure a suitable ship for his continued circumnavigation of the Australian continent. An outstanding navigator, Flinders managed to sail the ship's cutter the 1,120 km (700 miles) back to Port Jackson to obtain help for the ninety-four survivors of the wreck cast upon a fragile sandbank. The feat was regarded as one of Flinders's great achievements.*

Matthew Flinders, the remarkable navigator

Matthew Flinders, (1774–1814) was the first person to circumnavigate Australia and the first to adopt the name Australia for the continent as a whole.

The ill-starred but remarkable Matthew Flinders first served in the Pacific region with Bligh on his second voyage to gather breadfruit in Tahiti in 1791. Three years later he sailed for Port Jackson on HMS *Reliance* and, with the ship's surgeon George Bass, made two trips in open boats exploring Botany Bay and down the south coast of New South Wales. He later circumnavigated Tasmania in the sloop *Norfolk*, again with Bass, in 1798–9, proving it to be an island. After five years serving in New South Wales, Flinders returned to England, and, promoted commander, was appointed to HMS *Investigator* and commissioned to chart the 'Unknown Southern Coast' of Australia. As Britain was involved in the Napoleonic Wars, Flinders carried a special passport from the French Government commanding French officers not to hinder his expedition of discovery. The understanding was a two-way pact. The French expedition of exploration and discovery, under the command of Nicholas Baudin, was also in Aus-

tralian waters carrying out charting and scientific investigation, and Flinders and the French ship *Le Geographe* met in South Australian waters at Encounter Bay. Flinders's circumnavigation proved fraught with dangers. From Port Jackson, reached in May 1801, after carefully charting the southern coast, Flinders surveyed the Queensland coastline and the Gulf of Carpentaria, but the *Investigator* proving unseaworthy, he then sailed cautiously via Western Australia and the Bight back to Sydney. From Sydney he would try again. The second vessel of which he took command, the *Cumberland*, also proved a hazard. Although he sailed north through Torres Straits and southwards for the Cape of Good Hope to take his charts and papers back to England, Flinders was forced to take his leaky vessel to Mauritius where he was put under arrest as a prisoner-of-war for six long years. In failing health, he prepared his important work *A Voyage to Terra Australis*, published in London on 18 July 1814, the day before he died.

George Sound and Perth in Western Australia, and finally Melbourne on the south coast. By the mid 1830s the country's chain of future capitals was complete.

Most of these new settlements were isolated from one another by hundreds if not thousands of kilometres of unexplored country, and their only means of communication with Sydney and with one another was by sea. The problem was to link them up by land, and so we now have the explorers setting out on foot and on horseback from Sydney, each one penetrating a little further than the last. As in America, it was largely a matter of pushing out to the west where it was hoped new grazing lands would be found, perhaps mountains and rivers as well. In fact, in Australia there is no good country in the centre; the further you proceed from the coast the more barren the land becomes, until you end at last in absolute desert. The colonists did not know this, and perhaps it would not have made much difference if they had, for the zest for discovery was now very great. And so they kept on trying to penetrate into the interior, and to establish links from one side of the continent to the other.

These early explorers were an extraordinarily tough lot, mostly young English army officers who had come out to administer the penal settlements but preferred the freedom of the bush. Of them all, Edward John Eyre is perhaps

Flinders's charting had revealed Spencer's and St Vincent's Gulf, Kangaroo Island and Investigator's Strait; and others were filling in names on the great coastal landscape of Australia. There was also much speculation on the imagined inland river systems of the country. The map, dated c. 1827, pinpoints known coastal landmarks and demarks a mountainous and well watered inland scenario for Australia. In fact, as later exploration proved, there was no good country in the centre.

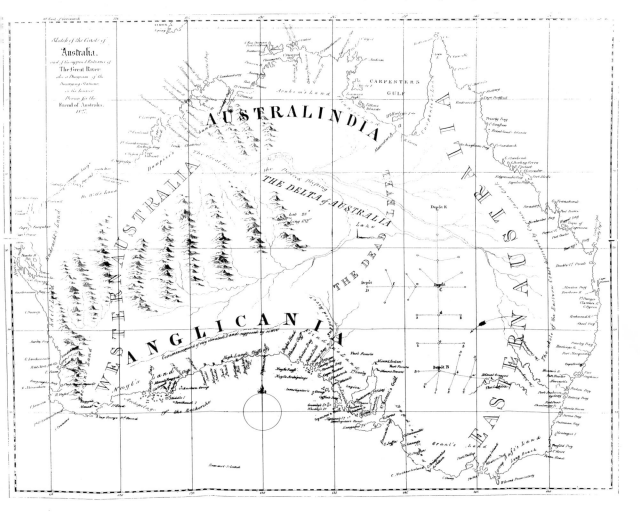

the most remarkable, if not intellectually, at least in his sheer persistence and the extent of his achievements. His tremendous march along the Great Australian Bight is more revealing of the true nature of Australian exploration than any other exploit of the day, and it complemented by land a great deal of what Flinders had already accomplished by sea.

Like Cook, Eyre was a Yorkshireman, and he was only seventeen when he came out to Sydney to seek his fortune. Since he had no other trade he entered into exploration as a practical business. His speciality was 'overlanding', the driving of cattle and other stock from Sydney to the distant settlements where the animals could be sold at profitable prices. By the time he was twenty-five he had travelled further through the bush than any other man in Australia. He had gone south from Sydney to the Murray River and Port Phillip Bay, he had crossed from Melbourne to Adelaide, he had taken a ship to King George Sound and had broken a trail up to the new colony of Perth on the Swan River, and he had ventured farther into the arid centre of the continent than any other explorer. No other colonist knew more about the bush and its black inhabitants than he did, and as a recorder of his experiences he was as accurate and colourful as Banks. There remained for Eyre in 1840 one more achievement to be attempted: the opening up of a stock route around the Great Australian Bight from Adelaide to King George Sound.

Overlanding stock, a practice that would push out the settled boundaries of the Australian colonies. Sketch by G. Hamilton.

Now this was an impossible proposition; even today no man in his right senses would attempt to make this journey on foot. Most other parts of Australia are succumbing little by little to civilization, but not this part. It is the

Edward John Eyre, explorer

Eyre's exploration of the southern reaches of Australia accomplished by land a great deal of what Flinders had accomplished by sea. Eyre had already opened up considerable tracts of the continent before he set out on his terrible journey from Adelaide to Albany near King George Sound. He had emigrated to Australia in 1833 at the age of seventeen and briefly took up land near Queanbeyan, NSW, with Robert Campbell. Overlanding sheep engrossed him and gave him that taste for exploration that was to mark him. The year 1839 found him exploring in the Flinders Ranges, naming Lake Torrens and opening up the Eyre Peninsula. The following year he was driving sheep overland from King George Sound to the Swan River settlement. In June 1840, Eyre set out on an expedition, partly funded by the South Australia Government, to 'discover the interior of the country', a venture that was to lead him finally across the Nullarbor Plain. For this incredible journey, Eyre was awarded the founder's gold medal of the Royal Geographical Society in 1847. In 1841, Eyre accepted an appointment as resident magistrate and protector of Aborigines at Moorundie on the River Murray, an area densely populated by Aborigines and where severe conflict had broken out between the local people and stockmen overlanding sheep. The successful relations Eyre built with the people resulted in an illuminating account of their manners and customs which he included in his *Journals of Expeditions of Discovery into Central Australia and Overland from Adelaide to King George Sound, 1840–1*, published in 1845. Eyre's work marked him for more luminous posts and he became successively Lieutenant-Governor of New Zealand, of St Vincent in the West Indies and acting Governor of the Leeward Islands and later of Jamaica.

Brisbane began its life as an outpost of convict settlement in the colony, at Moreton Bay. Queensland did not gain self-government until 1859. Its sturdy buildings, drawn here in 1846, clung to the Brisbane River named after a governor of New South Wales.

loneliest region imaginable. For almost 1,600 km (1,000 miles) there is no good anchorage, and the Southern Ocean beats up to the coast directly from the Antarctic. On the calmest day a strong wind blows, and occasionally the ocean swell will build itself up into a specially big roller than can be seen 1.6 km (1 mile) or more away, and it dashes itself against the shore with the effect of a tidal wave. Where the coast is flat the salt water sweeps inland; where there are cliffs – and they are immensely high and run for hundreds of kilometres – the wave hurls itself into their hollowed-out bases with a wild, ungovernable fury. Sometimes, unseen and unheard by anyone, great masses of rock come hurtling down to the sea from the 150 m (500 ft) heights above, and it is like the crashing of an avalanche.

Inland the country is flat and deserty; here and there a patch of rough scrub, but mostly an endless plain covered with coarse saltbush and with never a tree to shade one from the overpowering sun. They call this plain the Nullarbor. If you want water you have to dig for it among the sand dunes along the shore, a wearisome labour since the hole tends to keep falling in upon itself, and all has to be begun again. In this wilderness everything runs to excess; the excessive noonday heat is followed by outrageous cold by night, rainstorms burst with cyclonic force, and when the rain fails the blown sand is suffocating; even the flies and mosquitoes are in mad abundance. There are moments of grace sometimes in the evenings when extravagant sunsets sweep across the sky and then fade slowly behind enormous stars, but in the main the Nullarbor has an implacable sterility and the Aborigines used to believe that it was inhabited by demons. They would not chase a kangaroo there.

This then was the terrible region into which Eyre plunged with a party of six men, half of them natives, in the hope of opening up a stock route to the west. He began at Port Lincoln, the harbour on the western shore of Spenser Gulf that Flinders had discovered forty years before, and it seems to have been rather a forbidding place. Ashore the local settlers were carrying on a guerilla

LEFT, ABOVE
'Overlanding'. A freshly representative portrait of the Australian countryside by artist John Lewin. From a watercolour 'The Campbell River', 1815.

LEFT, BELOW
Melbourne, established in 1835 was growing as a wool port, a frontier town and a rising place of settlement when this sketch was made in 1839.

warfare with the natives who were raiding their cattle, while in the bay, resting briefly from their endless and ruthless battle with the sea, were a group of French and American whalers, with their polyglot crews, men who lived the most brutal of lives, deprived of women and every sort of comfort, even the comfort of decent pay. It was late in October (1840), with the summer coming on, but Eyre was a stubborn man and he set out resolutely into the unknown. Things did not go too badly so long as he had a little boat to accompany him along the coast, but after Fowler's Bay there were no further anchorages, and all their stores had to be carried on horses. The journey now resolved itself into a dull, insensate plodding on. Time and again Eyre reconnoitred ahead of his little party, walking enormous distances without water, only to be forced back again to Fowler's Bay. The New Year found him still there. Colonel George Gawler, the Governor of South Australia, sent out a boat with a message begging him to give up the venture, but he would not listen. Instead he decided to send back to Adelaide all his companions except his overseer, John Baxter, and three natives: Wylie, a man whom he had picked up on his earlier sea journey to King George Sound, and Neramberein and Cootachah, who were scarcely more than boys.

It is the behaviour of these three natives, who were no more than half civilized, that gives to the subsequent events a strange theatrical excitement. They were at home in these harsh surroundings, as Eyre and Baxter were not. So long as they could pick up grubs and lizards as they went along to supplement their rations, and so long as they could find water, they were quite ready to put up with the fearful heat and the interminable daily marches; indeed, they were almost inclined to regard the whole excursion as a kind of spree. The two white men had only their willpower to keep them going, and it was a progress of fits and starts. Eyre would discover from the wild natives they encountered how far the next waterpoint lay ahead 160 km (100 miles), perhaps 208 km (130 miles) – and then, while the others rested, he would go on ahead and lay out a series of caches of food and water. Then he would return to the base and the whole party would make a forced march, often for days and nights on end, to get through to the waterpoint. The whole weary business would then begin all over again.

Early in March 1841 they dragged themselves up the head of the Bight, and now they began to abandon such things as their greatcoats, pack-saddles, some of the firearms and ammunition, even their cooking pots. When the weaker horses could do no more they were either slaughtered and eaten or left to die. Sometimes they walked along the beach, sometimes they took to the scrub inland, and sometimes they followed along the dizzy heights of the cliffs; but whichever way they went they were always faced at the end of every day with the labour of digging for water.

In the midst of such a superhuman strain it is marvellous that Eyre was able to keep a fresh and lively diary. Peering over the cliffs he sees the spars and thwarts of sailing ships that, unknown to all the world, had been wrecked on this desolate coast, the shells of giant turtles and the carcasses of whales. He notes that the wild blacks have gathered near the coast because the mesembryanthemum is fruiting at this time of year, that ducks, pigeons and red-winged cockatoos manage to survive somehow in the desert, and that there are even kangaroos about. He observes that the male natives follow the practice of splitting the urethra and guesses that this is a form of birth control among the wild tribes; and when their women run away at the sight of his little party it strikes him that 'this might be the consequence of the conduct of the whalers and sealers with whom they might have come into contact on the coast'. He notes too how his own natives, when desperate for water, take bunches of fine grass and scrape the morning dew off the leaves of bushes, or hunt about until they find a certain shrub with a long tubular root from which a little moisture can be squeezed.

Towards the middle of April they had completed about half of the 1,600 (1,000 miles) to be covered, and there was still no sign of the country improving. They had passed the point of no return, but Baxter, the overseer, had had enough; both he and Eyre were suffering from dysentery, their rations had all but given out, and even the three natives were becoming sullen. He wanted to turn back. Eyre argued with him, cajoled him and encouraged him, and in the end they continued on their nightmarish way. They killed their last sheep, and one of their last horses, dipping the slices of meat into the sea to salt them and then hanging them out to dry. When Wylie and the two boys stole some of this meat Eyre put them on a ration, and in resentment the two boys took to the bush. But they came back after a few days, half-starved. All of them were now prepared to eat anything. They made a stew from an eagle that Baxter shot; very rarely they bagged a wallaby or managed to spear a stingray off the shore; and the natives, with the improvidence of small minds, could not understand why Eyre did not allow them to kill and eat all the remaining horses there and then. The journey by now had lost all meaning; obviously no stock route could ever be opened up around the Bight, and it was for all of them merely a matter of survival. On 27 April, Eyre notes in his diary: 'We had now entered upon the last fearful push, which was to decide our fate.'

April 29 was a hot sultry day. In the afternoon a hurricane blew up with heavy clouds, but there was no rain. However, they chose a place to camp where there were flat rocks which would catch water if rain fell in the night. They made their customary breakwinds of bushes, and Eyre took the first watch while the others slept. Their remaining arms and provisions were piled together under an oilskin, but Baxter kept his own gun beside him. The night was cold, with the wind blowing clouds hard across the moon, and after a time Eyre went off to gather in the horses which had grazed away through the scrub. He was returning with them around half past ten when he saw a sudden flash in the darkness and heard the report of a gun in the camp, about a quarter of a mile away. Thinking that Baxter must have awoken and fired so as to guide him back to the camp Eyre called out to him. There was no answer. In some alarm Eyre abandoned the horses and hurried on. Wylie came running out to meet him, calling for him to come quickly, and on entering the camp Eyre saw Baxter lying covered with blood on the ground. He had been shot through the left breast and the two boys had vanished. The cache of arms under the oilskin lay scattered about on the rocks, and both Eyre's and Baxter's double-barrelled guns were missing. Baxter was beyond help; he collapsed and died without a word. Wylie could explain nothing; he had been woken by the report, he said, and had found that the overseer had been shot.

The wind was now howling through the camp, and Eyre wrote later in his diary:

'Suffering and distress had well-nigh overwhelmed me, and life seemed hardly worth the effort to prolong it. Ages can never efface the horrors of this single night, nor would the wealth of the world ever tempt me to go through similar ones again.'

His chief concern was that he was now entirely in the power of the two boys, since they had taken away the only serviceable firearms; all that he was left with was a brace of pistols for which he had no cartridges, and a single rifle in which a bullet had jammed. There was no knowing where the two boys were lurking in the bush, or if they were going to shoot, but the horses had to be brought in and Eyre and Wylie set off after them. They found them at midnight after a long search, and at dawn drove them back to the camp. The corpse lay there rigid on the ground, the eyes still open, and it was now discovered that the two boys had also raided the stock of provisions. They had taken all the baked bread, most of the mutton, tea and sugar, Baxter's tobacco and pipes, a 4.5 litre (1 gallon) keg of water, some clothes and other articles. There remained some 18 kg (40 lb) of flour, a little tea and sugar, and an 18 litre (4 gallon) keg of water, enough at all events to sustain life for a few days longer.

Eyre took the barrel off the stock of his rifle and held it over the campfire. The jammed bullet whizzed out close to his head, and now at least they had one useful weapon. There was no question of burying the body – nothing but hard rock lay around them – but they wrapped it in a blanket, and then, after baking a little bread, packed their remaining provisions on the horses and set out again. They stopped at 11 a.m. to let the heat of the day go by, and Eyre questioned Wylie closely about the night's events. Baxter, it seemed evident, had woken and surprised the two boys when they were looting the camp, and in panic they had fired. Wylie still protested that he knew nothing of this, but Eyre had a feeling that he was lying, that he too had been involved in the plot and had planned to decamp with the others, but had taken fright when Baxter was shot. It was perhaps also significant that Wylie belonged to a different tribe.

Events now took a turn that irresistibly reminds one of some lurid movie of the American wild west. Late in the afternoon they were preparing to move on again when Wylie called Eyre's attention to two figures advancing towards them through the scrub. The boys were each wearing blankets and were carrying guns in their hands. Later Eyre recalled that he felt that he was a match for them by day but he feared an ambush by night. He wrote:

'As these impressions passed through my mind there appeared to me to be but one resource left to save my own life and that of the native with me: that was to shoot the elder of the two [boys]. Painful as this would be I saw no alternative if they still persisted in following us.'

As the boys came closer he went on quietly packing up his few belongings and putting them on the horses. Then he gave the bridles to Wylie to hold and with his rifle ready to shoot advanced upon the boys.

'They were now tolerably near, each carrying a double-barrelled gun, which was pointed towards me, elevated across the left arm and held by the right hand. As I attempted to approach nearer they gradually retreated. Finding that I was not likely to gain ground upon them in this way, I threw down my weapons, and advanced un-

armed, hoping that if they let me near them I might suddenly close with the eldest and wrest his gun from him.'

Now it had been one thing for Cook (and Phillip) to walk up unarmed to excited and menacing natives; this was another. In those earlier encounters fear and resentment had to be overcome by a show of confidence and friendliness. But these natives were half civilized, and guilt was involved as well; it could easily have been that, having shot once at a white man, they felt that they might somehow cover up and justify that crime by shooting once again. But it was fear that dominated their minds. The younger boy had been with Eyre for four years and the older for two and a half, and they had the habit of acknowledging his superiority. As Eyre came on they still fell back and they would not let him get nearer than 54–64 m (60–70 yds). Seeing it was useless to persist, Eyre now stopped and called out to them that they must go away; that they must return to Fowler's Bay, and that if they continued to follow him he would certainly shoot the elder of the two. They made no answer to this but instead began calling out to Wylie, hoping that he would desert Eyre and come over to their side. But Wylie too was frightened of Eyre. He stood quietly with the horses and did not reply.

Dusk was now falling, and Eyre decided that he must push on at all speed; since the two boys still had food they were bound to stop and eat, and it might be possible to outdistance them in the night. Moreover they had now been four days without finding water, and it would have been suicide to remain where they were. He ordered Wylie to go on ahead with the horses while he drew up in the rear. Eyre says:

'As soon as the two natives saw us moving on, and found that Wylie did not join them they set up a wild and plaintive cry, still following the brush parallel to our line of route, and never ceasing in their importunities to Wylie, until the denseness of the scrub, and the closing in of night, concealed us from each other.'

Eyre pushed on for 29 km (18 miles) that night before resting briefly, and then made another 45 km (28 miles) the following day. The horses had now been five days without water and clearly could not continue much longer, but there was no choice but to keep driving them on. On 2 May they crawled on for another 46 km (29 miles), and they were now 220 km (138 miles) from the last waterhole. Yet there was some hope to be had. Gradually, almost imperceptibly, the nature of the country was changing. The banksia, the shrub with the tassel-like flowers which Banks had discovered at Botany Bay, had begun to appear, and they came on tracks of wild natives going west and the ashes of fresh fires. Eyre also knew from Flinders's chart that the vast cliffs that had prevented them from getting down to the sea for the last few weeks would soon break up if they could keep going a little longer. On 3 May the horses were still alive, and like automatons, hardly knowing what they were doing any more, the little party dragged themselves on until at last they found a track leading down to the shore. And here they found a native waterhole. The frantic horses were given at first just a bucket of water each lest they should kill themselves with drinking. For the next three days they rested, taking care to sleep at a little distance from the waterhole in case the two boys should ambush them there in the night. By 6 May Eyre was convinced that he had thrown them off, and that they had either died of thirst or were somehow making their way back to Fowler's Bay. ★

And now as they moved slowly onwards again the country continued to improve. The banksia shrubs that had been stunted before became larger, leafier and more numerous, and there were other small trees of a variety which Eyre knew to exist at King George Sound. Black cockatoos and pigeons flew by, and although it was maddening that they could not be shot with the rifle at least it was an assurance that they were now entering a region where there was water. On 8 May they killed a horse and Wylie sat up eating all night long. Three days later they came on the first hill they had seen for many hundreds of kilometres, and it was apparent that the worst part of the journey was over. Yet paradoxically this was a moment of despair. Eyre had injured his hand and it was hurting him badly, the horseflesh had given him stomach pains, they had been nearly seven months on the road, and now exhaustion was becoming stronger than the will to go on:

'I felt . . . that I could have sat quietly and contentedly, and let the glass of life slide away to its last sand. There was a kind of dreamy pleasure which made me forgetful or careless of the circumstances and difficulties by which I was surrounded . . .'

Apart from their horses and a little flour they were now absolutely dependent upon living off the land, and it was a tremendous event on 18 May when Wylie shot a kangaroo and they found a dead penguin on the beach. Wylie's digestive powers were stupendous. Eyre watched him with fascination while he ate the flesh, the entrails, the tail and hind legs of the kangaroo. The penguin was then consumed whole. Having gorged himself into a stupor Wylie rested for a few hours and then rose again to fall to work on the kangaroo's hide, which was all that was left of the beast.

Wylie could never get enough to eat. The occasional stingray they speared in the sea and the shellfish they picked up served him only as appetizers. It was the sort of greed that overmasters every other feeling. One day he caught two opossums. One he cooked and ate immediately, the other he carefully put by, close to his sleeping place. When Eyre, who had gone without, asked him what he was going to do with it Wylie explained that he was going to eat it in the morning, when he would again be hungry. Eyre says:

'Upon hearing this I told him that his arrangements were very good, and that for the future I would follow the same system also; and that each should depend upon his own exertions in procuring food; hinting to him that, as he was so much more skilful than I was, and we had so very little flour left, I should be obliged to reserve this entirely for myself, and that I hoped he would have no difficulty in procuring as much food as he required. I was then about to open the flour-bag and take a little out for my supper, when he became alarmed at the idea of getting no more, and stopped me, offering the other opossum, and volunteering to cook it properly for me.'

It was now the end of May, and it was no longer heat and thirst they had to contend with, but cold and rain. The horses, however, had so much improved in condition that the two men were able to take turns at riding them – an immense relief for Eyre, since one of the animals had fallen on him and had

★In fact he never saw or heard of them again.

bruised his thigh. Every day the scrub grew thicker and the grass less dry, and they had even come on their first sign of civilization: the words 'Ship Julian, 1840. Haws 1840. C. W.' cut into a tree; no doubt the record of some whaling ship that had passed by in the previous year. It was the harbinger of relief at last. On 2 June, when they were approaching Lucky Bay, one of Flinders's old anchorages, some 480 km (300 miles) from King George Sound, Eyre thought he saw a small boat at sea. In intense excitement he scrambled with Wylie down to the shore only to be confronted by the empty ocean. But then, within half an hour, two boats appeared far out across the bay and he rushed to light a fire and to shout and wave. But it was useless; the boats vanished out to sea.

Eyre was not altogether despondent. He realized that these were whaling boats and that the mother ship must be somewhere along the coast. They pushed on to the west and there she was, a fine barque riding close to the shore and about 10 km (6 miles) away. Desperate that she might set sail before he could reach her Eyre jumped on the strongest horse and rode as fast as he could to the bay. The sailors on board were busy dealing with some fouled cables and they did not notice him at first. But then:

'I now made a smoke on the rock where I was, and hailed the vessel, upon which a boat instantly put off, and in a few moments I had the inexpressible pleasure of being again among civilized beings, and of shaking hands with a fellow-countryman in the person of Captain Rossiter, commanding the French whaler Mississippi. *Our story was soon told, and we were received with the greatest kindness and hospitality by the captain.'*

Both travellers moved on board – 'a change in our circumstances so great, so sudden and so unexpected it seemed more like a dream than reality'.

Eyre's arrival with his Aboriginal companion Wylie, at King George Sound, on 7 July 1841, after their overland endurance trek from Port Lincoln, South Australia. The Aborigines of the region greeted Wylie, wrote Eyre, 'with wordless, weeping pleasure'.

That night Eyre lay in a bunk while the wind and the rain roared outside the porthole, but he could not sleep. Most of the next day he spent reading old English newspapers.

Upon several counts it was an extraordinary meeting. Though Rossiter was English, his owners at Le Havre and his crew were French, and because he feared that war had broken out once more between England and France, he had not put into King George Sound, but had anchored surreptitiously here, 480 km (300 miles) away, to await the westward migration of the whales at the end of June. Rossiter was one of those men whose only home is the sea, and it is rather sad that many years later, when he was old and blind and ashore in Kent, he wrote to Eyre asking for help in getting a pension, and that Eyre by that time was himself disgraced and out of favour with the authorities and could do nothing for him; doubly sad indeed, for Rossiter was overwhelming in his generosity now. For twelve days, while the storm raged along the coast, Eyre remained in his snug berth in the *Mississippi*. He rested, he made excursions to the shore with Rossiter to see the vegetable garden he had planted and the little island where he kept his stock of sheep, pigs and tortoises; he went out hunting ducks and kangaroos, he fed on the delicious mackerel and barracoota the sailors were catching in the bay, he had wine to drink and he was dry and warm. Rossiter clothed him from his own chest, and gave him all the provisions he could possibly want for his onward journey to King George Sound: 18 kg (40 lb) of flour, 2.7 kg (6 lb) of biscuit, 5.4 kg (12 lb) of rice, 9 kg (20 lb) of beef, 9 kg (20 lb) of pork, 5.4 kg (12 lb) of sugar, 450 g (1 lb) of tea, a Dutch cheese, 2.3 kg (5 lb) of salt butter, salt, two bottles of brandy, two saucepans for cooking, tobacco and pipes, and for Wylie some canteens filled with treacle. The ship's smith worked up some old harpoons into horseshoes, and shod Eyre's horses. Rossiter would accept no payment for Eyre's and Wylie's stay on board (and Wylie had struck the crew dumbfounded by his capacity for consuming ship's biscuit), and since Eyre had no money he readily accepted an order on the English agent at King George Sound for the provisions – an order which, incidentally, Rossiter never presented.

On 14 June Eyre landed his stores, all got up securely in canvas bags, and the next day went back on board for a last breakfast. Rossiter returned with him to the shore to see him off, and made a last gift of six bottles of wine and a tin of sardines. Eyre took with him some letters for France to be posted in King George Sound, and promised he would not mention the *Mississippi*'s presence on the coast if war between England and France had actually broken out. And so the two men parted, never to meet again.

In parenthesis one feels here that Herman Melville was stretching the facts only a little too far when he wrote in *Moby Dick*:

'That great America on the other side of the sphere, Australia, was given to the enlightened world by the whalemen. After its first blunder-born discovery by a Dutchman, all other ships long shunned those shores as pestiferously barbarous; but the whaleship touched there. The whaleship is the true mother of that now mighty colony. Moreover, in the infancy of the first Australian settlement the emigrants were several times saved from starvation by the benevolent biscuit of the whaleship luckily dropping an anchor in those waters.'

The rest of the journey was uncomfortable but at least not hazardous. The

rain streamed down, a campfire one night destroyed most of their new possessions and for three weeks they seemed to be forever floundering in mud and
swamps. On 7 July, nearly nine months after leaving Port Lincoln, they came
up to their goal at last in a heavy storm. At first no one noticed them as they
approached the little settlement of Albany on the Sound, but then a native who
knew Wylie appeared, and he uttered a shrill cry which brought his tribe out of
their huts. They greeted Wylie, Eyre says, with 'wordless, weeping pleasure'.
For Eyre it was a moment of great triumph. He soon found himself out of the
rain surrounded by the white settlers who had long since given him up for
dead, with dry clothes on his body, a fire before him, and a hot brandy and
water in his hand. He had come a long way. If he had, as he himself admits,
discovered nothing of importance, he had made the unknown known, and he
had put a girdle across the country from the east to the extremest west.

*The little settlement of
Albany, King George's
Sound, painted by D. E.
Cobper. From the early
1830s Albany served as
the key south coast port of
Western Australia until a
navigable harbour was
built at Fremantle at the
end of the nineteenth century. Goods and mail
were overlanded from
there to Perth.*

197

6

The acclimatization

MOST OF CENTRAL AUSTRALIA was an impossible place for the white man to live in — that fact was established by Eyre and his fellow explorers beyond all reasonable doubt — but elsewhere and especially on the coast the colonists were doing very well. Sydney continued to be the major settlement. By the time Darwin arrived there in 1836 the population had risen above 30,000, and it was nothing unusual to see in the harbour as many as twelve ships from England as well as traders from India and China, and whalers from the islands. Darwin wrote:

'On entering the harbour we were astounded with all the appearances of the outskirts of a great city: numerous Windmills — Forts — large stone white houses: superb Villas . . .'

The town, in fact, had become the principal outpost of civilization in the South Pacific, and most southbound vessels made a point of calling there. Darwin did not much like what he found; the colonists, he thought, lived miserably uncomfortable lives, everyone was out to get rich quickly, and the presence of the convicts working on the farms and in chain gangs along the roads was degrading. But he conceded that the place was prosperous: more than £12,000 was paid for half a hectare (1 acre) of land in the city.

At last, after fifty years of relentless effort, the country was being forced to conform to the European pattern. Everywhere around the new settlements the native bush was being torn down and replaced by English farms where European crops and plants were being made to grow, and even English oaks and elms were beginning to appear. It was true that most livestock, whether horses or pigs, dogs or poultry, tended to degenerate after three generations, and new blood had to be brought in from the home country, but already there were substantial herds of cattle in New South Wales and sheep were thriving wonderfully. Manufactured articles and such things as tea and sugar still had to be imported, but in all the more basic commodities of life the colonist was becoming self-supporting; he could eat his own bread, mutton and beef, pick his own apples off the trees, and even drink his own wine. Every settlement had its acclimatization society which studied the means by which imported animals and plants could best adjust themselves to the Australian climate.

The Aborigines fell back steadily before this invasion. They could not conform, they did not know how to adjust themselves to the new social climate that was closing around them. So far as the white settlers were concerned they were in the way, they were an obstacle to progress, they had to be removed. European diseases removed most of them, and violent death in their futile struggle against the settlers carried away a few more. The prostitution of their women to the white men led inevitably to sterility or what was almost as bad, a race of half-castes who had no place either in the tribal system or the new European society. And when their own tribal laws collapsed the Aborigines found they could not understand the new English laws by which they were governed, especially the law of property. They thought that their tribal hunting grounds were their own, and when they found that this was not so, that they owned nothing, that they had virtually no rights of any kind, that they were aliens in their own country, they were bewildered and resentful; and when all their protests failed they succumbed to listless serfdom.

Phillip had estimated that there were about 1,500 Aborigines around Sydney when he first arrived in 1788. By the 1830s only a few hundred remained. Darwin, in 1836, found them still trying to live their tribal lives among the colonists' farms on the outskirts of the settlement, but there were practically no wild animals left for them to hunt. A few years later even this last remnant had disappeared, and all that was left were a few beggars in the Sydney streets. Darwin wrote:

'Wherever the European has trod death seems to pursue the Aboriginal. We may look to the wide extent of the Americas, Polynesia, the Cape of Good Hope and Australia, and we find the same result . . .'

In Sydney it had been a wearing away of the wild tribes. In Tasmania it was a wholesale massacre. Tasmania, because of its cooler climate, attracted many of the newly arrived free settlers, and by the 1930s they numbered, together with the convicts there, about 13,000, all of them eager for land and none of them disposed to let the blacks stand in their way. But those mild and cheerful people whom Cook had visited half a century before did not prove so tameable as the Aborigines on the mainland; when their land – and there was not much of it – was taken over for farms they attacked the settlers with their spears, and an organized manhunt was begun against them. There was no particular secrecy or shame about this; it was supported by the government. John Batman, one of the early settlers, describes a look-out on his land which was designed 'to entrap natives'. He kept, he says,

'a number of domesticated Sydney natives for the more particular purpose of sending them out to trace our wild ones if any should happen to be reported as being seen.'

And John Glover, the son of the artist who had settled on the island, remarks soberly,

'The natives have been very troublesome and treacherous, spearing and murdering all they find in the least unprotected . . . the only alternative now is, if they do not readily become friendly, to annihilate them at once.'

So the manhunt had started, and it grew more savage as it went on. In 1830 Tasmania was put under martial law, a line of armed beaters was formed across the island, and an attempt was made to drive the Aborigines into a cul-de-sac. They succeeded in slipping through the net, of course, but by now the heart had gone out of the tribe, and their terror was greater than their desperation. Felix Maynard, the surgeon of a French whaling ship that was based in Hobart at this time, wrote that the natives were 'continually hunted and tracked down like fallow deer, and, once captured, are deported, singly or in parties, to the islands in Bass Strait.' In 1835 the last survivors, only a couple of hundred of the original 5,000, were shipped away. If there had ever been any intention of preserving the race it was now too late; they could not sustain

The young Charles Darwin

Darwin, naturalist to the *Beagle*, arrived in Sydney Harbour on 12 January 1836. 'In the evening,' he wrote in his journal, 'I walked through the town and returned full of admiration at the whole scene. It [Sydney] is a most magnificent testimony to the power of the British nation. Here, in a less promising country, scores of years have done many times more than an equal number of centuries have effected in South America. My first feeling was to congratulate myself that I had been born an Englishman.'

'Group of midshipmen aboard the Beagle *during the course of Fitzroy's voyage' by Augustus Earle. One artist who subsequently achieved fame, Conrad Martens, had left the* Beagle *at Valparaiso in 1834 and continued on, after a visit to Tahiti and New Zealand, to settle in Sydney.*

Bungaree, 'King of the Blacks'

Bungaree was one example of the 'anglicization' of the Aborigines. He had been taken up by Flinders and, accompanying him on the *Investigator*, became the first Aborigine to circumnavigate Australia. In 1817 he sailed north west on the *Mermaid*, with P. T. King, and helped to contact strange tribes. Both Flinders and King praised his equable nature and courageous conduct. Various governors and military officers gave Bungaree discarded uniforms and the cocked hat, and in this garb he lived and slept. Bungaree was a great mimic, had a good command of English and a merry sense of humour. Because of his seeming adaptation, the settlers regarded him as the leader of the 'township Aborigines' and gave him the title 'King of the Blacks'. But while Bungaree lived in seeming contentment, imitating British settlers, and died peacefully in 1830, the town-adapted Aborigines were, on the whole, a sad remnant of their people, giving exhibitions throwing boomerangs, doing odd jobs and begging for bread, liquor and tobacco. Portrait by Augustus Earle.

life away from their tribal hunting grounds and the instinct to survive very quickly flickered out. Within seven years their numbers were down to fifty. The last pure-blooded Tasmanian died in 1876.

Charles Darwin visited Tasmania in the *Beagle* during this holocaust, and he wrote, 'I fear there is no doubt that this train of evil and its consequences originated in the infamous conduct of some of our countrymen.' He was putting it mildly. It was a monstrous, unforgivable crime, worse even than the brutalities which were being committed against the white convicts in the Tasmanian prison of Port Arthur at that time. Even when one makes allowances for the hardships of the settlers, the loneliness and danger of their lives, it almost seems that a sadistic frenzy possessed them, a toughness and pitilessness that was beyond all reason. The setting of the tame Sydney natives against the Tasmanian primitives was especially horrible. The place to be allotted to the Aborigines in the new society was now becoming very clear. Only two alternatives lay before them: to resist and be killed, or to submit and to degenerate into caricatures of themselves, street-beggars and useless hangers-on.

Count Strzelecki, the Polish explorer who was in Australia in the late 1830s, was moved to write:

'A Native Family of
NSW sitting down on an
English Settler's Farm',
watercolour by Augustus
Earle. Darwin, travel-
ling overland to Bathurst
in January 1836, found
some Aborigines still
trying to live a tribal life
among the farms on the
outskirts of settlement.
He saw them as doomed
in the battle for the survival of the fittest.

RIGHT
The town-adapted Ab-
origines formed a pathetic
remnant of their people.
Governor Phillip esti-
mated that there were
about 1,500 in Sydney
when he arrived. By the
1830s the number had
dwindled to a few hun-
dred.

'Degraded, subdued, confused, awkward and distrustful, ill concealing emotions of anger, scorn or revenge, emaciated and covered with filthy rags; these native lords of the
soil, more like spectres of the past than living men, are dragging on a melancholy
existence to a yet more melancholy doom.'

Nowhere apparently in this process was anyone in particular to blame; it just
happened, one thing led to another, and in the disastrous ending the beginning
was forgotten.

Brutality towards the Tasmanian Aborigines

The treatment of the Tasmanian Aborigines remains one of the stains on the history of British settlement. Attrition began early, and the 'mild and cheerful people' Cook and the early French scientific expedition encountered, were strenuously hunted out of their tribal territory. In 1830, a line of armed beaters was formed across the island and an attempt made to drive the Aborigines into a cul-de-sac. While only one Tasmanian Aborigine was caught in this net, by 1835 the surviving Tasmanian Aborigines were rounded up and shipped to islands in Bass Strait. The Aboriginal woman, Truganini, 'the beauty of Bruni', lived on to become the last of her race in Tasmania. 'Her uncle had been shot by a soldier, her sister stolen by a sealer, her mother stabbed. Her man had had his hands cut off in life (and left to drown) and her last compatriot had had his hands cut off in death.' Such was the brutality racism excited. Truganini died in 1876. It was the end of a war, Bernard Smith has written, the only war that, unaided, Australians have won. It was a complete victory, none of the Tasmanians survived.

ABOVE
On the back of this photograph was written, 'The Last of the Native Race of Tasmania all dead'. This picture was taken for the Tasmanian Government obviously before they all died. Most notable is the contrast between the powerful women, Truganini (far left), Pattly (right) and Bessy Clark (far right) with Lanne, the sad, beaten man.

BELOW
An attempt to get a message of equal treatment for black and white across to the Tasmanian Aborigines. A Proclamation issued by the Lieutenant–Governor of Tasmania, Thomas Davey, in 1816. It was modelled on a similar pictorial message which Governor Phillip had earlier issued in New South Wales. It had strikingly little meaning in Tasmania.

Aborigines being driven to police courts for trespassing. Such pressures on the original inhabitants was the unconscious outcome of the belief that a man with a gun was superior to a man with a spear. Painting by W. A. Cawthorne.

Things were not so bad in the other new colonies on the mainland, mainly because the natives still possessed open country into which they could retreat, but they were bad enough. Along the Murray River, which divides New South Wales from Victoria, a series of pitched battles was going on between the settlers and the tribes, and it was nothing unusual for the whites to organize a day's sport in the bush – a kangaroo or a man, it did not matter much what you bagged. Smallpox and tuberculosis swept through the tribes whenever they came into contact with outlying farms, and soon missionaries who had gone inland were giving up their missions because there were no longer any blacks to convert. Now and again the government made inquiries into the extermination of the natives, but it was a half-hearted interest; a solitary policeman in a remote outpost did not stand a chance against a horde of angry settlers, and Strzelecki summed it all up bitterly as

'an inquest of the one race upon the corpse of the other, ending for the most part with the verdict of "died by the visitation of God".'

There were others too who protested, but Australia was still a convict settlement, and most people found their own lives too hard for them to bother

about the misfortunes of others; you might just as well have asked the slave drivers of Africa or the settlers pushing out west in America to take pity on the tribes they were exterminating.

Edward John Eyre fits oddly into this controversy; indeed, he is such a paradox that one wonders if we are ever going to know the truth about him. Later in life, when he was Governor of Jamaica, his name was to become a byword for the oppression of coloured people. His removal from office and his subsequent arraignment before a Royal Commission caused almost as much of a rumpus in England as the Dreyfus case was to do later in France. Yet now, as a young man in Australia, there was no stronger advocate for the blacks; he worked with them, he lived with them, and he compiled the first really thorough and reliable account of their tribal lives. After returning to Adelaide from his long walk he went up to Moorunde on the Murray River as 'Protector of the Aborigines', and within three years he had settled their differences with the white settlers and had won back their confidence. When he came to write his book on his great journey he gave up nearly half his pages to a description of the Aborigines and a plea for their survival. He lists case after case in which they have been maltreated, hunted and shot down like wild animals, sometimes with the connivance of the police. He wrote:

Daisy Bates, known as 'Kabbarli'

From the first years of this century Daisy Bates, an emigrant from Ireland, set out in intrepid fashion to understand, record and help the Australian Aborigines in a period of change. She began this work at Beagle Bay, north of Broome, Western Australia, and later at Roebuck Plains where she collected vocabularies and saw and recorded sacred and secret rituals. In 1904, the West Australian Government appointed her to research the tribes of the state and she worked on Maamba Reserve in south west Western Australia. By 1910, Daisy had completed a substantial manuscript on the Aborigines, but the arrival from England of A. R. Radcliffe-Brown to study the social anthropology of the Aborigines of the north west deflected her from pure anthropological work. She turned to welfare, moved by the miseries of sick and elderly Aborigines living in enforced exile on the islands of Bernier and Dorré, off Australia's northern coast. The Aborigines there named her 'Kabbarli', meaning 'grandmotherly person', a title that went with her all her life. In 1912, she established a camp at Eucla on the southern fringe of the Nullarbor Plain; she was later at Yalata, and in 1918 she moved her camp to Ooldea, a permanent watering-hole on the trans-Australian railway. In her long Victorian skirt, button-up boots, stiff collar, hat and gloves, she lived the lives of her Aborigines, caring for them, even as she objectively observed their customs and ceremonies and wrote numerous articles which caused lively interest in the press. Anthropologist Radcliffe-Brown compared her mind to a 'well stocked but very untidy sewing basket', but her work aroused such interest that her isolated and ragged camps received three visits from royalty and she was awarded the CBE. Daisy Bates published *The Passing of the Aborigines* in 1938, and died a pauper in 1951. One of Australia's rare operas, *The Young Kabbarli*, written by Lady Maie Casey with music by Margaret Sutherland, is based on her life.

'It is a most lamentable thing to think that the progress and prosperity of one race should conduce to the downfall and decay of another; and still more so to observe the apathy and indifference with which this result is contemplated by mankind in general . . .'

But everything was against him. Liberals and humanitarians in England acclaimed his book, but Australia was too far off for them to support it with effective action. Even his individual attempts at kindness came to nothing. He secured for Wylie a government grant of free rations, and that mighty eater soon degenerated into an idler and nuisance-maker in the little settlement in Albany. Then there were the three native boys he took back to England and introduced to Queen Victoria; one of them died, and the two others, being quite unable to achieve Omai's polish in their new surroundings, were shipped back miserably to Australia.

It was left to the indomitable figure of Daisy Bates to write the epitaph of the wild Aborigines in Australia. Her career in many ways reminds one of her near contemporary, Mary Kingsley, the blue-stocking who went out to West Africa and who raised a plea for the Negro in his native state, as 'a free un-smashed man – not a white-washed slave or an enemy'. Daisy Bates was brought up in rather grand circumstances, at first in Ireland and then in England, and was sent out to Australia, a petite and pretty girl, because she had a weakness in her chest. She soon married a prosperous cattleman and had a son by him, but domestic life was not for Daisy Bates; she was one of those women who have to have a cause, who have to embrace the world at large. After ten years in Australia she left both son and husband and returned to England, where W. T. Stead gave her a job on the *Review of Reviews*. Here in the society of the Fabians (Shaw and the Webbs were just launching themselves forth), she was a debutante among good causes, and one in particular took her eye: she read a letter in *The Times* which accused the white settlers in Australia of maltreating the blacks. She went to the editor of the paper, saying that she intended to sail to Australia to investigate the matter, and offering to write a series of articles. The editor said that he was interested and that was enough for Daisy Bates: she had found her career at last.

She travelled for years in the most distant parts of Western Australia, bought and managed a property there, and lived the incredibly tough and lonely life of a bushman in the 1890s. The more she saw of the Aborigines the more she was moved and touched by them, and in the end she gave up everything to serve them. She learned to speak their many dialects, she came to know all their habits, their legends and their tribal rites, she ate their food and nursed them when they were sick, and eventually she went to live alone with the remnants of the tribes in that loneliest and most forbidding region of the whole continent, the Nullarbor Plain on the Great Australian Bight. The Aborigines adopted her as one of their own; 'I lived,' she says, 'their lives, not mine.' But upon one point she would not compromise. She emerged each morning from her broken-down shanty wearing button-up boots, a long Victorian skirt and a blouse, a stiff collar with a blue ribbon around it, gloves and a hat with a veil, and that was her unchangeable costume among these semi-naked and naked men and women, whatever the temperature, whatever the time of year. And quite admirable she looked, anything but ridiculous.

By now, at the beginning of the twentieth century, a telegraph line had been built around the Bight along the line of Eyre's old route, and this had been followed by the construction of a railway, but Daisy Bates's camp at Ooldea, one of the stops along the line, was about as far away from civilization as you could get. The tribes knew she was there, they came from hundreds of kilometres away in Central Australia to see her, and she perhaps was the only European who was ever fully admitted to their most secret ceremonies.

Yet Daisy Bates does not quite fit into the accepted notion of dedicated, missionary zeal. She was a very brisk character indeed, she was well aware of the outside world, and she had a talent for writing about the people she loved without sentimentality or preaching. She writes only of what she knows, and flinches at nothing. She admits that the Nullarbor blacks, in their extreme hunger, sometimes killed and ate their own children, and she does not ask that you should admire them or even sympathize with them; she simply says, 'Here they are, this is the last of them, this is how they lived.' She does not want to reform them or evangelize them; she only wants them to live out their last years in peace.

Her *Passing of the Aborigines*, like all good books of the kind, is something more than a revelation of its own subject; it throws a light on the human condition everywhere. She writes:

'On their own country they [the Aborigines] were trespassers. There was no more happy wandering in the interchange of hospitality. Sources of food supply slowly but surely disappeared, and they were sent away to unfamiliar places, compelled to change their mode of life, to clothe themselves in the attire of strangers, to eat foods unfitted for them, to live within walls.

Their age-old laws were laid aside for the laws they could not understand. The young generation, always wilful, now openly flouted the old, and defied them, and haunted the white man's homes, protected by his policemen. A little while, and they resorted to thieving – where theft had been unknown – and sycophancy, and they sold their young wives to the depraved and foreign element. Half-castes came among them, a being neither black nor white, whom they detested. They died in their numbers of the white man's diseases, measles, whooping-cough, influenza and the results of their own wrong-doing.

In Tahiti the Polynesians had been taught to despise their own religion, and had torn down their *marae*. In the same way the Aboriginal gods and totems had been brought into contempt by the white man and had been destroyed and forgotten. To the proselytizing Christian this was a good and necessary thing, but it left the natives without a tradition or a past and they were like men who had lost their memories; they wandered about in a trance in the materialistic present and they could not in a moment be anchored to the new white god. Backwards as well as forwards the way was blocked.

Yet in their ignorance and bewilderment there continued to be a fumbling back to the instincts of the race:

'When the first half-caste babies appeared, the wild mothers believed that they were the results of eating white man's food, and rubbed them frantically with charcoal to restore their black health and colour, till they often died.'

From her isolated perch in the desert Daisy Bates saw the white invasion very clearly and through many things; the first English sparrows and rabbits

'Native Girls Going to
Trinity Church, Ade-
laide' by W. A. Caw-
thorne. Trinity Church,
North Adelaide, was the
first church in the colony
of South Australia.

which had been imported into New South Wales making their way towards
the west, the sandstorms that grew more frequent as more and more trees in
the east were cut down to make way for the grass and crops that died in the
summer heat, and then the increasing passage of the white man himself, the
prospecting miner, the itinerant trader, the railway worker, and finally the
train passengers from whom the Aborigines learned to beg for food and tobacco and liquor.

Daisy Bates implies (but does not say) that the *status quo* is not necessarily
stagnation, and that Australia, like Tahiti, was possibly a happier place before
the white man arrived there. She certainly agreed with Cook that the blacks
had found a way of life that was perfectly valid until it was broken into and
destroyed. Could the white man say he had adjusted himself to *his* environ-
ment as well as the Aborigines were once adjusted to theirs? In the Australia
that Daisy Bates knew the white settler was often a figure who was soured
by hardships and frustrations, and he was conscious of a superiority he could
not really enjoy – a sad sort of life when you compared it with the comfortable, polygamous, communal existence of the blacks who wanted to change
nothing and to govern nobody.

At Ooldea Daisy Bates found among her charges an intolerable nostalgia for
their half-forgotten past:

*'Often in the evening dream-echoes of native voices come, borne on the winds, singing
weird cadences that seem to take one's soul into a barbaric past in which it once lived and
moved. . . . If you are a Celt you can sense what the singer is unable to express and feel
the varied emotions passing through him. . . . His totem songs – a few words at most –
are sung with a wild abandon, the emotions they stir within him becoming stronger with
every repetition, until finally, from excess of feeling, the singer will often fall unconscious, to be roughly massaged into life again.*

The theme again seems to be, Nevermore.

'Ice Islands', by George Foster 1772–3, who described them as having 'the appearance of a spire or steeple; and many others gave full scope to our imagination, which compared them to several known objects, by that means attempting to overcome the tediousness of our cruise.'

PART THREE

THE
ANTARCTIC

I

The Resolution

IT WAS ON HIS SECOND VOYAGE that Cook, with his two ships, the *Resolution* and the *Adventure*, struck directly south in search of a southern continent. The Antarctic summer lasts only four months at the most, and Cook timed his arrival to make the most of it. He left Capetown on 23 November 1772, and already in early December they were in 'pinching cold', with every man wearing his Fearnought jacket. On 10 December, in latitude 50 degrees 40; they saw the first of their 'islands of ice', and soon they were surrounded by them. One of the ships' diarists records:

'Excessive cold, thick snows, islands of ice very thick, sometimes forty in sight at once, the people numb'd, ye ropes all froze over with ice, and ye Rigs and Sails all covered with snow.'

As with everyone who has since followed them to the Antarctic seas, these first explorers were awestruck by the size, the grandeur and the extraordinary shapes of the icebergs with their marvellous translucent shades of blue and green, and the sea birds circling round them and the occasional whale surfacing to blow; and in foul weather the waves dashing against their menacing black sides. They saw icebergs 'as high as the dome of St Pauls', others that looked like castles and fortresses, and others again that had melted into the forms of monstrous animals. An iceberg looks infinitely solid and serene as it glides

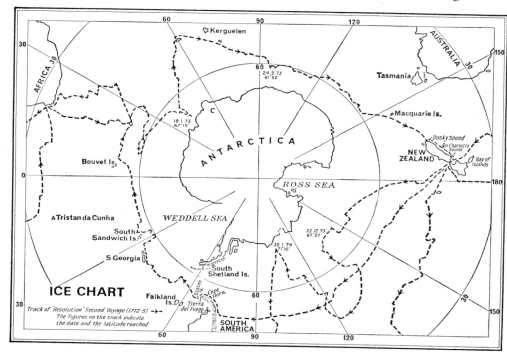

ICE CHART

Track of 'Resolution' Second Voyage (1772-5)
The figures on the track indicate
the date and the latitude reached

Map labels: Kerguelen, AFRICA, AUSTRALIA, Tasmania, Macquarie Is., Dusky Sound, Qn Charlotte Sound, NEW ZEALAND, Bay of Islands, Bouvet Is., ANTARCTICA, ROSS SEA, Tristan da Cunha, WEDDELL SEA, South Sandwich Is., S Georgia, South Shetland Is., Falkland Is., Cape Horn, Tierra del Fuego, SOUTH AMERICA, 24.2.73 61°52', 18.1.73 67°15', 22.12.73 67°27', 30.1.74 71°10'

silently by on a calm sea, but in fact, as Cook soon discovered, it is not very stable. When it drifts into less frigid seas the great bulk beneath the surface is eaten away and the equilibrium is lost. Then in an instant the whole mass turns over on itself and as it wallows about from side to side, huge chunks of ice break off and with a roar like a cannon shot come cascading down into the sea. Such upheavals could be very dangerous if one happened to be sailing near, and in a fog or a storm it was not always easy to steer clear.

Hodges, the artist on board the *Resolution*, made a series of drawings of these scenes, and he reveals very well the fragility and littleness of the two sailing ships among so many threatening towers and pinnacles of ice, and over all, a strange, subaqueous, milky light. Quite apart from the discomforts of being there at all, these bizarre surroundings, so wildly remote from normal life, must have created a sense of deep uneasiness and unreality, and Cook's crews had to live with this feeling day after day and week after week without knowing when it would ever cease.

But even this frozen wilderness had its Ultima Thule. In mid December they were stopped by 'an immense field of ice' to which they 'could see no end' – the ice pack. In fog so thick they could not see one end of their vessels from the other, Cook kept tacking about in search of an opening that would take them further south. The cold was now so intense that the men were given an extra dram of brandy in the morning, and some red baize cloth was found to lengthen the sleeves of their jackets. On Christmas Day they all got drunk.

Cook had the feeling that he was near land, or that at any rate this field of ice was attached to land, and he kept thrusting his way into it whenever an open

Resolution and Adventure, *4 January 1773. 'Taking in Ice for Water. Latitude 61 S' by William Hodges. 'We hoisted out three Boats,' writes Cook, 'and took up as much [ice] as yielded about 15 Tons of Fresh Water.'*

channel appeared. On 17 January 1773 they crossed the Antarctic Circle, the first ships ever to do so (though Cook makes no particular celebration of it), and then, when the weather cleared a little, moved on steadily to the south and east. The icebergs had been bad enough, but nothing in all Cook's voyaging can have been more resolute than this. Even at the present time it can be a hazardous thing for a ship to steam into these frozen seas and see ice forming in its wake and blocking its way of escape. But to do this in a small sailing ship with no other means of power but the unpredictable wind, and not to know what lay ahead or how thickly the ice would form behind, or indeed have any clear notion of what was going to happen – this must have required an extreme of courage and perseverance. Strangely, one of the things they minded most

THE ICE ISLANDS , feen the 9ᵗʰ of Janʸ 1773.

'The Ice Islands' seen by the Resolution on 9 January 1773. The ships had crossed the Antarctic Circle, the first vessels to do so. For their part, the men were struck by the size and the extraordinary shapes of the icebergs, with the sea birds circling and an occasional whale surfacing to blow. The ships themselves seemed very small amid the encircling towers. Engraved by B. T. Pouncy from a drawing by William Hodges.

was the shortage of water; before they could wash themselves or their clothes they had to go through the labour of cutting up ice into chunks and melting it in the ships' coppers.

On 18 January they reached latitude 67 degrees 15, which was much further south than any man had been before. But now once again solid ice blocked their progress and even Cook, for the moment, had had enough. He turned his ships around and sailed east by north into warmer water.

All this time they had been in perpetual daylight, but now, in lower latitudes, they began to get three or four hours of darkness each day, and for the first time in many weeks saw the stars and the moon again. On calmer days there must have been moments of great beauty, the sails filling, the two little ships sliding silently onward with albatrosses and petrels swinging about in their wake; and then, in the brief darkness, the strange, lurid lights of the aurora forming so brightly over their heads that the sailors' shadows were cast on the decks.

But the good weather did not last. On 8 February fog closed in again and the

ABOVE
'A Man Killing an
Albatross' by Augustus
Earle. The albatrosses
kept them company and
provided occasional food.

LEFT
Although the icebergs
looked solid, Cook soon
discovered that when they
drifted into less frigid
seas, the great bulk be-
neath the surface was
eaten away and the equi-
librium lost. Then, in an
instant, the whole mass
turned over on itself.
Such upheavals could be
very dangerous.

Resolution lost contact with the *Adventure*. This was not a disaster; Cook had envisaged such a happening and had given her captain, Furneaux, a rendezvous for the end of the summer in Queen Charlotte Sound in New Zealand. Still, it was not really safe for a ship to be alone in these waters, and for some days the *Resolution* cast about, firing her guns every few minutes and showing flares on her masthead, before the search was given up.

A little of the summer still remained and Cook struck south again; we soon have him recording in his journal that everywhere around them icebergs were capsizing and splitting up, and a white pall of mist hung about day after day. It was a scene that filled the mind, Cook says, 'with admiration and horror'.

In 1798 Coleridge's *Ancient Mariner* was published, and one cannot easily believe that it was written without knowledge of this voyage; indeed, there are passages in which it seems that Cook's own words have been cast into poetic imagery. Take, for example, the following:

> *And now there came both mist and snow,*
> *And it grew wondrous cold:*
> *And ice, mast-high, came floating by,*
> *As green as emerald.*
>
> *And through the drifts and snowy clifts*
> *Did send a dismal sheen:*
> *Nor shapes of men nor beasts we ken –*
> *The ice was all between.*
>
> *The ice was here, the ice was there,*
> *The ice was all around:*
> *It crack'd and growl'd, and roar'd and howl'd,*
> *Like noises in a swound!*

And then again:

> *The ice did split with a thunder-fit;*
> *The helmsman steer'd us through!*

When finally they reached New Zealand in March they had been nearly four months at sea, and without waiting to go on to Queen Charlotte Sound Cook put in directly to Dusky Bay in South Island to recuperate his men. No one was really ill – hardly a man on board had scurvy – but the strain of the eerie Antarctic fogs had been very great, and one can imagine with what delight they set up their tents on the green shore and went off hunting and fishing for their dinners. They had no trouble with the cannibalistic Maoris, and this seems to have been due to Cook's manner of approaching them without the slightest show of aggression or fear. He walked up boldly to the first warrior who appeared and rubbed noses with him. On another day when he was approached by a man armed with a spear he sat down on the ground and quietly threw beads and trinkets at him until he was won round.

After six weeks they sailed on to Queen Charlotte Sound where Furneaux was awaiting them, and the two ships then went off on their winter sweep through the Pacific to Tahiti. October 1773 found them heading south again for the next season in the Antarctic. At this stage there was an air of well-being about the voyage – 'We live at present,' wrote Clerke, the *Resolution*'s

second lieutenant, 'a very jolly life' – but they were on too hazardous an undertaking to expect good fortune all the way. The *Resolution* again lost contact with her consort in a severe gale off New Zealand, and Cook, having waited there for three weeks in vain, gave her up for good and continued alone.★

This second season in the Antarctic was even more testing than the first. By 12 December they were among icebergs again – icebergs 60–90 m (200–300 ft) high and some of them were several kilometres long – and fog, snow and wind dogged them all the way. Cook's entries in his journal lose nothing by being laconic:

'In the PM a squall of wind took hold of the Mizen Top-sail and tore it all to pieces and rendered it forever useless . . . the ropes like wires, sails like board or plates of metal . . . cold so intense as hardly to be endured.'

The blocks froze, making it impossible to shift the sails, and lumps of ice were constantly falling from the rigging to the decks. Their second Christmas Day was spent in surroundings of frozen gloom and danger, with 100 icebergs or more floating round the ship. They had their carousal and felt more cheerful, but the crew were reaching the limit of their endurance. Even Cook looked wan and could not eat.

★It will be recalled that the *Adventure* made her own way back to England.

Dusky Bay, New Zealand. Here the Resolution *came to shelter after four months in Antarctic waters. Cook found it 'one of the most beautiful [places] which nature unassisted by art could produce.' 'The sloop was no sooner in safety,' Cook recorded in high spirits, 'than every sailor put his hook and line overboard, and in a few moments numbers of fine fish were hauled up on all parts of the vessel, which heightened the raptures we had already felt at our entrance into this bay. The real good taste of the fish, joined to our long abstinence, inclined us to look upon our first meal here as the most delicious we had ever made in our lives.'*

'View in Pickersgill Harbour, Dusky Bay by William Hodges. The Resolution's outline is seen to the right of the painting with a crudely fashioned gangway linking the ship and 'the antediluvian forests which clothed the rock'.

Cook seldom gave any hints of his plans; perhaps he himself did not always know what precisely he was next going to do. So now when he turned the *Resolution* into warmer latitudes a rumour got about the ship that he was heading for home, and it was a moment of utter dismay when, after a few weeks, he ordered the helmsman to turn about and to make south again. 'A gloomy, melancholy air,' George Forster writes, 'loured on the brows of our shipmates and a dreadful silence reigned among us.' One almost detects the tones of the Ancient Mariner. They loathed the salt meat and the weevilly bread, they were sick of gales, they longed for home.

But Cook was adamant. What he was doing – what he was privately determined to go on doing – was to keep moving round the Pole in an easterly direction until he had circumnavigated it or had actually succeeded in reaching it; and it must be remembered that this last was not thought to be impossible. No one knew what was at the pole or around it. There could be solid land. There could be a gulf of warmer water reaching through the ice towards it. One simply had to go on trying to find out.

And now in fact, in January 1774, they did come on calmer, more ice-free seas roughly along longitude 110, and they sailed on, down and down, through persistent fog, until on 30 January, when the mist temporarily cleared, they were on latitude 71 degrees 10. This was the farthest south they were ever going to get. Solid pack ice blocked the way ahead, and great white clouds merged with icy mountains on the southern horizon. Could that be land? Could that be the edge of the southern continent? There was no way of knowing definitely but Cook had his ideas:

'I will not say it was impossible anywhere to get farther to the south, but the attempting it would have been a dangerous and rash enterprise, and what I believe no man in my situation would have thought of. It was indeed my opinion, as well as the opinion of most on board, that this ice extended quite to the Pole or perhaps joins to some land to which it has been fixed from the creation . . . I, who had ambition not only to go farther than anyone had done before, but as far as it was possible for man to go, was not sorry at meeting this interruption . . .'

The Resolution *among the ice on her second excursion to the Antarctic in late 1773. 'The ropes like wire, sails like board or plates of metal,' Cook reported of his faithful vessel, 'cold so intense as hardly to be endured.' The journeys into the ice packs were feats of endurance for officers and crew. From William Hodges's painting 'Ice Islands'.*

So he turned north again. Yet he could not quite bring himself to give up. He consulted his officers and they agreed – Cook says willingly – to protract the voyage by one more year; they would now cruise for the nine winter months in the tropical Pacific, breaking into unknown seas wherever possible, and then come back to the Antarctic for a third and final attempt at the end of 1774.

It took all of those nine months in a warm climate to get the men back into condition again. Cook himself fell seriously ill with an acute infection of the gall-bladder, and this was the occasion when Forster's dog was killed to provide him with a little fresh meat and broth. Without Cook they all felt lost, and there was consternation in the ship. When he eventually recovered and re-appeared on deck, John Marra (the marine who was so often flogged for his misdemeanours) says that one could read the delight on everyone's face, 'from the highest officer to the meanest boy on board the ship'.

After three and a half months out of sight of land they reached Easter Island, and then followed the tremendous cruise through the Marquesas, the Society Islands, the Friendly Islands, the New Hebrides, New Caledonia, Norfolk Island and so back to New Zealand – a series of discoveries which, by themselves, make this voyage forever memorable. The unhappy Marra was still in trouble: in Queen Charlotte Sound he got another twelve lashes for drunkenness and for being absent without leave in search of women on shore. Cook remarks drily that he would have let him stay there had he been sure that the Maoris would not have killed and eaten him before morning. For the rest, the crew, though tired and homesick, were much improved in health by the fresh fruit and meat they had eaten in the tropics, and in fairly good heart they turned south for the last time.

Sea lions (which the company called sea bears). Here, a female with her young.

From New Zealand, on 10 November 1774, Cook set a course on latitude 55 for Cape Horn – a route never traversed by a ship before – and they made the

crossing in five weeks, averaging a remarkable 256 km (160 miles) a day. He then set about exploring the islands of Tierra del Fuego, South Georgia and the Sandwich Group. Although he did not get so far south this time, it was in many ways the most interesting part of the whole voyage, for they were constantly in sight of land and surrounded by living creatures; schools of whales and seals and sea lions (which they called sea bears), penguins (which they called Jumping Jacks), geese and sea birds of every kind, and their steady fellow-travellers through all these years, the great *Diomedea exulans*, the Wandering albatross. It was always there, each morning at first light moving up to the ship and wheeling around it without so much as a flicker of its immense 4.2 m (14 ft) wings, a lovely thing, the perfection of effortless motion. No distance wearied it, no storm deterred it; when the gale became too fierce it took shelter with outspread wings in the hollows of the waves. It was a most reassuring bird, as friendly as a dolphin, and even more beautiful to watch. One doubts of course that Cook's men saw it in quite so poetical a light as Coleridge did – still less as a symbol of man's guilt – but at all events they did not shoot it now. They preferred instead to shoot the geese, and on their third Christmas Day afloat they had enough to provide a third of a bird for every man. Their madeira wine had improved in quality during the voyage, and they caroused for two days. Cook had to put the bulk of the crew ashore to recover.

The marine life seethed around them. Clerke wrote:

'There are a greater abundance of whales and seals rowling about these straits than I supposed were to be met with in any part of the world; a fair account of them would appear incredible – the whales are blowing at every point of the compass and frequently taint the whole atmosphere about us with the most disagreeable effluvia that can be conceived.'

Christmas Sound, Tierra del Fuego, which Cook discovered along with South Georgia and the Sandwich group, on his epic journey into deep southern latitudes in December 1774. All of these he claimed for Britain. The Sound he named on Christmas Day, his ship dwarfed by the barren rock in a place he judged 'doomed by Nature to everlasting sterility'. Engraving by W. Watts from a drawing by William Hodges.

ABOVE
On his second period of reprieve from Antarctica in 1874, Cook reached Easter Island and saw the great stone carvings that had long ago been mysteriously erected by the inhabitants. William Hodges depicted them in his 'A View of the Monuments of Easter Island'.

RIGHT, ABOVE
A silver-grey petrel.

RIGHT, BELOW LEFT
The blue petrel was a native of the lush shores of Dusky Bay.

RIGHT, BELOW RIGHT
The Bearded Penguin found in New Zealand waters. To the crew they were know affectionately as 'Jumping Jacks'.

On Staten Island and the nearby coasts they made a great killing among the fur seals, the bellowing sea lions and the birds. Cooper, the *Resolution*'s second lieutenant, noted in his diary:

'*Observed the small island covered with seals, sea lions and birds of different kinds. Hoisted out the boats and sent them on shore with several of the officers and ship's company to kill sea lions and seals to make oil for the use of the ship. At 8 the boats returned on board loaded with sea lions, seals, geese, shags and penguins, the shores of the island being entirely covered with them, some of the lions weighing 1000 lbs weight [454 kg]. AM. Hoisted the launch out (again) and sent her with the other boats to bring off those amazing animals whilst hands are employed on board taking off the skins and blubber.*'

'We have seen a male (sea lion) with 20 or 30 females about him,' wrote Cook, 'and he was always very attentive to keep them all to himself by beating off every other male.' They also saw others which 'would suffer neither male nor female to come near them; we judged these to be old and superannuated.' Here, in this extreme isolation, where the penguins bobbed about in thousands and the sea birds 'darkened the air', nature had achieved a state of balance: 'It is wonderful to see how the different animals which inhabit this little spot are reconciled to each other; they seem to have entered into a league not to disturb each other's tranquillity.' They mixed together 'like domesticated cattle and poultry in a farmyard'. Even the eagles did not attack the young gulls.

Kerguelen's Land. The Resolution*'s crew went ashore at whatever landing spots availed, to collect food or to kill sea lions and seals to make oil for the ship's use. 'At 8,' wrote Lieutenant Cooper, after one of these forays, 'the boats returned on board loaded with sea lions, seals, geese, shags and penguins, the shores of the island being entirely covered with them.'*

Next they came up with the icy mountainous coast of South Georgia, a place which Cook found 'savage and horrible', a desolation without a tree. Nevertheless he claimed it for Britain. The Sandwich Islands, the most southerly land Cook discovered on this voyage, were no less bleak – 'the most horrible coast in the world', according to Cook's journal. The extraordinary thing about these desolate places was that the cold sea supported such a wealth of marine and bird life. Even on the lushest tropical island Cook had not seen such teeming abundance: whales spouting about the ship in every direction, seals inhabiting every frozen rock, and always the myriad birds wheeling overhead. Until now no man had ever visited these islands; these were their last few years of peace.

Now at last they had circumnavigated the Pole, and Cook, without regret, turned for home:

'I have now done with the southern ocean and flatter myself that no one will think that I have left it unexplored or that more could have been done in one voyage . . .'

And perhaps, in that age so long before steam navigation or aircraft, he can be forgiven for adding:

'The risk one runs in exploring a coast in these unknown and icy seas is so very great that I can be bold to say that no man will ever venture further than I have done and that the lands that may lie to the south will never be explored.'

In so far as it was impossible for any ship, steam or sail, to reach the Pole he was right.

His last word on the great object of his journey, the discovery of a southern continent, was this:

'That there may be a continent or large tract of land near the Pole I will not deny, on the contrary I am of the opinion that there is, and it is probable that we have seen a part of it.'

'A Shooting Party from the Resolution killing Sea Lions'. The ship and its crew were the harbingers of human predation in the Antarctic.

For the time being, however, nothing more could be done; the *Resolution*'s rigging had become so rotten that some part of it gave way every hour, scurvy was threatening on board – they were even reduced to eating penguins – and Cook, in one of his rare moments of approbation, conceded that the behaviour of his crew throughout the voyage 'merited every indulgence which was in my power to give them.'

On 21 March 1775 they anchored off Capetown in Table Bay, it being two and a half years since they had had any contact with civilization. They were so weary, so grateful to get off the *Resolution*'s heaving deck, they lay down by the roadside when they got ashore and fell asleep. To stretch the legs, to breathe fresh air full of the smell of the country, to drink tea and eat fresh food, to get news of home, to be idle, to be safe – these things were pleasures beyond dreams. On the voyage from the Cape to England, an easy, coasting time, they called at St Helena, and it is interesting to note that in 1775, forty years before Napoleon's imprisonment, they found there a flourishing British settlement with a garrison of 600 soldiers and 1,400 slaves.

At the end of July 1775 they anchored at Plymouth. They had been away three years and eighteen days. They had sailed more than 20,000 leagues – three times the circumference of the earth – and Cook had lost no more than four men, and only one of them by sickness. If there had been any doubt before, this voyage established him as one of the greatest navigators of all times.

The bloodstained ice

'. . . all my means are sane, my motive and my object mad.'
CAPTAIN AHAB

ONCE AGAIN it was Cook's fate to bring disaster in his wake. He had stumbled upon what was probably the largest congregation of wildlife that existed in the world, and he was the first man to let the world know of its existence. One would have expected the Antarctic seas to be as barren as the frozen land, but the remarkable thing is that they are in fact extraordinarily rich in mineral food and in small forms of marine life. Sponges, for instance, are more prolific here than in tropical waters, and if a chunk of pack-ice is turned over it will often be found to be stained yellow with algae. This richness of vegetable matter in the sea was the explanation of the tremendous number and variety of the animals and birds that Cook saw on his voyage.

Every year the 30 m (100 ft) blue whales, the largest animals in creation, came down here to the Antarctic during the summer months in tens of thousands to feed on the red krill, a minute shrimp; and they were followed by other leviathans as well, the humpback and the right whales, and by the smaller carnivorous killer whale, which preyed upon them. In March when they had grown fat and were heavily encased in blubber the whole horde turned north to warmer seas. The migratory habits of whales are still a mystery; no one knows how they navigate, perhaps they follow the stars, but at all events the month of May found them thousands of kilometres away to the north. In August 1699 Dampier had come upon them far up the coast of Western Australia:

'We had in the night abundance of whales about the ship, some ahead, others astern, and some on each side blowing and making a very dismal noise . . . indeed the noise they made by blowing and dashing of the sea with their tails, making it all of a breach and foam, was very dreadful to us, like the breach of waves in very shoal-water, or among rocks.'

A favourite breeding ground of the right whales, one of many in the southern Pacific, was the estuary of the Derwent River in Tasmania. Cook found none there when he visited the place on his third voyage in 1777, but that was because he arrived in January; they came up from the Antarctic in great numbers a little later in the year. In 1804 a clergyman who had settled at Hobart town observed that it was positively dangerous to go up the river in a small boat since there were so many right whales about, forty or more within a stretch of a few kilometres. Here the females gave birth, and the calves were suckled at sea as they cruised on again to the north. Killer whales swam with them, hoping to grab a child when a mother grew careless.

Here too in these warmer waters the whales caught up with the porpoises or

dolphins, those most fascinating of all animals in the sea. Like the albatross, they always seemed to be about the *Resolution* on her voyage; they liked the company of man and trusted him. The porpoise, Melville was to write later on,

The Resolution *and* Adventure *among Antarctic icebergs during the voyage of 1772–3, by William Hodges.*

'*always swims in hilarious shoals, which upon the broad sea keep tossing themselves to heaven like caps in a Fourth-of-July crowd. Their appearance is generally hailed with delight by the mariner. Full of fine spirits they invariably come from the breezy billows to the windward. They are the lads that always live before the wind. They are accounted a lucky omen.*'

Sometimes the ship would come upon the green turtle, the one that makes the soup, flopping about in the waves, and it too was migratory. The seals and the sea lions which Cook saw in such abundance about the Horn and the frozen islands off the Antarctic coast were, as he said, 'all so tame, or rather so stupid, as to suffer us to come so near as to knock them down with a stick.' Then again there were the penguins, the little black and white Adélie and the 27 kg (60 lb) Emperor with a splash of yellow on his jowls, and they also were not afraid, they did not see an enemy in man.

At the time of Cook's voyages very little was known about these creatures or their habits. Some of them had been observed in the Northern Hemisphere, but the south Pacific and the Antarctic waters had never been fished by white men, and many of the species there were entirely new to science. Unobserved and until now unknown, the great cavalcade – the whales and the dolphins, the penguins and the seals – moved on from the cold water to the warm during the southern winter, and then back to the Antarctic again in the summer, breeding and feeding, and it knew no enemies except those that were created by nature in the sea itself.

Since it was almost totally unknown the Antarctic was then an even more frightening place than it is now. In fact it was a vast sheet of ice and frozen rock covering an area of more than 13 million km² (5 million sq miles), which is nearly half the size of Africa. At places great mountains pushed their black lava peaks out of the surrounding whiteness, but nearly all the rest of the land had been pressed below the surface of the sea by the great weight of permanent ice that lay above it.

The South Pole itself lay about 1,600 km (1,000 miles) inland from the coast, and it was quite unlike the North Pole (where there are open seas); it was very high – some 3,000 m (10,000 ft) above the level of the sea – and it was surrounded by an immense flat plateau of ice that was 3.2 km (2 miles) thick. Nothing there would grow or survive; it was the coldest, most desolate place on earth.

For nine months of the year it was shrouded in continuous night in which, apart from the moon and the stars, the only light to appear was the aurora with its fantastic curtain-shapes and spiralling, coloured rays, flickering briefly in the sky. Towards the end of each year an orange band formed around the circular horizon, and this grew stronger day by day until at last the red rim of the sun appeared, and it gradually circled higher and higher until there was continual daylight where there had been only night before.

Within three months the sun descended again to the horizon, casting immensely long shadows on the ice, and then again, with a last glow of orange light, it vanished entirely. Except for the raging blizzards it was a world of utter stillness and silence.

On the coast things were very different. Here, through the summer months at least, there was life and movement. The landscape had great splendour: glaciers with their surfaces curiously puckered up like a quilt reached down from the mountainsides into the sea, and on the sea itself the floating ice-pack broke up and drifted away in the form of tremendous icebergs, some of them over 105 m (350 ft) high.

Yet there was relief here from the prevailing whiteness; the greenness in the sea itself, the dark shapes of whales and seals, the penguin colonies, and in the ice itself, especially in the icebergs drifting in the sunshine, that lovely shade of bluish-green which was to be found nowhere but in polar seas. It was a very delicate and limpid colour but it filled the eye, and it had a quality of absolute purity and permanence, the cold fire of the diamond.

But the sun so seldom shone; the icy fog was all-pervading.

The mirages in the Antarctic had a clarity that was almost beyond belief, and made it difficult for an explorer to know whether he was seeing land or not. Second ranges of mountains appeared to be built on top of the real mountains lying below, and these false ranges were immensely high and clear in outline. They hung there in the pale sky for a few minutes and then vanished only to re-form themselves again, so that the sailing ships drifted about in an atmosphere of ghostly fantasy. It was both awe-inspiring and beautiful. There it was, the great unknown continent, immaculate, untouched, relating itself to nothing else on this earth and utterly indifferent to man. It was hostile and yet it beckoned the explorer on, impressing him with his littleness, but at the same

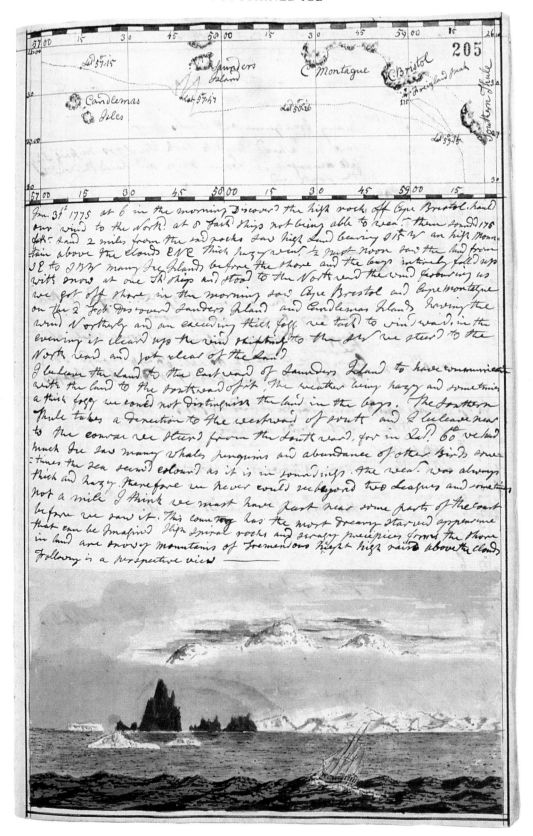

time creating in his mind a sense of almost spiritual purity and of heightened living. It was frightening, but it was not malign; one walked, as it were, through this valley of the shadow of death and feared no evil. Running through the explorers' journals there are two themes: their frustration, their feeling that they ought to be doing more, and then their reverence – it is hardly too strong a word – for the mighty works of nature all around them. The vast icebergs drifted by, menacing, implacable and serene.

Nothing decayed in this pure, icy air, nothing rusted. It was a petrified world, and what Cook saw almost 200 years ago we can still see today. Had Cook landed some of his wooden casks on the ice they would still be there, and the food they contained might be eatable. A century after Cook (when the Pole itself had still not been visited by any man), Edgar Allan Poe wrote a novel about the Antarctic which he called *The Narrative of A. Gordon Pym*, and he peopled it with savage tribes and with polar bears that roamed about in primeval forests. He may not have been absolutely wrong, for there are indeed traces of fossilized trees to be found in Antarctica, and clearly there may have been a past age when the ice-cap did not exist. In the present millennium, however, there was no place for man in this frozen desert.

It was too cold for him to live there, and since there was no ground to cultivate he could contribute nothing. A case could have been made out for the invasion of Tahiti and Australia; they were a part of the inhabitable world. But here in this icy wilderness there was nothing man could usefully do. It was impossible for him to blast away the ice and get at the land beneath, and even if he did there was no known plant that could grow there. He could come to the Antarctic in one way only, and that was as an invader, as a conqueror come to pillage and then go away again.

And this, of course, is what happened. The results of Cook's intrusion into

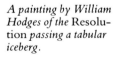

A painting by William Hodges of the Resolution *passing a tabular iceberg.*

Tahiti and Australia had been bad enough for the native peoples: for the Antarctic animals it was a holocaust. His account of his voyage in the *Resolution* was naturally of intense interest to the whaling and sealing industry in the Northern Hemisphere, where the catch was already diminishing in the closing years of the eighteenth century. Here now was news of a magnificent hunting ground in the far south: seals and whales by the million, all ready for the taking. From Le Havre in France and Hull in England, and from New Bedford and Nantucket in America, the whaling and the sealing fleets set out.

No one will ever know how many whales and seals were killed in the southern ocean in the ensuing fifty years. Was it ten million or fifty million? Figures become meaningless; the killing went on and on until there was virtually nothing left to kill, nothing at any rate that could be easily and profitably killed.

The sealers came first. With the aid of Cook's charts they found their way down to the desolate islands he had discovered, and then went on to explore many new coasts and islands on their own account. There was a devastating simplicity in their methods: they clubbed the animals to death. The usual practice was to wait offshore until a sufficient number of seals had gathered on the beach, and then the ships' crew landed in small boats and cut off their retreat to the sea. The club that was used was a thick wooden stave about 1.2 m (4 ft) long and its end was studded with nails. One quick blow on the head as the animal reared up was enough to knock it senseless, and the *coup de grâce* was

Seals being clubbed to death at a Seal Rookery at Beaucheene Island.

231

delivered with a skinning knife. It is horribly easy to envisage the carnage – the blood, the mess of entrails, the barking and roaring of the terrified animals as they tried to get away – enough, one would have thought, to make any normal man turn sick, but no doubt the sailors got used to it.

In the South Shetlands a single ship would expect to take as many as 9,000 seals in three weeks, and there is a record of two ships and sixty men de-molishing 45,000 in one season. And since every pelt was worth a guinea – in some markets like Canton in China very much more – there was every induce-ment for the slaughter to go on to the bitter end. An end, however, there had to be; and by the 1830s fur seals in the southern ocean were virtually extinct, and sea lions and sea elephants were dying out as well.

The main attack was now diverted to the whales, and in an age that needed oil for its candles (not to speak of the whalebone for such articles as umbrellas and women's corsets), this was an even more profitable trade than sealing. Whaling was an ancient business – it had been going on in the Northern Hemisphere for 1,000 years – but nothing so rich as 'the southern fishery' had ever been discovered before. The first comers in the south Pacific hardly needed to go to sea at all; the whaler simply set up a shore factory in some estuary where the animals were known to breed and then attacked them from small boats. There were dozens of such places: the Bay of Islands in New Zealand, the Derwent Estuary in Tasmania, all the coves and inlets along the deserted coasts of southern, western and eastern Australia. Each year, follow-ing an immemorial instinct, the whales would arrive from the south, travelling sometimes in small groups and sometimes in hundreds, and directly they cruised into these quiet bays where they had never met an enemy before they were set upon like Gulliver among the Lilliputians, by midgets armed with murderous arrows. Like the Lilliputians the whalemen were very brave, and no doubt excitement led them on. A warning cry from the look-out post on the cliffs would send the men running for the boats and they would row away madly towards the incoming leviathans. Each boat had a harpooner in the prow, and he would sink his shaft with its attached line from 5.5 m (6 yds)

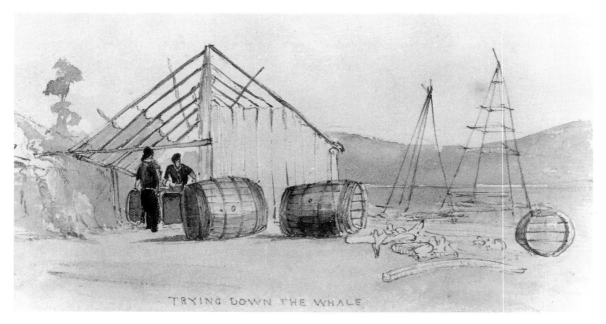

TRYING DOWN THE WHALE

FLINCHING THE WHALE

away. Then, when the whale dived, the line would run out, perhaps a couple of hundred fathoms of it, and away the boat would go on a wild career through the waves until the line slackened and the beast surfaced again to breathe; and again the whalemen would strike, this time with lances, and again the whale would sound, and this would go on for an hour or an entire day until at last the quarry was exhausted, and its life's blood gushed out from its blowhole. Then the carcass would be towed ashore and its blubber peeled off like the skin of an orange and rendered down into oil in furnace-heated vats on the beach.

In the Derwent River estuary where it had once been dangerous to sail in a small boat because of the numbers of right whales there – mostly pregnant mothers either calving or about to calve – a massacre went on year after year until the animals were wiped out. And so the hunt went on from May to October in all the breeding and mating grounds along the New Zealand and Australian coasts.

The whales never seemed to learn from their experiences; the survivors came back again and again, even those which had escaped from earlier encounters and now had harpoons and broken lances sticking in their backs. It is true that later on there was some evidence that the animals began to recognize men as their mortal enemies; we have Melville's revengeful *Moby Dick*, and it is even reported that some whales could recognize the difference between a normal vessel and a whaling ship with its harpoon mounted in the prow, and that they had some means of communicating to their companions so that all could dive to safety together. But habit and instinct were very strong. The sperm whales, the most valuable of all because of the reservoir of pure oil in their great square heads, travelled in packs – a male and a number of females. If the

ABOVE
'Flinching the whale'. Watercolour by Owen Stanley.

LEFT, ABOVE
Whales occasionally had the edge on seamen. Here, two sportive animals frolic across the pinnace of HMS Rattlesnake *during her voyage in southern waters, to the considerable surprise of the crew. Watercolour by Owen Stanley.*

LEFT, BELOW
The whale, the great monarch of the southern latitudes, reduced to bones and blubber in a process known as 'trying down the whale'. Watercolour by Owen Stanley.

Whalemen took large risks and excitement led them on. Here, a harpooned whale overturns a boat; men and lances scatter in the churning waves.

male was attacked the cows and the calves took off, but if a cow or a calf was struck the whole pack turned back to try and render help, and all would be destroyed. In this the sperm whales remind one of the elephants which were soon to be shot in tens of thousands in central Africa.

Then too, by the very nature of their size, these sea monsters were extremely vulnerable. They cruised no faster than a ship under canvas could sail, and when they dived it was easy enough to note their direction and be waiting for them at the point where they surfaced again a kilometre or two further on. They did not proliferate rapidly: a cow's pregnancy lasted about a year, and only one calf was born at a time. It was suckled for periods of five to ten months, and two or three years would elapse before another calf was born.

In these conditions it was not long before bay whaling – the taking of whales in their offshore breeding grounds – was practically finished and the hunt was then continued in the open sea. Pelagic whaling – the taking of whales in the ocean – was a more arduous business. You needed a ship about the *Resolution*'s size, 305 or 306 tonnes (300 or 400 tons), with a crew of thirty or more and six whaling boats that could be launched in any weather. The whales that were killed were towed alongside the mother ship and their oil was rendered down on brick furnaces on board. When the hunting was good a great red glow from

the fires lit up the sails all night. Sometimes a whaling ship would be gone from its home port for three or even four years before all her oil casks were full, but the great advantage of pelagic whaling was that you could follow the whales' migratory routes around the world and you delivered the cargo directly to the market.

It was a primitive business, absurdly so when one compares the look-outs on the mastheads and the hand harpoon with today's great whaling ships with their spotting aircraft, their radar, and their explosive guns; but it was effective because it was on so wide a scale. By 1846 America had 735 whalers operating out of the New England coast, and each of them averaged 100 whales, or 304 tonnes (300 tons) of oil, on every voyage. They came south round the Horn and out into the Pacific where their bases in the tropics were Hawaii and Tahiti, and in the south, the Bay of Islands in New Zealand, Sydney and Hobart town in Tasmania. It was a tremendous killing. Eyre on his walk along the Great Australian Bight found the shore at Fowler's Bay 'literally strewed in all directions with the bones and carcasses of whales', and he estimated that there were 300 American and French vessels operating on that coast alone. For meat they killed the kangaroos on Kangaroo Island, and for women they raided the native tribes ashore.

'Flinching a young sea elephant'. The hide of the bull elephant was used for shoe leather while the softer fur of the pups was made into caps.

237

One has but to visit the reconstructed whaling village at Mystic, Connecticut, USA, to see what a vast industry whaling had become through these middle years of the nineteenth century. They could build a ship at Mystic, and everything she needed for a long voyage could be supplied on the spot by the chandlers' shops, the blacksmiths and sailmakers, the carpenters and the ropemakers, the butchers and the flour millers. Mystic provided boots and clothing, compasses, maps and anchors and splendid figureheads – often a rather ample nymph with a scaly breast and fluttering veils – and of course, the sailors themselves. It is a pleasant and peaceful place to visit, a sort of recreation of nineteenth-century cottage industries, and at the height of the whaling days it must have been a very lively and engaging sort of place. The blood and guts and the dangers of the whale hunt in the southern ocean were very far away.

A great romance was made out of whaling, and so it was romantic if one thought of the tropical islands the ships called at, and the peculiar plaintive harmonies of the whaling songs, and of the adventure of breaking into undiscovered seas and of the headlong excitement of the whale hunt itself. The owners grew rich. 'In New Bedford,' Melville wrote, 'fathers, they say, give whales for dowers to their daughters and portion off their nieces with a few porpoises a-piece.' Melville lifted whaling into the realm of high tragedy and set it up as something apart, a relic from the heroic age. His masterpiece, *Moby Dick*, incomparably the best book on whaling ever written, is Shakespearean in its language, in its zany humour and in its rhetoric reveries; and its characters, the Lear-like Ahab and the poor little fool Pip, are symbols of a myth. But for the man actually sailing before the mast whaling was a degrading and brutal existence; he earned next to nothing, he was frequently in danger, and his food and the conditions of his life were so appalling that he often deserted his ship whenever he could, preferring exile among natives on some lonely Pacific coast rather than face the horrors of the long journey home. It was the emptiness of these immense, hardly-explored seas that was so forbidding. A ship would travel 16,000 km (10,000 miles) or more merely to get to the southern whaling grounds, and a year might go by before she sighted another vessel. When you signed on you put civilization behind you and condemned yourself to a life of being constantly wet, dirty and cold, constantly in the dark gaol-like confines of the fo'c'sle with twenty other men whom you might distrust or loathe. You were absolutely in the captain's power; if you disobeyed him he could bind you and flog you.

'I love to sail forbidden seas,' Melville wrote, 'and land on barbarous coasts.' But you also had to expect to be 'alone, in such remotest waters, that though you sailed a thousand miles and passed a thousand shores you would not come on any chiselled hearthstone . . .'

Or, of course, the society of women.

This was worse, far worse, than sailing with Cook, despite all the rigours of eighteenth-century naval discipline. The gullible farmer's boy who came hopefully to Nantucket from the middle west, dreaming of a life of adventure at sea, was soon disillusioned, and he was quite likely to become a decrepit and drunken beachcomber or a hanger-on along the docks if he continued in the trade too long. Most whaling crews were a polyglot collection picked up wherever they could be found in the course of a voyage; escaped convicts from Sydney, mutineers like the *Bounty* men, Australian Aborigines and South Sea

LEFT, ABOVE
The Australian colonies, particularly New South Wales, took a prominent part in whaling in the South Seas. The NSW entrepreneur Benjamin Boyd established a whaling station beside his pastoral estate at Boyd Town near Twofold Bay and other whaling establishments operated from the area. In this drawing by J. Carmichael, 'Bay Whaling off the Boyd Town Lighthouse', the great whales surface to make easily located prey just off the shore.

LEFT, BELOW
The remains of the fight. An old whaling station, painted by J. S. Prout. Herman Melville, author of Moby Dick, an experienced whaler himself, lifted whaling into the realm of high tragedy and set it up as an epic of a heroic age. But for the man actually sailing before the mast, whaling was a degrading and brutal existence. The captains of whaling vessels knew this and preferred their crew to have as many different nationalities as possible, and no questions asked.

islanders, men who wanted to hide for a time and half-starved illiterates ejected from Europe by the potato famine. The Portuguese were particularly numerous among the whaling crews. It was like the French Foreign Legion: you signed on and no questions asked, and the captains preferred their crews to belong to as many different nations as possible since they were then less likely to combine together and raise a mutiny. Thus there were few loyalties other than those created among the men by common hardship, and it was customary for a sailor to use an assumed name – probably to cover up his past.

It was not in *Moby Dick* but in the lesser-known *Omoo: a Narrative of Adventure in the South Seas*, that Melville revealed the real sordidness of the whaling life. It will be recalled that he deserted his ship, the *Acushnet*, in the Marquesas in July 1842, and he relates in *Omoo* how, after weeks of apparently idyllic existence among the islanders, he was taken off by the Sydney whaler, *Lucy Ann* (though Melville calls her the *Julia* for some esoteric reason of his own). In her he sailed to Tahiti, where he mutinied with other members of the crew and was arrested. The mutiny appears to have been more than justified, for the *Lucy Ann* was a former privateer which, long since, should have been condemned. Her hull and spars were 'a dingy black', she was infested with rats and cockroaches, her rigging was rotten, and such food as she carried had become uneatable. Vinton, the captain, was an irresponsible weakling, and he had given over effective command to the drunken mate, a man named John Jermin. At the time Melville joined her the ship's filthy and reeking fo'c'sle was filled with sick and dying men, and on the 1,600 km (1,000 miles) trip to Tahiti two men did die. The crew seems to have been a piratical lot; merely to read the list of their names conjures up the idea of some hell-ship on the Spanish Main. There was the surgeon, Melville's particular chum, Doctor Long Ghost, a tall thin man, 'a tower of bones'; Bembo, the tattooed Maori harpooner from New Zealand (the original Queequeg in *Moby Dick*?); Van, Navy Bob, M'Gee, Jingling Joe, Antone, Pat, Wymontoo, Bungs, Long

The Bay of Islands, New Zealand. After Cook's experience of witnessing cannibalism there, the place had a bad reputation. It was to gain another. By 1802 it had become 'a sort of piratical nest where the only law was the law of the gun'.

Jim, Salem, Black Dan, Flash Jack, Beauty and Blunt Bill alias Liverpool. Melville was Typee, so called from the valley he had inhabited in the Marquesas.

For weeks on end they lurched and zigzagged across the ocean to Tahiti, the days punctuated by fist fights and drunken brawls, and the burial of the dead. When at last they reached Papeete sixteen of the men, including Melville, drew up a round robin in which they declared that the ship was unseaworthy, that scurvy was rife amongst them and that they refused to sail in her any more. In short, they proposed to desert unless something was done. This document was sent ashore to the acting British consul, Charles Wilson, who seems to have been a mean-spirited sort of man; at all events, he came on board and decided against the mutineers. When they still refused to sail, Wilson solicited the aid of Rear Admiral Dupetit-Thouars, who had recently arrived at Papeete in his flagship *La Reine Blanche*. The Admiral obliged him with the loan of a cutter and twenty French sailors armed with cutlasses and boarding pistols. With this force Wilson, now wearing his consular cocked hat, returned to the *Lucy Ann* and arrested the mutineers. They were conveyed to *La Reine Blanche* and kept there in irons between decks for three days. Finally they were brought onshore and imprisoned for six weeks, as we have already seen, in the Calabooza Beretanee, the local gaol. Later on Melville sailed in a whaler to Honolulu and eventually reached home in an American man-of-war.

The interesting thing about this lurid tale (which Melville relates very gaily) is that it does not seem to have been particularly unusual. Mutinies or near mutinies were happening on whale ships all the time, and desertions were a commonplace. Half of the *Acushnet*'s crew deserted her during her four and a half years' voyage.

Melville speaks of the bad reputation of Australian whaling men and it does seem that they created little hells on earth wherever they made port. The Bay of Islands in the north island of New Zealand became a notorious place. As far

241

back as 1769 Cook had had a brush with the cannibalistic natives there, and
Banks had noted gloomily in his diary 'the almost certainty of being eat as
soon as you come ashore adds not a little to the terrors of shipwreck'. The
whalers, however, mostly Americans and Australians, were not deterred – it
was a marvellous place for hunting seals and the sperm whale – and by 1802
the Bay of Islands had become a sort of piratical nest where the only law was
the law of the gun. With equal ferocity the sailors killed the whales at sea and
the Maoris on land. The Maoris, at least, were able to strike back, since the
whalemen were so foolish as to supply them with firearms in exchange for
their women and their foodstuffs. In 1809 they captured the vessel *Boyd*, further
up the coast, and killed and ate its crew; and we hear of other affrays in which
white women and children as well as the whaling crews were seized from their
ships and either eaten or held as prisoners of war. Even as late as 1835 when
things had somewhat settled down Darwin speaks of the white population
there as 'the very refuse of society', and he adds, 'I believe we were all glad to
leave New Zealand. It is not a pleasant place.'

Hobart, too, was known for its spectacular drunkenness, and nightly brawls
between rival whaling crews were the accepted thing in the town's innumerable grog-shops. There was even gunfire at sea when two ships disputed the
possession of a whale or a sealing ground, and a death here and there was
simply another nameless body cast into the sea. In the Recherche Archipelago
in Western Australia – the place where Eyre was rescued by Captain Rossiter –
lawless bands of sailors, some of whom were wanted for murder in Sydney,
set themselves up in the islands, and they were ruled over by a savage and
ridiculous Negro named Black Anderson. He flourished his pistols, he went
about with his harem of grubby wives who were stolen from the Aboriginal
tribes, and he scraped along in his little reign of terror, eating wild geese and
seal meat, and exchanging sealskins for flour in King George Sound. Eventually he was murdered.

If there was precious little glamour in these men's lives there was still less in
the trade they followed. For all the bravery involved and the skill with which
they pursued the chase, it was the most wasteful business imaginable, since it
doomed not only the whales but the trade itself to extinction. They killed
everything, the young whale and the old, the pregnant mother and the calf;
and every living thing in the sea that could serve for food or be sold in the
market was hunted down in its breeding grounds. The poor green turtle,
flopping about helplessly in the warm tropical sea, and landing, even more
helplessly, to lay its eggs in the sand, was an easy quarry, and became steadily
more rare.

There were, of course, respectable whaling firms like the Enderby Brothers
in England; and the Quaker whale ship owners in Nantucket, though hard
men, and out for cash, saw to it that their vessels were properly equipped and
handled. But nobody contested the rightness of what they were doing, and
any protest about the cruelty and wastefulness of the whole enterprise would
have been met, then as now, with incredulity. The oil was wanted, and the
whales were there for the taking; it was just a question of getting ahead of one's
rivals and of bagging as many as you could. Then as now the London alder-
man, in the midst of consuming his good turtle soup, was not likely to be
much moved by the news that the turtles in the Pacific were being decimated;

indeed, one fears it would have increased his appetite for more. The whalers felt that way about the whales. Nobody at this stage dreamed of putting limits on the catch, of trying to prevent the killing of pregnant or nursing mothers, or of adopting any of the laws which would have allowed the trade to survive. Such restrictions could never have been enforced, and every whale ship was a law to itself. And so the southern ocean was pillaged to the limit throughout these years without a protest, or indeed without the outside world really knowing anything about it, since the captains were naturally secretive about their whaling grounds.

Their persistence was immense, and it is marvellous that in a period of little more than fifty years – roughly from the 1790s to the 1840s – these little ships with their casually gathered crews could have combed these vast icy oceans so thoroughly that no large marine animal was to be easily found there any more. Only the Antarctic coast itself – the coast that Cook had glimpsed through the icy haze – was still safe from their ravages.

Antarctica in the summer: 'That lovely shade of bluish-green which was to be found nowhere but in polar seas . . . a delicate and limpid colour [which] filled the eye. It had a quality of absolute purity and permanence, the cold fire of the diamond.' From a painting by Sir Sidney Nolan from his private collection. The author flew to Antarctica with Nolan in 1964 as he prepared this book and observed the strange landscape of Cook's journey at first hand.

243

BIBLIOGRAPHY

Relating to the text

The Journals of Captain James Cook on His Voyages of Discovery. Vols I, II and III. Edited by J. C. Beaglehole. Hakluyt Society and the Cambridge University Press, 1955, 1961 and 1967.

The Life of Captain Cook by J. C. Beaglehole. Hakluyt Society and the Cambridge University Press, 1974.

The Endeavour Journal of Joseph Banks, 1768–1771. Two vols. Edited by J. C. Beaglehole. The Public Library of New South Wales and Angus and Robertson, 1962.

A Voyage to the Pacific Ocean, London, 1784. Three vols: Vols I and II by Captain James Cook, Vol III by Captain James King.

A Journal of the Second Voyage of HMS Dolphin *Round the World under the Command of Captain Wallis RN in the years, 1766, 1767 and 1768, by her Master, George Robertson*. Edited by Hugh Carrington. Hakluyt Society, 1948.

A Voyage Round the World by Louis Antoine de Bougainville. Translated from the French by John Reinhold Foster. London, 1772.

A Voyage Round the World by George Forster. Two vols. London, 1777.

A Journal of a Voyage to the South Seas by Sydney Parkinson. London, 1784.

Journal of the Resolution's *Voyage, 1772–1775* by John Marra. Newbery, London, 1775.

Dampier's Voyages by Captain William Dampier. Two vols. Edited by John Masefield. Grant Richards, 1906.

The Voyage of Captain Bellingshausen to the Antarctic Seas, 1819–1821. Translated from the Russian by Frank Debenham. Hakluyt Society, 1945.

The Voyage of the Beagle by Charles Darwin. Dent, 1906.

The Southwest Pacific to 1900 by C. Hartley Grattan. University of Michigan Press, 1963.

European Vision and the South Pacific by Bernard Smith. Oxford Press, 1960.

Typee: A Peep at Polynesian Life, or Four Months' Residence in a Valley of the Marquesas by Herman Melville. New York, 1846.

Omoo: A Narrative of Adventures in the South Seas by Herman Melville. New York, 1847.

Moby Dick, or the White Whale by Herman Melville. New York, 1851.

Melville in the South Seas by Charles Roberts Anderson. Columbia University Press, 1939.

Intimate Journals by Paul Gauguin. Translated by Van Wyck Brooks. Crown, New York, 1936.

Terre Napoléon by Ernest Scott. Methuen, 1910.

Australian Discovery by Sea by Ernest Scott. Dent, 1929.

My Own Destroyer by Sidney J. Baker. Angus and Robertson, 1963.

Waterless Horizons by Malcolm Uren and Robert Stephens. Robertson and Mullens, 1941.

Journals of Expeditions of Discovery into Central Australia and Overland from Adelaide to King George's Sound 1840–1841 by John Edward Eyre. Two vols. Boone, 1845.

The Passing of the Aborigines by Daisy Bates. Murray, 1938.

'Mrs Bates and the Aborigines'. Article in the *Cornhill Magazine* by H. J. Samuel. Spring, 1964.

The Road to Xanadu by John Livingstone Lowes. Constable, 1927.

The Sea Hunters by Edouard A. Stackpole. Lippincott, 1953.

Narrative of A. Gordon Pym by Edgar Allan Poe. Kegan Paul Trench and Co., 1884.

Antarctic Penguins by G. Murray Levick. Heinemann, 1914.

The Whalers by Felix Maynard and Alexandre Duman. Translated by F. W. Reed. Hutchinson, 1937.

The Australian Aboriginal by Herbert Basedow. Adelaide, 1925.

Sydney's First Four Years by Captain Watkin Tench. Angus and Watson, 1961.

The Voyage of Governor Phillip to Botany Bay. London, 1790.

Whalemen Adventurers by William John Dakin. Angus and Robertson, 1934.

The White Road: a History of Polar Exploration by L. P. Kirwan. Hollis and Carter, 1959.

The World of the First Australians by Ronald M. Berndt and Catherine Berndt. Ure Smith, Sydney, 1964.

The Western Invasions of the Pacific and Its Continents by A. Grenfell Price.

A History of Australia, Vol I, from the earliest times to the age of Macarthur by C. M. H. Clark. Parkville, Victoria, Melbourne University Press, 1962.

BIBLIOGRAPHY

Relating to the boxed information and captions

Darwin and the 'Beagle' by Alan Moorehead (London, Hamish Hamilton, 1969).
Aboriginal Australian Art. A Visual Perspective by R. M. Berndt and Catherine Berndt. (Methuen, Australia, 1982).
Early Tahiti As Explorers Saw It by E. N. Ferdon (University of Arizona Press, 1981).
Tahiti. A Paradise Lost by David Howarth (N. Y. 1984).
Australian Dictionary of Biography. 1788–1850 Vols 1 & 2; and 1891–1939 Vol 7. (Parkville, Victoria, Melbourne University Press, 1966, 1967, 1979).
The Australian Aborigines. A Portrait of their Society by Kenneth Maddock (Penguin, Australia, 2nd. edn 1982).
The Spectre of Truganini, by Bernard Smith (Boyer Lectures, 1980, Australian Broadcasting Commission, Sydney, 1980).
The Art of Captain Cook's Voyages, by R. Joppien and Bernard Smith (Melbourne, Oxford University Press, 1985).
Other works referred to are listed under the 'text bibliography'.

Relating to the illustrations

Antarctica. Reader's Digest Services Pty Ltd, 1985.
European Vision and the South Pacific by Bernard Smith. Harper & Row, 1984 (2nd edn).
Great Voyages of Exploration by Jacques Brosse. Doubleday, 1983.
Le Grand Livre du Pacifique by Roselene Dousset and Etienne Taillemite. Edita Vilo, 1976.
The Art of Captain Cook's Voyages by Rüdiger Joppien and Bernard Smith. Vols I & II, Oxford University Press, 1985.
The People from the Horizon by Philip Snow and Stefanie Waine. Phaidon, 1979.

SOURCE OF ILLUSTRATIONS

Abbreviations

BL British Library; BMNH British Museum, Natural History; DG Dixson Gallery; DL Dixson Library; ML Mitchell Library; NL National Library of Australia; NMM National Maritime Museum, Greenwich.
L = left; R = right; T = top; B = bottom.

p.2, 3 William Westall, *Port Jackson*, ML V1/1804/1; p.6, 7 George Foster, *Ice Islands*, ML PXD11 f.30; p.10, 11 John & James Cleveley, *A View of Moorea*, ML ZML101; p.12T James Webber, *Oheitepeha Bay in Otaheite, 1784*, DG189; p.12 BL Sydney Parkinson, *Otaheite View Along Shore, 1769*, BL Add. MS23921 f.9(a); p.14 Nathaniel Dance, *Portrait of Cook*, NMM B1355; p.15TL William Hodges, *Tainamai Princess of Raiatea*, NL; p.15TR William Hodges, *Hiti Hiti, Raiatea*, NLA; p.15B Sydney Parkinson, *The Tree On One Tree Hill*, BL Add MS 23921 f.6(a); p.16 Samuel Wallis, *A Ground Plan and Perspective View of the Queen's House at King George's Islands, 1767*, ML PXD 72 f.1; p.17 G. B. Cipriani, *A Dance in Otaheite*, DL PXX2 f.14; p. 18T Charles Praval, *Household Furniture Weapons and Tools Used by the Inhabitants of the South Sea Islands, 1771*, p.18 BL Add MS 7085 f.9; p.18B *The Artist of the Chief Mourner, Musicians of Tahiti, 1769*, BL Add MS 15508 f.10(b) no.11; p.19 John Barralet, *View in the Island of Otaheite, c.1772*, DL PXX2 f.45; p.21 James Cook, *Chart of the West Coast of Newfoundland*, ML ZM4 621/1770/1; p.22 William Hodges, *Captain James Cook*, DG ZDG 214; p.23 *A Page of Cook's Holograph Log*, 13 July 1769, BM Add 27956; p.25 Benjamin Wise, *Sir Joseph Banks*, NL NK265; p.26T From Sydney Parkinson's '*A Journal of a Voyage to the South Seas . . .*', 1773, f'piece, ML Q980/P; p.26B Thomas Luny, *The Bark, Earl of Pembroke, Later Endeavour, Leaving Whitby Harbour in 1768*, NLA; p.27 Alexander Buchan, *A View of the Endeavour's Watering Place in the Bay of Good Success*, BL; p.29 George Tobin, *Matavai Bay, Tahiti, 1792*, ML PXA 563 f.36; p.30 William Hodges, *A View of Point Venus and Matavai Bay, Looking East, 1773*, NMM; p.31 William Hodges, *Matavai Bay, Tahiti*, Yale Center for British Art, Paul Mellon Collection, B1981.25.343; p.33 *The Natives of Otaheite Attacking Captain Wallis the First Discoverer of that Island*, NLA NK 147; p.34 Joseph Banks, '*Atlas of Account of Voyage . . .*' No.22, ML X980/26; p.37T Sydney Parkinson, A Op cit [plate IV f.p.16] *Venus Fort*, ML Q980/P; p.37B Charles Praval, *A Plan of Fort Venus in Royal Bay*, 1771, BL Add MS 7085, f.8d; p.39 Sydney Parkinson, Op cit [plate VIII f.p.26] *Heads of Divers Natives of Otaheite*, ML Q980/P; p.40T Sydney Parkinson, Op cit [plate V f.p.23], *A Woman and Boy of Otaheite*, ML Q980/P; p.40B George Tobin, *In the District of Whapiano, Island of Otahytey*, ML PXA 563 f.38; p.41 J. F. Miller, *Different Sorts of Fish Hooks From Otaheite, 1771*, BL Add MS 23921, f.56(b); p.42 George Tobin, *Breadfruit, Tahiti, 1792*, ML PXA 563 f.2; p.43 *Tattooing Designs on Buttocks*, BL Add MS 23921 f.51c; p.44 William Hodges, *View of Otaheite, c.1776*, NMM 1583; p.47L & R Sydney Parkinson, *Distortions of the Mouth Used in Dancing*, 1769, BL Add MS 23921 f.51 (a-c, cv); p.51 *Captain Bougainville & Other Officers Taking Fruit From a Native*, NLA NK 5066; p.52 *Portable Observatory used by Cook on His Voyage and Observation of Transit of Venus*, Archives Nationales, Fonds Marine; p.53BL In '*Philosophical Transactions of the Royal Society*', 1771; p.54TL & R Sydney Parkinson, '*Zoological Drawings*', L *Moorish Idol*, R *Tropic Bird*, BMNH; p.54B Sydney Parkinson, *Erythrina Indica*, BMNH; p.55T J. R. Forster, *Barringtonia Speciosa*. BMNH; p.55B *Gold-Throated Bird of Paradise* from '*Oiseaux Lores*', 1802, Museum National D'Histoire Naturelle, Paris; p.56 George Tobin, *On Matavai River, Island of Otahyay, 1792*, ML DXA 563 f.32; p.57 Sydney Parkinson, Op Cit [plate IX f.p.66], *The Lad Taiyota*, ML Q980/P; p.61 Sydney Parkinson, Op cit [plate XIII f.p.75], *Various Instruments and Utensils of the Natives of Otaheite*, ML Q980/P; p.67 Francis Holman, *The Resolution and Adventure in the Downs*, DG ZDG 22; p.70 William Hodges, *The Resolution and Adventure in Matavai Bay*, NMM A7756; p.72 J. W. Lewin, *Otoo, Present Sovereign of Otaheite*, ML PX*D379 f.2; p.73 G. B. Cipriani, *A View of the Inside of a House in the Island of Ulieta*, DL PXX2 f.14; p.76 Sydney Parkinson, Op cit [plate VI f.p.24], *from A Part of a House and Plantation of a Chief of the Island of Otaheite*, ML Q980/P; p.78 William Hodges, *War Galleys at Tahiti*, NMM C3409; p.80 William Parry, *Sir Joseph Banks, Omai and Dr Daniel Solander*, Parham Park, Sussex; p.81T *Omiah the Indian from Otaheite, Presented to Their Majesties*, NLA NK10666; p.81B William Hodges, *Omai*, Royal College of Surgeons, London; p.84 John Webber, 'Drawings on Cook's Third Voyage', fol.16, *A Human Sacrifice at Otaheite*, ML PXX2 f.10; p.85 J. Rickman, 'Journal of Captain Cook's Last Voyage to the Pacific Ocean', London, 1781, [f.p.136], *Omai's Public Entry on His First Landing at Otaheite*, ML Q910.8/CO4/RIA1; p.86 John Webber, *King of Owyhee Bringing Presents to Captain Cook*, DL PXX3 f.35; p.87 William

246

Hodges, 'A Collection of Drawings...', Vol 1 Fol 95, *The Landing at Middlesburgh, One of the Friendly Isles*, BL; p.88T George Carter, *The Death of Captain Cook*, NLA NK2; p.88B J. Zoffany, *The Death of Cook*, NMM 1484; p.91 Phillipe Jacques de Loutherbourg, *Oberyan Enchantress*, NLA; p.92 John Webber, *Poedooa Daughter of Orea, King of Ulaitea*, NLA NK5192; p.93 T. Gosse, *Transplanting of the Breadfruit Trees from Otaheite*, NLA NK2010; p.96 'Atlas of the Voyage of La Pérouse', *Massacre of Fleurnot de Langle*, ML X980/3; p.97 *La Pérouse*, ML Portrait File; p.99 James Wilson, 'A Missionary Voyage...' p.77, *A Missionary House at Matavai*, ML Q989/14B2; p.100 'Missionary Sketches', October 1818, *The Family Idols of Pomare*, ML 266.05/7; p.101 Ibid, July 1819, *Destruction of the Idols of Otaheite*, ML 266.05/7; p.102 Robert Smirke, *The Cession of Matavai*, 1820, The School of Oriental and African Studies, London, Courtesy Council for World Mission; p.103 Op cit October 1837, *The Offering of a Human Sacrifice in Tahiti*, ML 266.05/7; p.104 T. Bellingshausen, 'Izyskaniia V. I'Uzhnom Led Ouotorn Okenne, *Thaddeus Von Bellingshausen*, NLA; p.106 L.F. Lejeune, *King Pomare III's Guard*, Service Historique de la Marine, Vincennes; p.107 G. Baxter, *Pomare IV Unable to Watch the French Landing in Tahiti*, Courtesy of Council for World Mission, London; p.110 Jean Randier, 'Hommes et Navires...' p.89, *L'Artémise Being Careened in Tahiti*, 1839, Service Historique de la Marine, Vincennes; p.111 J.O. Eaton, *Herman Melville*, Fogg Art Museum, Harvard University, Cambridge, Massachusetts; p.112, 113 Paul Gauguin, *Nevermore*, Courtauld Institute Galleries, London; p.114 Philip Snow and Stephanie Wame, *L'Artémise*, 'The people from the Horizon'; p.116,117 Joseph Lycett, *View On the Illawarra River*, DG DI DA f.6; p.118 Sydney Parkinson, Op cit, [plate XXIII f.p.116], *The Heads of Six Men, Natives of New Zealand*, ML Q980/P; p.119 Sydney Parkinson, *New Zealand War Canoe Bidding Defiance to the Ship*, BL Add MS 23920, f.50; p.120 Sydney Parkinson, *The Endeavour at Sea*, BL Add MS 9345 fol 16V; p.121 Joseph Lycett, *Aborigines Spearing Fish*, NLA R5686; p.122T Sydney Parkinson, Op cit [plate XXVIII f.p.134], *Two of the Natives of New Holland Advancing to Combat*, ML Q980/P; p.122B T.R. Browne, *Aboriginal Tools and Weapons*, ML PXA 555 f.56; p.123 Sydney Parkinson, *Two Australian Aborigines and Other Drawings*, BL Add MS 9345 f.14; p.125 Augustus Earle, *Cabbage Tree Forest, Illawarra, NSW*, NLA NK12/37; p.126 G. Perry, 'Arcana', Vol 1, 1811, opp p.81, ML 570.7/D; p.127L G. Barrington, 'History of NSW', London, 1802 opp. p.443, ML 991/B; p.127R *The Peppermint Tree*, ML; p.128 T.R. Browne, *Fish of Eastern Australia*, ML ZPXA 555 f.45; p.128B T. R. Browne, *Black & White Cockatoo*, ML ZPXA 555 f.14; p.129 James Phillip, 'The Voyage of Governor Phillip', Stockdale, London, 1789, *Port Jackson Shark*, ML 990/P; p.131 Sydney Parkinson, *The Endeavour Beached at the Mouth of the Endeavour River*, NLA; p.133 'Hawkesworth's Voyages of Captain Cook' Vol 3, p.157, *Kangaroo*, NLA NK2851; p.134T T. R. Browne, *Butterflies*, ML PXA 555 f.50; p.134B J. Gould, *Black-Gloved Wallaby*, NLA NK4050/9; p.135T T. R. Browne, *Insects*, ML PXA 555 f.52; p.135B John Hunter, *Waratah*, NLA RNK; p.137 Thomas Watling, *A Group on the North Shore of Port Jackson*, BMNH; p.138 A. Browne, *Natives Fishing in a Boat Canoe, NSW*, 1819, DGA3f.1; p.139 W. A. Cawthorne, *Boomerang and Cutta Wirri*, ML PX*D70 f.20; p.140 Port Jackson Painter, *Method of Climbing Trees*, BMNH; p.145 Nicholas Martin Petit, *A Young Australian Aboriginal Woman*, Museum D'Histoire Naturelle, Le Havre, 20035; p.146 Augustus Earle, *Desmond, A New South Wales Chief*, NLA NK12/61; p.147 Yakaduna, *Views of a Corroboree and a Battle*, DGSSV*/AUS/ABO/5; p.148 John Glover, *Aborigines Dancing at Brighton, Tasmania*, Queen Victoria Museum & Art Gallery, Launceston; p.150 Nicholas Martin Petit, *A Group of Tasmanian Aborigines*, Museum D'Histoire Naturelle, 20024-2; p.151 W. F. E. Liardet, *Natives Stalking Emus*, 1871, NLA NK157; p.156 George A. Robinson Papers, Part 2, p.171, ML A7084; p.158 S.T. Gill, *Native Sepulchre*, NLA NK 7063/2; p.159 W. A. Cawthorne, *A Native Woman Mourning for the Dead*, ML PX*D70 f.11; p.162 William Bradley, *The First Fleet Entering Port Jackson*, ML Safe 1/14 opp f.65; p.163 *Governor Arthur Phillip*, ML124; p.165 William Bradley, *First Interview with the Native Women*, ML Safe 1/14 opp f.70; p.166 Jean Ravenet, *Convicts of New Holland*, DG D2 f.5; p.167 *Captain Watkin Tench*, ML; p.168 William Bradley, *Sydney Cove Port Jackson 1788*, ML Safe 1/14 opp f.84; p.169 J.S. Prout, *Norfolk Island*, ML PXD 75 f.16; p.170 *Rosehill 1791*, DG SVIA/24; p.171 John Gould, 'Birds of Australia', Vol 5 plate 27, *Rosehill Parakeet*, ML X598.2/5; p.172 William Bradley, *Taking of Colbee and Benalon*, ML Safe 1/14 opp f.182; p.173 *Bennelong*, ML SPF; p.174 John Hunter, 'An Historical Journal of the Transactions at Port Jackson...', London, 1793, F'piece, ML 990/H; p.175 The Port Jackson Painter, *The Hunted Rushcutter*, BMNH Banks MS34; p.176 William Bradley, *Wreck of the Sirius, Norfolk Island*, ML Safe 1/14 between ff194 and 195b; p.178 Jean Ravenet, *Settlers of New Holland*, DGD2 f.4; p.179T William Bradley, *Government House, Port Jackson 1791*, ML Safe 1/14 opp f.225; p.179B Museo de Naval, Madrid; p.180 John Hunter, *Sketch of Sydney Cove Port Jackson, July 1788*, ML; p.181 'The Voyage of Governor Phillip', London, Stockdale, 1792, ML 990/P; p.183 William Westall, A. Flinders, 'A Voyage to Terra Australis', 1814 p.312, ML Q980.1/37A2; p.184 *Matthew Flinders*, NLA; p.185 T.J. Maslen, 'Friend of Australia', London, 1830, ML 980.1/58A1; p.186 G. Hamilton, *Bushman's Halt*, ML V*/BUSHLIFE/1b; p.187 Edward John Eyre, ML P1/E; p.188T J. W. Lewin, *Campbell River*, 1815, ML SVIB/BLUEM/9; p.188B *Melbourne*, 1839, ML SPF; p.189 *Brisbane, Moreton Bay*, 1846, ML ZPXX30 f.7/(c); p.195 E.J. Eyre, 'Journal of Expeditions in Central and Southern Australia...' Vol 2, p.109, ML 983.7/20A2; p.197 D. C. Cooper, *The Harbour, Albany, King George's Sound*, NL NK 10163/6; p.200T *Charles Darwin*, ML P1/D; p.200B *Midship Aboard Beagle*, NMM B2630; p.201 Augustus Earle, *Bungaree*, NL NK118; p.202T NLA NK12/45; p.202B Augustus Earle, *Natives of NSW in Sydney Town*, ML; p.203T *Tasmanian Aborigines*, ML SPF; p.203B Cover, NLA; p.204, 205 W. A. Hawthorne, *Natives driven to police court for trespassing*, 1845, ML V*/AUS

INDEX

Key

Text in roman type; Boxed information in bold type; Captions in italic type.

Aborigines *121, 122, 123, 137, 140, 143–*
59, 146, 151, 152, 174
  arts and symbols **156**, *156*, 156–8
  Bennelong *172*, 172–3, **173**
  circumcision 147–8
  Colebe *172*
  contact with colony 171–5, *172, 175,*
202, 208–9, *209*
  Daisy Bates **206**, 207–9
  dances *147*, 153–6
  described by Dampier 121–3
  'dreamtime' **141**, **156**
  Eyre's account of **187**, 190, 192–4,
205–7
  food 139
  funeral ceremony **158**, *159*
  language and religion 157–9
  marriage **144**, 149
  menace to penal colony 168–9
  misrepresented by painters *181, 182*
  observed at Endeavour River 136–
42, *138*
  origins 143, 143n
  reception of Cook 120–1
  Tasmanian *150*, 199–201, **203**, *203*
  tribal life **141**, 143–59, **158**
    destroyed 173–4, 198–209, *202,*
204–5
    wars 153–4
    weapons *122, 139*, 153–4
    women **144**, *145*, 149
Adelaide *186, 187*, 190, 205
Adventure 10–11, 67, 70, **81**, *213, 227*
  Cook's first voyage 67–78
  Cook's second voyage 79–87, 212–
17
  Raleigh 66
  see also Resolution
Aguila 71, 82
Albany *197*
Ancient Mariner 90, 216, 218, 221
Antarctica 71–2, **104**, 212–43, *243*
  emperor penguins *232*
  sea lions *220*
  see also sealing; whalers and whaling
Aotourou **51**
arioi 18, 19, **19**, 46, 74, 76, 83, 92, 102
Arnould, M. 90
L'Astrolabe 96, **97**, *164, 210–11*
Australia 118–209, *125*
  animals, birds and plants *127*, 132–6
    black and white cockatoo *128*
    butterflies *134*

    emu *127*
    fish *128*
    insects *135*
    kangaroo 132, *133*, 136, 156, 194
    peppermint tree *127*
    Port Jackson shark *129*
    rosella *171*
    wallaby *134*
    waratah *135*
    wombat *126*
  Bligh charts coast **93**
  Botany Bay named 128
  British claims unchallenged 183
  circumnavigation 182–3, **184**, *184*
  colony at Port Jackson 164–80, *168*
    becomes self-supporting 198
    famine 168, 175
    relations with Aborigines *165,*
171–5, *172, 175*, 208–9
    settlers of NSW *178*
    Tench's account of **167**
  convicts 160–2, **163**, *166*
  Cook claims for George III **62**, 142
  Cook explores east coast 118–42
  Daisy Bates 206–9
  Eyre's exploration of Great Austra-
lian Bight 185–97
  First Fleet 161–4
  Flinders' expedition 181–3
  French expedition 181–3
  Great Barrier Reef 136–7
  inland unknown 183
  landscape 123–4, 181
  Melville on whaling influence 196,
239–41
  name adopted by Flinders 183, *184*
  new capitals set up 183–5
  Phillip takes over new colony 165
    Second Fleet 177
    Third Fleet 177
    vegetation and fish 136
    whaling and sealing 231–43

Banks, Joseph **25**, *25*, **26**, 34–58, **60**,
80, 81
  attitude to Tupia 57
  background 24–8
  Burnett affair 68
  death of **60**, 103
  describes Maoris **119**
  director, King's Royal Garden,
Kew **60**
  first sight of kangaroo 132

  gold-throated bird of paradise *55*
  in Tahiti 13–58, *56*
  journal **25**, 28, 34–5, 38–9, 41, 45,
48, 65, 120, 124, 130, 132–7,
138–9, 142
  launches Omai 79–80
  marries 92
  on convicts 108
  president of Royal Society **60**, 92
  robbed 50
  satirized 63–4
  sends Bligh to Tahiti 92–4
  shoots albatrosses 118–19
  sights Australia 120
  suggests convicts be sent to Botany
Bay **60**, 160
  supporter of Flinders 181–2
  withdraws from second voyage 67
Banksia 127, 193
Baré, Jeanne 56
Basedow, Herbert 143n, *157, 159*
Bass, George **184**
Bates, Daisy **206**, 206–9
Batman, John 199
Batts, Elisabeth
  see Cook, Mrs James
Baudin, Nicholas *150*, **184**
Baxter, John 190–1
Bay of Good Success, Patagonia *27*
Bay of Islands *240–1, 241*
Beagle 106, **200**, *200*, 200–1
Beaglehole, Dr J. C. 63, 65, 66, **66**, 67,
68
Beaucheene Island 231
Bellingshausen, Baron Thaddeus 102–
3, **104**, 105, 107
Bennelong *172*, 172–3, **173**
Bennett, Frederick Debell 108
Berndt, R. and C. 143n
Bernier **206**
Black, Anderson 242
Blake, William 181
Bligh, Captain William 22, 79, **93**, *93*,
177, 181–2
  Bounty 13, 92–5, **93**
  governor of NSW **93**
Bootie, John 29
Boswell, James 60n, 63, 65, 89, 177
Botany Bay 121–8, *122*, 132, 160, 161,
162, 169, 170, 175, 177, 181, 193
  Stingray Bay *129*
Boudeuse, La **51**, *51*
Bougainville, Louis de

account of voyage 62
  in Tahiti 13, **51**, *51*, 64
    calls Tahiti New Cythera 20, **51**
    describes Tahitian women 46–7,
      46–8
    on venereal disease 49
bougainvillea **51**
Bounty 13, 92–5, **93**, 99, 239
Boussole, La **97**, 164
Boyd, Benjamin *238*
Boyd Town *238*
breadfruit *42*, *93*
Brisbane 183, *189*
Bruce, James 92
Bryant, Mary 177, **177**
Buchan, Alexander **26**, 26–8, 38
Buckley, William **153**
Bungaree **201**
Burney, Fanny 63, 68, 80, 95
Burney, James 68
Byers Island *233*
Byron, Lord 90, 128
Byron, Commodore John 90, 128

Cape Byron 128
Cape York 142
Carolines **104**
Carpentaria, Gulf of 182
Christian, Fletcher **93**, 94
Clark, Bessy *203*
Clerke, Charles 68, 74, 79, 83, 86,
  216–17, 221
Colebe *172*
Coleridge 90, 216, 221
Commerson, Philibert 46, 56, 57
Cook, Captain James 21–4, *22*, 65
  Antarctic voyage 212–25, *213*, 231
  appointed to Greenwich 79, **79**
  Australia 118–42
    claims NSW **62**, 142
    contact with Aborigines 123–9,
      132–42
    Endeavour strikes reef 129–31
  biography **66**
  circumnavigates Pole 224
  claims South Georgia 224
  crosses Antarctic circle 214
  cruises the Pacific 220
  deals with deserters 58
  death of 35, 87–9, **88**, *88*
    effect in England 89
  discovers Antarctic animals
    226–8
  Endeavour strikes reef 129–31
  Endeavour voyage 13–58
  in Hawaii *86*
  in Tahiti 13–58, *56*, 69–78, 82–7
    attitude to Tahitian women 49
    European influence on 71, 86–7
    Fort Venus *30*, 31, 36, *37*
    presents cattle 83
    sees human sacrifice 83, *84*, *103*
    venereal disease 50, 71
  in Tonga 87
  journals *23*, 63, **66**
  Lord Howe Island 170
  loses contact with *Adventure* 216
  Newfoundland, map of *21*
  Norfolk Island 169n
  on Tasmania 151

pantomimes about him 90–1
portable observatory *52*
punishments he inflicted 39, 49, 58,
  72, 76–7, 84, 86, 220
relations with Banks 27
Resolution
  first voyage 67–78
  second voyage 79–87, 212–25
  return of Omai 84, 85
  returns to England 61, 78–9
  sails to New Zealand 216
  sees first icebergs 212
  transit of Venus **14**, *14*, 50, *52*, **52**,
    53
Cook, Mrs James 24, 65, **79**
Cook Islands **104**
Cooper, Lieut 222
Crozet, Julian 95
Cumberland **184**

Dalton, – 28
Dampier, William 121, 123, 127, 143,
  159, 226
Dance, Nathaniel 21, 80
Darwin, Charles **43**, 87, 105, 106,
  108–9, 151, 154–5, *168*, 198, 199,
  200, 201, *202*, 242
Davey, Thomas *203*
Death of Captain Cook, The 67
Defoe, Daniel 90
Diderot, – 62, 63, 84, 94, 111, 114
Discovery 79, 86, 87, **88**
Dolphin 13, 20, **20**, 21, 24, 28, 33, 46,
  49, 50, 56, 67, 90, 128
Dorré **206**
Douglas, Dr John 91
Drake
  see *Resolution*
Duff 97, 98, **98**, 101, *102*, *103*, 107
Dupetit-Thouars, Admiral 109, 110,
  110, *241*
d'Urville, Dumont 210–11
Dusky Bay 217, *217*

Earl of Pembroke
  see *Endeavour*
Easter Island 222
L'Embarquement pour Cythère 63
Endeavour 120, 160, 162
  Banks' plans for voyage **25**
  damaged on reef 129–31, *131*
  Earl of Pembroke 26
  explores east coast of Australia *2–3*,
    118–42
  illustrations from voyage **60**
  in Tahiti 13–58, *15*
  official account of voyage 63
Endeavour River *131*, *133*, 139
Enderby Brothers 242
Erebus, HMS 232
L'Etoile **51**, *51*
Eucla **206**
European Vision and the South Pacific
  89n
Eyre, Edward John **187**
  exploration of Great Bight 186–97
    crisis with native boys 192–3
    murder of Baxter 191
    reaches King George's Sound 195,
      197

saved by whalers 195
governor of Jamaica 205
on Aboriginal dances 155
on whaling 237
overlanding 186, **187**
protector of Aborigines **187**, 205
tried for oppression 205
Wylie 190–7, 207
Eyre Peninsula **187**

First Fleet 161–4, *162*, **163**
Flinders, Matthew 181–3, *183*, 184,
  184, *184*, 185, 189, 193, **201**
Flinders Ranges **187**
Forster, George 68, 69, 70, 72, 74, 75,
  75, 77, 89, 218, 220
Forster, John Reinhold 67, 72, 74, 75,
  75
Fowler's Bay 190, 193, 194, 237
Frazer 178
Fresne, Marion du 95
Friendly Islands 94
Furneaux, Lt Tobias 66, 70, 71, 76, 79,
  80, **81**, 83, 95, *119*, 216

Garrick, David 63, 80, 90, *91*
Gauguin, Paul 64, 112–13, 115
Gawler, Col George 190
Geographe, Le **184**
George III 59, 78, 79, 82, 142, 170
Gibson, Sam 58, 58n, 63, 76
Glover, John 199
Gore, John 24, 31, 39, 50, 79, 132
Grattan, C. Hartley 97
Great Australian Bight 184, 186–9,
  190–1, 207, 237
Great Barrier Reef 136–7
Green, Charles 24, 36, 38, 45, 50, 52,
  52, **53**, 59
Greenwich Hospital **79**
Grey, Sir George 149
Grindall, Richard 68
Gulliver's Travels 90

Haitaa *51*
Halley, Edmund **52**
Hawaii 35, 65, *86*, *88*
Haweis, Thomas 96
Hawkesbury River 170, 180
Hawkesworth, Dr John 63, 64, 65, 66
Hicks, Zachary 24, 45, 58, 59, 120
Hobart 183, 226, 242
Hodges, William *22*, 67, 76, 78, 89,
  90, *213*
Hooker, Joseph 65
Horrocks, Jeremiah **52**
Huahine 71, 84, 85, 86
Humbolt, Alexander von 68

icebergs 6–7, 212, *214*, *215*, 217, 227,
  230
Investigator 182–4, **184**
Investigator's Strait *183*

Jeffs, Henry 39
Johnson, Dr 59, 63, 80, 89, 91, 160

'Kabbarli'
  see Bates, Daisy
Kangaroo 132, *133*, 136, 156, 194

Kangaroo Island *183*
Kealakekua Bay 87, 88, **88**, *88*, 89
Kerguelen's Land *224*
King, P. T. **201**
King, Philip Gidley *169*
  idealized sketch of Aborigines *182*
King George Sound 154, 182, 183,
  185, 194, 195, *195*, 196, *197*, 242
King George the Third's Island
  see Tahiti
Kingsley, Mary 207
Kotzebue, Otto von 105

La Pérouse 89, 95, *96*, **97**, 164, 169,
  177
Lady Juliana 176
Lake Torrens **187**
Lanne *203*
Lewin, John William 183
Livingstone, Dr 24
London Missionary Society
  see missionaries
Lord Howe Island 170
Louis XVI 89
Loutherbourg, Philip de 90
Lucky Bay 195
Lucy Ann 240, 241

Magnetic Island 129
Malthus, Thomas Robert 92
Mamelukes 19
Maoris **119**, *119*
  war canoe *118*
marae 17, 18, **19**, *19*, 53, *84*, 101, 103,
  115, 208
Maria Island *150*
Marquesas 74
Marra, John 76–7, **77**, 89, 220
  on Tayeto *57*
Marsden, Rev. Samuel *100*
Martens, Conrad *200*
Mary Anne 177
Matavai Bay 13, *15*, 20, *29*, 30, *31*, 32,
  36, *40*, 50, 53, *57*, 69, 70, *70*, 74,
  76, 82, 90, 98, 99, 101, *102*, 103,
  109
Matavai River *56*
Maynard, Felix 199
Melanesians 74
Melbourne 185, 186, *188*
Melville, Herman 226, 235, 239, 240
  account of Tahiti **111**, 111–15
  Moby Dick 196, *238*
  Omoo **111**, 240–1
  on Pomare II *100*
  on porpoises 227
  on the Pacific 119
  on whalers 240
  Typee **111**
M'Entire, – 175
Mermaid **201**
missionaries 96–113, **98**, *99*, *100*
Mississippi 195, 196
Moby Dick 196, 226, 235, *238*, 239, 240
Molyneux 59
Monboddo, Lord 65
Monkhouse, Jonathan 130
Monkhouse, Dr William 35, 49, 50, 59
Moorea 32, 50, 76, 83, 84, 101, 110,
  114

Moreton Bay 189
Mort du Capitaine Cook, La 90
Mystic, USA 239

Nantucket 107, 231, 239, 242
'Nevermore' 112–13, 115
New Caledonians 74
New Hebrides 177, 220
New Holland
  see Australia
New South Wales 142, 160, 181, 198,
  204
New Zealand 95, 109, 118, 160, 168,
  216, 220, 232 240
  flora and fauna
    bearded penguin *223*
    blue petrel *223*
    silver-grey petrel *223*
  Maoris **119**
  see also Maoris
Newfoundland
  Cook's map of *21*
Niger, HMS **25**
Norfolk **184**
Norfolk Island 169, *169*, 169n, 175,
  177, 220
  Sirius wrecked *176*
Nott, Henry 103, 104
Nullarbor Plain **187**, 189, 207

Obarea, Queen 33, 34, *34*, 39, 46, 49,
  53, 58, 63–4, 71, 82, 83, 90
  house on Tahiti *16*
Oedidee *15*
Omai 33, 71, 76, 79, *80*, **81**, *81*, 82,
  84–5, 86, 90, 96, 151, 172, 207
  returns to Tahiti *85*
Omoo 111, **111**, 240
Ooldea **206**, 208, 209
Orton, Richard 129
Ossory, Countess of 63
overlanding 186, *186*, 188
Owhaa *31*, 37

Pandora 95
Papeete 33, 103, 109, 110, 112, 241
Parkinson, Sydney 27, 60, 65
  'Crucifix' painting *123*
  death 26, 59
  in Australia 126, 129, 132
  in Tahiti *26*, 29, 36, 38, 39, 51
Parramatta 170, *170*, 177, *179*
  Rose Hill 170, *170*
Parry, William 80
Passing of the Aborigines, The 208
Pattly *203*
Perth 185
Phillip, Governor Arthur 161–77,
  163, *165*, 172, 174, 193, 199
  death *163*
Picasso, Pablo 157
Pickering, Charles 151, *152*
Pickersgill, Richard 68
Pitcairn Island 94
Poe, Edgar Allan 230
Poedooa *92*
Point Hicks 182
Polynesians 74
Pomare 99
  see also Tu

Pomare II 100–1, 103–4
  family idols *100*
Pomare Vahine III, Queen 107, **107**,
  109–10
Porpoise, HMS *183*
Port Arthur 201
Port Bowen, Queensland *116–17*
Port Jackson 128, 162, *162*, 164, 168,
  181
Port Lincoln 189, 197
Port Phillip Bay 186
Possession Island 142

Queen Charlotte Sound 216, 220
Quiros 13

Radcliffe-Brown, A. R. **206**
Raleigh
  see Adventure
Raratonga **104**
Rattlesnake, HMS *234*
Reine Blanche, La 110, **110**, 241
religion 208
  Aboriginal 208
  effects of missionaries 97–104, **98**
  Tahitian 208
  see also missionaries
Resolution 10–11, 67
  Cook's first voyage 67–78
  Cook's second voyage 79–87, **88**,
    89, **93**, 212–25
  Drake 66
  in Antarctic 212–25, *213*, *214*, *219*,
    224, *225*, 227, 230
  in New Zealand 217
  in Tahiti 69–78, *70*, 82–7
  Marra's account of voyage **77**
Reynolds, Joshua 59, 80, 90
Richmond, – 28
Robertson, George 33, 46, 50
Robinson, George Augustus *156*
Robinson Crusoe 90
Rose Hill
  see Parramatta
Ross, Sir James Clark *232*
Rossiter, Captain 195, 196, 242
Rousseau, Jean-Jacques 59, 95, 111,
  174
Royal Society of London 24, **25**, 60

St Helena 225
St Vincent's Gulf *183*
Samoa *96*
Sandwich Islands 221, *221*, 224, *229*
sealing 231, 231–2, *233*, 237
Sirius, HMS 161, *169*, 170, 175
  wrecked at Norfolk Island *176*
Smirke, Robert 101
Smith, Bernard 89n
Society Islands *56*
Solander, Dr Daniel Carl 27, 35, 36,
  45, 51, 59, 67, 78, 80, *80*, *81*, 128
South Georgia 221, 224
South Pole 224, 228
Spanish exploration in Tahiti 67, 82,
  105, 109
Spencer's Gulf *183*
Staten Island 222
Stead, W. T. 207
Stingray Bay

see Botany Bay
Strzelecki, Count 201, 202, 204
Stubbs, – 132
Supplement au Voyage de Bougainville 62
Supply 161, 162, 169, 175
Sutherland, Forby 127
Swift, Dean 90
Sydney 128, 164, 170, 171, 172, 173,
    176, 177, 180, *180,* 182, 183,
    185, 186, 198, 199
    Government House *179*
Sydney, Lord 160

Tahiti and Tahitians 13–115, *39, 40*
    annexed by France 110, **110**, 114
    as seen today 32–3
    Bounty mutiny 92–5, **93**
    condition in 1777 82
    Cook's first visit *12,* 29–58
    Cook's second visit 69–70
    Cook's third visit 71–2
    dancing *17, 47, 73, 92*
    dependent on Europe 94
    described by George Forster 74–5
    described by La Pérouse 95–6
    described by Melville 111
    described by William Wales 73–4
    eager to sail with Cook 78
    first explorers 13
    flora and fauna 55
    food 41
    funeral ceremony *19*
    Gauguin in 115
    human sacrifice 83, *84,* **98,** *103*
    huts *12*
    idealized by Europeans 65–6, 89,
        90–1
    missionaries 96–7, 97–104, **98,** *99,*
        208
    morals 46
    musicians *18*
    'Nevermore' *112–13,* 115

opinion of Bougainville on 7
pantomimes about 90, *91*
Parkinson in **26,** 29, 36, 38, 39, 51
population figures 107
portrayed by European artists 89
reaction in Europe 62–5
reaction to Europeans 31, *76*
red parrot feathers 72, 83
seen by Darwin 108–9
surfing 41
tattooing 16, **43,** *43,* 43–4, *44*
thefts by 35
traditional life 13–20, *61, 76*
    breadfruit *42, 93*
    European influence on 71, 95,
        102, 105–15, *106,* *112–13,* *114*
    fish hooks *41*
    household objects, weapons,
        tools *18*
    uncorrupted 76
    Wallis visits 33
    war canoes *31, 76, 78*
Tainamai *15*
Tasmania 151, 181, 183, 199, 201, 226,
    232, 237
tattooing
    see Tahiti, tattooing
Tayeto **57,** *57,* 58, 59, 69, *70*
'Te Atua' **19**
Tench, Captain Watkin **167,** 167–8,
    169, 172, 174, 175, 178
Terror, HMS *232*
Tierra del Fuego 28, *155*
    Christmas Sound *221*
Tonga *87*
Tootaha, Chief *45*
Truganini **203,** *203*
Tu 71, 72, *72,* 73, 76, 79, 82, 83, 99,
    100, 114
Tubourai *39,* 45
Tupia **57,** *57,* 58, 59, 69, *70,* 76
    warns against Maoris **119**

Tutuila *96*
Typee 111, **111**

Urville, Dumont d'
    see d'Urville, Dumont

Vaipopoo River 36
Vancouver, George 68
venereal disease 49, 50, 58, 71, 94, 107
Venus, transit of **14,** 20, **20,** *31,* 32, 36,
    44, 50, **52,** *53,* 60
Vostok **104**
Vostok Island **104**

Wales, William 68, 73–4, 78
Wallis, Captain Samuel 13, 21, 24, 28,
    48, 49–50, 56, 59, 63, 67, 71, 82,
    83
    in Tahiti **20,** 31, 33, *33, 34,* **51**
Walpole, Horace 63, 64, 67, 91, 97
Watteau 63
Webb, Clement 58, 63, 76
Webber, John 79, 83, 90, 101
whalers and whaling 94, 107, 108,
    177, 190, 195–6, 226–43, *233, 234,*
    235, 236
    Twofold Bay, NSW *238*
Wheeler, Daniel 106–7
Wilson, Captain 101, *102*
Wilson, Charles 241
Wolf, Archibald 49
World of the First Australians, The 143n
Wreck Reef *183*
Wylie 190–7, *195,* 207

Yalata **206**
York, Cape 142

Zelee, La 210–11
Zoffany 22, 67, 89